THE SECRETARY OF DEFENSE

The Secretary of Defense

DOUGLAS KINNARD

THE UNIVERSITY PRESS OF KENTUCKY

Copyright © 1980 by The University Press of Kentucky

Scholarly publisher for the Commonwealth,
serving Berea College, Centre College of Kentucky,
Eastern Kentucky University, The Filson Club,
Georgetown College, Kentucky Historical Society,
Kentucky State University, Morehead State University,
Murray State University, Northern Kentucky University,
Transylvania University, University of Kentucky,
University of Louisville, and Western Kentucky University.

Editorial and Sales Offices: Lexington, Kentucky 40506

This book was written under the auspices of the
Center of International Studies, Princeton University.

U.S. Army Photographs, pages iii, 8, 44, 72, 192
U.S. Air Force Photograph, page 113

Library of Congress Cataloging in Publication Data

Kinnard, Douglas.
    The Secretary of Defense.

    Bibliography: p.
    Includes index.
    1.   United States. Dept. of Defense—History.
I.   Title.
UA23.6.K56   353.6   80-5178
ISBN 0-8131-1434-9

To My First Wife

CONTENTS

ACKNOWLEDGMENTS

In writing this book I have received a great deal of assistance of various kinds which I would like to acknowledge. Three of my colleagues at the Woodrow Wilson School at Princeton during my 1976–1977 stay were most helpful: Junius J. Bleiman for his insightful comments on portions of the draft of the McNamara chapter, Stephen H. Strom and Franklin C. Miller for their extensive research assistance on the Laird and Schlesinger chapters respectively.

The basic research for the book was conducted while I was a Visiting Fellow at the Center of International Studies at Princeton, and the American Philosophical Society provided financial support for the many research trips from Princeton to Washington that year.

Finally I want to acknowledge a special indebtedness to the seventy-four persons, all of them busy in their own affairs, who granted interviews. Their names are listed in the Bibliography. Twenty-seven of these were in connection with earlier research of mine which was also relevant to this book, and the remaining forty-seven were directly related to this work. Dr. Henry S. Gaffney, Department of Defense, was very generous of his time in helping me select potential interviewees for this latter group.

INTRODUCTION

In 1947 Congress passed the National Security Act which, among other things, established the cabinet position of secretary of defense. In the intervening years, the position has increased in significance to the point where it is perhaps second only to that of the president. This book is concerned with the evolution of that office from the incumbency of James Forrestal, the first secretary, until the departure of Secretary James Schlesinger in late 1975. It is not a history of the office, nor is it an attempt to build social science theory. Rather, it is designed to provide insight on the office to those who are interested in the process of American defense/foreign policymaking, as well as to those with broader interests in national government affairs.

It is relevant at the outset to ask what the secretary of defense does. He plays several important roles in the American political system. First, he plays a major role in the development of national strategy and defense policy. Second, he is responsible for management of the defense establishment, including formulation of the defense budget, which is more than 25 percent of the total federal budget and whose size and distribution have enormous impact on many sectors of American society. Third, when crisis leads to the use or potential use of force, he must act as a crisis manager, negotiating between the Joint Chiefs of Staff and other military advisers and the president, who faces political constraints that may be at odds with a rational military solution to the crisis. Finally, he is the civilian leader to whom the military services look for guidance and who represents the military to other parts of the bureaucracy, the Congress, the media, the public, and other nations.

The problem of a civil-military relationship is of central importance to the institution of the secretary. Normally articulated in terms of civilian control of the military, the problem is not one of de jure civilian control—which has always existed in America. The problem is rather one of de facto civil control over the military. For while some secretaries have understood the military and handled them effectively, others clearly have not. Before describing the structure of this book, I will provide some historical perspective on the office.

The experiences of World War II were the major impetus for creation of the National Military Establishment, as it was initially called, as a kind of federation of the military departments under a secretary of defense. The first secretary, James Forrestal, soon discovered that he lacked authority commensurate with his responsibilities. His problems were recognized by the Hoover Commission on government organization which concluded, in 1948, that the problem was a deficiency in the authority of the secretary over the defense establishment. The commission's report along with Forrestal's own recommendations, together with his own untimely death, brought about the amendments in 1949 to the National Security Act. These amendments increased the power of the secretary, particularly over the budget, and at the same time reduced the service secretaries to subcabinet level positions.

When Dwight D. Eisenhower became president in 1953 he reorganized the Department of Defense so as to further centralize the functions of the secretary, with a corresponding reduction in the power of the military services. By 1957 public furor over what was perceived to be excessive rivalry among the military services influenced Eisenhower to propose a more drastic reorganization of the department. This time the changes he had in mind were sufficiently extensive to require specific statutory authority. While he did not secure all that he desired, Eisenhower's 1958 reorganization was a major step toward a truly unified defense establishment. It represented a final subordination of the military departments to the defense secretary, and reduced the service secretaries' role to administrative functions within their departments.

This was the last major legislative reorganization of the department. It was not, however, until Secretary of Defense Robert McNamara assumed office under President John F. Kennedy in

1961 that the full statutory authority of the act was implemented. Using the authority available to him, McNamara introduced a number of new managerial techniques designed to further centralize administration of the department, in budgetary areas in particular, but in overall management as well.

Many of McNamara's management reforms resulted in objections from the military and were modified by the subsequent secretaries, especially Melvin Laird, who served throughout the first Nixon administration. Nonetheless, the preeminent position of the secretary over the Defense Department that McNamara established remained, and the office is vastly greater in influence and authority today than was conceived in 1947 when James Forrestal was sworn in as the first secretary.

Concomitantly with the organizational evolution of the Department of Defense American military strategy evolved in response to a rapidly changing world, and in particular to the perceived challenges of the principal adversary, the Soviet Union. Since a primary function of the secretary of defense is to develop strategy, as well as to manage the resources necessary to implement that strategy, it will be useful to review briefly that strategic evolution.

By 1947 the Truman administration had adopted the containment policy, the principal thesis of which was that if Soviet expansion could be halted, the USSR would in time lose its desire to expand. The accompanying defense strategy of the period focused largely on the problem of large-scale Soviet aggression into Western Europe. The American atomic monopoly was viewed as the principal safeguard of European security. By 1949 the North Atlantic Treaty Organization had come into being in the belief that an American commitment to defend Europe (considering the United States nuclear monopoly) would be sufficient to deter Soviet aggression.

By 1950, however, events dictated a new evaluation of United States defense policy. The Soviets had, by this time, become a nuclear power themselves. Also, in 1950 came the Korean War. This event caused an enormous increase in the U.S. defense budget and also raised the question of the operational utility of nuclear weapons in wars with limited political objectives.

Before all this could be resolved Dwight Eisenhower became president with a commitment to end the Korean War, which he did, and to reduce the federal budget, especially the defense portion. To accomplish this latter objective, as Eisenhower saw it, required a nuclear heavy strategy with reduced emphasis on the manpower-expensive ground forces which had evolved during the Korean War. The resultant defense program that Eisenhower began to implement by 1954 was called the New Look.

Eisenhower's strategy raised too many questions not to be fair game for critics. They argued that American capability below the nuclear threshold (i.e., limited warfare) had to be improved to meet situations in which the employment of nuclear weapons would not be appropriate. These arguments made little impact on Eisenhower, but Kennedy made much of them in his successful 1960 campaign against Richard Nixon.

With the arrival of John Kennedy in the White House and Robert McNamara at the Pentagon, United States defense strategy shifted to one of Flexible Response, i.e., an increase in conventional forces, with the ability to fight wars below the nuclear threshold. Simultaneously, the new administration continued Eisenhower's emphasis on development of America's strategic nuclear arsenal.

Thereafter, preoccupation with the Vietnam War led to a virtual hiatus in United States strategic development until the arrival of the Nixon administration in 1969. Nixon's program continued to provide forces for the defense of Europe but eliminated American ground forces from future Asian involvements, relying instead on indigenous forces which would be supported by United States naval and air forces.

Late in the Nixon administration, and certainly by the Ford administration, Vietnam had receded sufficiently to permit rebuilding and reorienting the American military establishment so as to give it a more worldwide focus. Simultaneously, the secretary of defense, James Schlesinger, worked on developing a more flexible nuclear strategy and increasing the capability to meet a limited nuclear provocation.

With this perspective of the organizational and strategic framework within which the role of the secretary of defense evolved, I would like to turn to the structure of this book. Each chapter (with one exception) is devoted to an analysis of the tenure of one secretary whose course in office distinctively affected the evolution of the institution of secretary of defense. The chapters

begin with a brief overview of the domestic and international contexts that circumscribed the secretary under consideration. Although the period covered is only thirty years, the domestic and
international contexts changed rapidly during those years. Next
comes a discussion of pertinent organizational factors and of the
perceived roles and relationships of the national security leadership,
including the president, the secretary of defense, and the secretary
of state. The assumption here is that the bureaucratic world in
which the secretary of defense functions has at least as much bearing
on the manner in which he performs as does the domestic and
external environment. With this stage thus set, an important case is
examined in terms of its origins, opposing views of the leadership,
the role of the secretary of defense, and the outcome. Chapters
conclude with observations of the role of the secretary concerned.

Some explanation seems in order at this point about the defense
secretaries selected for inclusion, and the case selected for each. No
study of this institution could omit the first secretary of defense,
James Forrestal. As secretary of the navy, and victor in the battle to
curtail the proposed defense secretary's power, he then inherited
the new job himself. Clearly his central problem was the continued
power of the individual services and the ongoing interservice competition, especially between the navy and the air force. His experience gave impetus to the 1949 organizational changes.

The three brief secretarial terms of Louis Johnson, George Marshall, and Robert Lovett that followed Forrestal are not included.
Their impact on the institution of the secretary of defense was,
relatively speaking, negligible.

The role of the secretary of defense during the Eisenhower
period was unique. Eisenhower was, in effect, his own defense
secretary. While his two functionalist secretaries, Charles Wilson
and Neil McElroy, had titular responsibility for managing the Pentagon and keeping the lid on the defense budget, neither man had a
sophisticated understanding of strategic policy—which is one reason
Eisenhower chose them for the office. On strategic policy matters,
Eisenhower dealt directly with the chairman of the Joint Chiefs of
Staff. Holding down the defense budget, however, was central to
Eisenhower's conservative fiscal notions. His determination to do so
was based on the belief that a balanced budget was vital to United
States economic strength and security, and here Wilson and McEl-

roy did play significant roles. The tenure of these two men covered
seven of the eight Eisenhower years. The last year of the
Eisenhower presidency, when Thomas Gates was secretary of defense, was different in one respect—Gates achieved a better working relationship with the Joint Chiefs than had his immediate predecessors. His secretaryship, however, was a short one and is not
treated here.

Of all the secretaries to date, Robert McNamara has had the
greatest impact on the Pentagon. For the first time, true civilian
control—some would say overcontrol—of the Pentagon was
achieved below the presidential level. The hallmark of the McNamara style was an analytical mode of thought, introduced first into the
Defense Department and later adopted by all the military services.
Primary devices of this mode of operation were the Planning Programming Budgeting System and a novel independent systems
analysis role at the assistant secretary of defense level.

I have selected Vietnam as the case for the McNamara period,
rather than some hardware issue that might better illustrate his
analytical apparatus, because Vietnam was the principal case in
which McNamara's decisions were central. Relatively speaking,
there is little importance to some piece of McNamara-approved
equipment as compared with the $150 billion spent on Vietnam, or
the almost 50,000 American troops killed there. This is not to say his
incumbency must be judged solely on his Vietnam-related decisions. Indeed, there is good evidence he became disenchanted with
the war before most other senior decision-makers. Nevertheless, the
importance of this case and the wealth of material now available
make it the most logical to examine.

It would be interesting to look at Clark Clifford's part in modify-
ing the Johnson administration's Vietnam policy in 1968, but his
period in office was so relatively short that inclusion is not war-
ranted.

Clifford's successor, Melvin Laird, served as secretary during
the entire first Nixon administration and played the central role in
the Vietnamization program. Evidence seems to indicate that Laird,
rather than the White House, set the pace for this program. He had
other major problems—the all-volunteer force, for example—but
Vietnamization is the major case by which his Pentagon days should

be judged. His successor, Elliot Richardson, served less than six months and exerted little influence on the department.

James Schlesinger, the final secretary to be considered, is the first post-Vietnam holder of that job. As such, his main efforts were directed toward reversing the drop of real dollars appropriated for defense—a decline in appropriations caused in large part by the public disillusionment with defense matters that had begun in the late stages of the Vietnam War. Schlesinger based his argument ultimately on two cornerstones: the threat posed by the Soviets' increasing capabilities, and the need to develop a strategy to counter that threat. It is his strategy—i.e., improved United States nuclear capability to give more options for employment of nuclear weapons, together with increased conventional capability to raise the threshold of nuclear warfare—that we most associate with his name. Neither of these strategic ideas was novel, but his forceful and fairly successful public presentation of them and the subsequent increase in defense budgets constitute his major legacy.

1

The Embattled
James Forrestal

On September 17, 1947, James Vincent Forrestal was sworn in as the first secretary of defense. He held that position until March 1949. Those were turbulent years for an America still emerging from World War II. On the international scene the cold war, which, by whatever title, had entered the consciousness of many United States officials in the final months of the European conflict was intensifying. At home the effort to reconvert the economy from war to peace continued as the central issue. To place the period of Forrestal's tenure as defense secretary in perspective, we should first recall the most significant events following the end of the war up until the new office was established.

The most dramatic event, which set the stage for much of what followed, was the demobilization of the American armed forces. When the war ended, those forces numbered over 12 million, more than half of whom were deployed outside of the United States. Planning for the release of military personnel had gotten under way about a year before the war ended. It was based upon the assumption that the demobilization would be orderly and gradual and would eventually result in a total force of 2.5 million. The assumption took into account both the difficulties of redeploying such vast numbers of people and the need for the United States to retain a credible strategic posture during the demobilization period. Of equal importance was the perceived necessity for the economy to absorb the influx of veterans in terms of jobs, housing, and other necessities.

The assumption that the demobilization would be orderly and

gradual proved highly unrealistic in the political atmosphere that developed. Neither the service personnel nor their families were persuaded by the strategic argument that the United States needed to retain a credible military force. The war was over and the veterans wanted to return to civilian pursuits. As for the physical problems of redeployment, the services did a magnificent job. For example, the three million military in the European theater in June were reduced to only one million by November 1, 1945.

Even these efforts were not sufficient to halt the pressure to "bring the boys home." In addition to the torrent of mail received in Washington from parents and service personnel, the world was treated to protests by United States forces in Europe and the Pacific. What was happening was not demobilization, but, as Truman himself termed it, disintegration. By the end of June 1947, when the demobilization officially ended, the 12 million force at the war's end was down to 1.5 million, of whom about half were on occupation duties in Europe and Asia.

During these demobilization years of 1945–1947, all officials, from the president down, faced tremendous domestic difficulties engendered by the struggle over who would get what from the postwar economy. After a war economy in which everyone had benefited, business, labor, and agriculture were now faced with the uncomfortable need to curb their requirements, a dilemma that each group attempted to avoid. Labor wanted increased wages to substitute for wartime overtime. Agriculture wanted higher subsidies and business wanted higher profits and an end to price controls. Whatever the merits of the policies that the president followed, the result was an inflation that by 1947 had sent prices up a third over what they had been at the end of the war.

In the course of this inflation there occurred a large number of labor strikes, and in time the public and the Republican-controlled Congress were in the mood for some kind of labor control bill. The result was the Taft-Hartley Act of 1947, which Truman to safeguard his own political future played no part in developing. In fact, he vetoed the bill, with the veto being overridden by Congress. Truman's veto message was in effect the beginning of his 1948 campaign, as Taft-Hartley gave him his big domestic issue against the Republicans.

In certain areas there was presidential agreement with conservative elements in Congress. Of major interest here was the president's commitment to a balanced budget, which meant cuts in defense spending and a tightly controlled defense budget. This commitment was to have profound implications for Forrestal's tenure as defense secretary.

There is one other domestic matter that should be highlighted—Universal Military Training. Late in the war period, military planners perceived the need for a large reserve during peacetime that would be available for mobilization in event of another war. President Truman raised the issue at a press conference in June 1945, and in the same month the House Postwar Military Policy Committee began hearings on universal military training.

Truman presented his plan to a joint session of Congress on October 23, 1945. In essence the plan called for each male citizen to receive one year of training, beginning at age eighteen. After completion of the year of training, the trainee would revert to a reserve status for six years and thereafter to a secondary reserve status.

The notion was never a popular one with Congress, and no positive action was taken as a result of Truman's message. In his State of the Union message of January 1946, he reminded Congress of the need for action on universal training.[1]

Subsequently, in December 1946, Truman appointed an advisory commission to study the problem. Predictably the commission, when it reported to the president the following May, recommended establishment of a universal military training program. With the price tag estimated at $2 billion annually, the Republican-controlled Congress was not receptive to the idea and it was never enacted, although it remained an issue as late as 1949.

The international environment of 1945–1947 from the American perspective has been the subject of an enormous body of literature. Interpretations of what happened cover a wide spectrum, from traditionalist to revisionist.[2] There is no need to enter the lists here. My purpose is merely to highlight the international environment in the two years preceding Forrestal's assumption of the office of secretary of defense.

When the European war ended in May 1945, the Soviets had achieved de facto control of Eastern Europe and had no intention of relinquishing it. It was, among other things, a buffer zone between the Soviet Union and Germany. Included in this empire was eastern Germany. The territorial and political realities of a divided Germany and a Soviet-controlled Eastern Europe set the stage for much of what happened in subsequent years.

Another reality, although a temporary one, which influenced events, although not decisively, was the United States monopoly of the atomic weapon. There was considerable talk of international control of atomic weapons through the medium of the United Nations, but it became evident in time that neither the United States nor the USSR really wanted that. The Russians for reasons of their own could never agree to the verification conditions the Americans required, which would have put observers inside the USSR. The monopoly was difficult to use as leverage in political bargaining with the Soviets. In those years, however, it was the only real military deterrent the United States had, in view of the demobilization.

In the fall of 1945, there was still ambivalence among American officials and the public as to how to handle the former ally who now seemed a threat to a prostrate Western Europe. Was the USSR bent on a program of unlimited expansion or did it share with the United States sufficient international interests to make cooperation possible?

By the beginning of 1946 the ambivalence was rapidly disappearing, and in January a startled secretary of state, James Byrnes, was treated to a presidential outburst for having made too many concessions to the Soviets and not getting enough from them at a December meeting of the Council of Foreign Ministers.[3] Truman was in fact hardening toward what he perceived to be expansionist tendencies on the part of the Soviets in Iran and elsewhere. He was also aware of the increasingly tough approach of leading Republicans, such as the influential Senator Arthur Vandenberg. He was in addition aware that the American public was becoming increasingly apprehensive about Soviet aims, and 1946 was an election year.

A series of events took place in February and March 1946 that mark this period as a definite turning point toward a tougher United States policy toward the Soviet Union. On February 9, 1946, Stalin made a public speech in which he established the goal of three five-year plans directed toward economic development. In the course of the speech he stressed the conflict between the com-

munist and capitalistic systems and implied that until the former
supplanted the latter, conflict was inevitable. Whatever the motives
of the speech—and it probably was directed internally—
Washington interpreted them as warlike.

In that same month, there was received in Washington the famous long cable from George Kennan, at the moment chargé d'af-
faires in Moscow. His analysis of the situation vis-à-vis the Soviet
was sobering. The opposition of Russia's leaders to capitalism, he
hypothesized, was necessary for internal reasons, as a means of
justifying their autocratic rule. Washington, suggested Kennan, had
to resist Soviet attempts to expand their influence and hope that
internal changes in the Soviet Union would eventually come about
that would shift the direction of Soviet foreign policy. The message
was widely read in Washington.

In that same month of February, Senator Vandenberg was on
the floor of the Senate attacking the Truman foreign policy as being
too conciliatory toward the Russians. Truman had, however, already
decided on a new approach, which was articulated the day after the
Vandenberg attack by Secretary Byrnes, speaking in New York.
Byrnes's speech was a strong one and the first open pronouncement
by the administration of a tougher policy toward Moscow.

Within a week, on March 5, Churchill made his famous Iron
Curtain speech in Fulton, Missouri. The speech delineated a bleak
international situation and called for a stronger position toward Russia. During March also, the Iranian question was settled. In the war
years the Soviets had moved troops into Iran to protect the oil fields
from the Axis powers, with the understanding that they would vacate
the country six months after the end of hostilities. The deadline
passed in early March without any Soviet withdrawal. With United
States support, the Iranians submitted the issue to the Security
Council. In the end, the Soviets backed down and agreed to remove
their troops by May. All in all, it was an interesting period in the
development of the cold war, and one that set the stage for an even
more dramatic series of happenings one year later.

There were a number of intervening events of significance, but
for our purposes we can omit most of them. A few, however, should
be mentioned. In August 1946 the United States resisted Soviet
efforts to revise the Montreux Convention so as to allow for joint
Turkish-Soviet defense of the Dardanelles. This was a major Soviet

thrust toward the Mediterranean. Second, in a speech at Stuttgart on September 6, 1946, Secretary Byrnes in effect ended the occupation of West Germany and began the process of its development as a sovereign state, while still adhering to the principle of German unification. Third, on the domestic scene the Republicans won control of both Houses in the 1946 congressional elections. Of interest, many of the winners had campaigned on a 20 percent tax cut—a threat to Truman's budget, including his foreign policy programs.

In February 1947 there occurred an event that set in motion United States reactions that in retrospect marked the beginning of the cold war, if indeed it was not already under way. On the twenty-first of that month, the British government officially informed the State Department that because of internal economic problems, it would have to end economic aid to Greece and Turkey. The Turks, under pressure from the Soviets, did not have an economy that could sustain armed forces of requisite size. The Greeks, for their part, were in the midst of a civil war between communists and monarchists.

Truman, with advance support from Vandenberg and others, was to go before Congress on March 12, 1947, and ask for economic and military aid for the two countries. This was a new and untried approach, since neither Greece nor Turkey had been depicted before as important to the United States' national interest. The speech had ideological overtures that went beyond the two countries in question and later became known as the Truman Doctrine. It was not without its opponents, but the specific aid request received overwhelming congressional support.

Meanwhile, Western Europe was in an economic crisis of serious proportions. The problem was given intense consideration by an able group of State Department planners, with George Marshall, who in January 1947 had replaced Byrnes, also supplying his own ideas. The outcome was the Marshall Plan, first publicly articulated by the secretary at the Harvard commencement on June 5, 1947. Of basic importance, it would be a European undertaking and would treat Europe as an entity with America supplying the economic help that Europe could not provide itself. As articulated, the concept did not exclude Eastern Europe or the Soviet Union, but when the Soviets, headed by Molotov, attended the opening sessions in Paris, they opted against participation—which meant that no other East-

ern Europeans joined—although Poland and Czechoslovakia tried.
Subsequently, the Western Europeans came forth with their plan
and the European Recovery Act was signed by the president on
April 3, 1948.

There remains one more event to recall, the now famous article
by "X" that appeared in *Foreign Affairs* in July 1947, entitled, "The
Sources of Soviet Conduct." "X" was George Kennan, the author of
the long cable of early 1946. It was evident that the article represented a statement of American policy toward the Soviet Union. In
this public articulation, an important word was added to the American political vocabulary—*containment*. The thoughtful observer,
Kennan argued, had no cause to complain about the Kremlin threat
"which, by providing the American people with this implacable
challenge, has made their entire security as a nation dependent on
their pulling themselves together and accepting the responsibilities
of moral and political leadership that history plainly intended them
to bear." The cold war now had its theoretical as well as its operational justification. These then were the circumstances, domestic
and international, when James Forrestal was named as the first
secretary of defense during the summer of 1947.

Prior to World War II, the president had three cabinet officers
concerned with national security affairs who reported directly to
him: secretaries of state, war, and the navy. During the war, there
was created in addition a nonstatutory Joint Chiefs of Staff (JCS),
consisting of the military chiefs of the army, navy, and the
semiautonomous air force.[4] Subsequently, Roosevelt appointed
Admiral William D. Leahy as chief of staff to the commander-in-
chief, and Leahy joined the JCS. Leahy signed papers on behalf of
the group, but he had no more authority than the others. Roosevelt
dealt directly with the chiefs on major matters—Leahy on a daily
basis and the others when required. It is interesting to note that the
secretaries of war and the navy were bypassed by this process.

When the war ended in 1945, the wartime organization for managing defense was no longer appropriate, and for a variety of reasons
the prewar arrangements also had to be changed. First, it was evident that the United States had a new and vastly more important
role to play in world affairs than it did before the war. This required
a united foreign policy. It was an area in which a busy president
would require coordinated help and, in fact, a full-time deputy in

national security matters, such as he already had in the person of the secretary of state for foreign policy matters.

The military forces themselves would also be larger and require greater coordination than the simple army-navy division at the shoreline that had come about in the prewar period. Warfare in the future was obviously going to be an integrated affair, involving unified efforts by sea, land, and air forces. The concept of forces being prepared to fight rather than merely serving as a cadre for mobilization was new and necessary. This concept required peacetime forces on a scale never before maintained by the United States.

The new world role would in time mean allies, if the United States was not going to bear all the costs—which it could not do in any case. Also, alliances require coordinated positions and a unified voice. Allies are not interested in army positions or navy positions, but rather the government position or policy.

Finally, there was the need for economy, including the avoidance of duplication among the services. There was no question that the technological revolution had introduced the potential for a host of competing weapons systems, especially in the case of aircraft and missiles. Everything each service wanted could not be produced. Some official, below the presidential level, had to determine priorities and make selections among competing service claimants.

The first proposal for postwar unification was made by army Chief of Staff Marshall in the fall of 1943.[5] The proposal, while differing in some details from later army proposals, remained consistent—a single department with ground, naval, and air components, with a civilian secretary and a single military chief of staff. The proposal as such got nowhere but did result by the following spring in the establishment of a special committee to study the question that was headed by retired Admiral James O. Richardson.

Meanwhile, the House of Representatives had established a Select Committee on Post-War Military Policy headed by Congressman Clifton A. Woodrum, on which twenty-three members of the House served. The army plan was presented to the committee by army Lieutenant General Joseph T. McNarney. In content it was similar to the Marshall concept. Soon thereafter the navy witnesses, led by Under Secretary James V. Forrestal, began to appear. It became quite clear that the navy wanted no strong single secretary to head up the defense effort, although their approach at this point was one of raising questions rather than outright opposition. When the committee submitted its report that spring of 1944, it merely deferred the issue until after the war.

The JCS-sponsored Richardson committee, however, was busy at work throughout the summer and into the following winter gathering the opinions of high military officers in Washington and throughout the world. Their report in the spring of 1945 (with Richardson dissenting) favored a single department of the armed forces with army, navy, and air force components. The Joint Chiefs could not agree on this, there being the usual split that found the army and air force in favor of a single department and the navy opposed.

In June 1945 James Forrestal, by now having replaced Frank Knox as secretary of the navy, set his own study in motion. This was one that was to have an important effect on the unification outcome. Forrestal had become convinced that it was not enough simply to object to the army's proposal for a single department but that the navy needed to set forth a proposal of its own. He commissioned an old friend, Ferdinand Eberstadt, to head the study group. The report, which was completed in September 1945, included the following recommendations: add a Department of Air and continue the Departments of War and Navy; continue the Joint Chiefs of Staff by statute; establish a National Security Resources Board (NSRB) whose concern would be industrial mobilization; establish a Central Intelligence Agency (CIA); establish a group to coordinate overall policies on foreign and military affairs called the National Security Council (NSC), with the president as chairman, and the secretaries of state, war, navy, and air, and the chairman of the NSRB as members and with the JCS in attendance.

The following month the Senate Military Affairs Committee began hearings on unification. During the course of the hearings, army Lieutenant General J. Lawton Collins presented the War Department's plan, which became known as the Collins plan.[6] It was, in effect, the earlier army plan of having a secretary and a chief of staff of the armed forces, with army, navy, and air each having its own chief of staff, but no secretary. Forrestal was the first navy witness and in general he favored the Eberstadt report. He and the navy witnesses who followed him offered many arguments against the Collins plan. It was quite evident that the navy was not going along with any plan whereby it lost its cabinet-rank secretary with direct access to the president and the Congress.

Shortly after the close of the Senate hearings in December 1945, President Truman sent a message to Congress recommending establishment of a Department of National Defense with a cabinet-level secretary and an overall military chief of staff. The land, naval, and air forces would each be headed by an assistant secretary and a military chief. Reception of the message by Congress was mixed and depended upon which side of the army-navy cleavage one stood on.

It was quite clear that the president and his navy secretary had different opinions on how unification would come about. We cannot examine here all the hearings or intraexecutive branch and congressional-executive branch bargaining that went on over the next eighteen months. In the summer of 1946, Truman did secure a major concession from Forrestal in getting his public agreement to a single secretary of common defense. Forrestal, however, remained convinced that there should not be a strong secretary of defense but rather a loose or federated arrangement, wth the services maintaining much of their autonomy. After two years of controversy, the National Security Act was passed on July 25, 1947.

These are the major provisions that the act provided for: 1) Separate army, navy, and air departments, each with its own secretary, who would have cabinet rank. These departments would be administered separately and would retain all powers not specifically conferred upon the secretary of defense. 2) A secretary of defense, who would head the National Military Establishment (NME).The secretary would establish general policies and programs and exercise general direction, authority, and control over the NME. He was to be the principal assistant to the president in all matters relating to national security. The secretary was to be provided with three special assistants and civilian personnel, as needed. 3) Statutory Joint Chiefs of Staff, who were also the chief military officers of their services, were to be principal military advisers to the president and the secretary of defense. The JCS were to be assisted by a Joint staff of not more than 100 officers. 4) Within the NME, a Munitions Board would be responsible for certain supply functions, and a Research and Development Board would be responsible for certain research and development functions. 5) Within the NME would be a War Council, chaired by the secretary of defense and composed of

the service secretaries and the military chiefs of each service. 6) A
National Security Resources Board would be created, with a chairman responsible for developing industrial and civilian mobilization
plans, the chairman reporting to the president. 7) A Central Intelligence Agency would be created, with a director who would be
responsible to the National Security Council. 8) A National Security
Council, presided over by the president and composed of the secretaries of state, defense, army, navy, and air, the chairman of the
National Security Resources Board, and others designated by the
president, would advise the president with respect to the integration of domestic, foreign, and military policies relating to national
security. Provision would also be made for an executive secretary
and a small supporting staff.

On July 26, on board his plane, the "Sacred Cow," at
Washington National Airport, President Truman signed the act, as
well as the nomination of James Forrestal to be secretary of defense.
His first choice had been the secretary of war, Robert P. Patterson,
but Patterson wanted to leave the federal service for financial reasons.

James Forrestal, first secretary of defense, was an enigmatic,
courageous, and tragic figure. He eventually paid the highest price,
his life, in establishing the new department and in achieving the
first steps toward unification of the armed forces.

Forrestal was born in the Hudson River town of Matteawan,
New York, in 1892. His father had emigrated from Ireland as a
young boy and as an adult developed his own construction business.
He was also active in the Democratic party and as a result served for
four years as the Matteawan postmaster. Forrestal's mother was a
staunch Catholic and insisted that her sons be equally devout. For a
few years after high school, young Forrestal worked in the newspaper business, but he was ambitious and soon decided he wanted a
college education.

He went first to Dartmouth for a year, and then to Princeton,
ending up in the class of 1915. Sometime in those years he became
estranged from his religion and family. At Princeton he was editor of
the *Daily Princetonian* and developed an identification with the
university that was both intense in feeling and active up to the time
of his death.

After graduation Forrestal held two or three jobs before joining the New York investment firm of Dillon, Read and Company. Beginning as a bond salesman, his rise in the firm was spectacular: in less than three years he was head of sales; in seven, a partner; in ten, a vice president; and in 1938, at age forty-six, he became the firm's president.[7] Such a rise does not happen without driving ambition and willingness to work, and those who speak of Forrestal during those years, or later during his government service, always mention those characteristics.[8]

In 1940 President Roosevelt was looking for an assistant with a background in finance and banking. Not a New Dealer, Forrestal was nonetheless a registered Democrat and was favorably known to Harry Hopkins, one of Roosevelt's key advisers. Forrestal was offered and accepted the $10,000 a year job in June 1940, but he soon felt it was not sufficiently challenging. About that time a new post, under secretary of the navy, was created and Forrestal made clear his interest in the position, to which he was soon nominated by the president. He held the post until 1944 and on the death of Frank Knox became the secretary of the navy.

As under secretary, Forrestal became the business manager of the navy; in a vastly expanding navy, this meant procurement and deep involvement in contract problems. It also meant some conflict with traditional navy procedures, which were designed for a less turbulent time. There were conflicts of authority with the chief of naval operations, Admiral Ernest J. King, and Forrestal managed to prevail. Other conflicts arose between the two; and when Forrestal became navy secretary, he never was able to form the close relationship with King that Marshall and Stimson had developed in the War Department.

The picture one gets of Forrestal in the days of his government service, during and after the war, is of a tight-lipped, tough, pipe-smoking, skilled bureaucrat. He emerges as highly competent and hard-working—a master of the concepts as well as the details associated with his tasks. In appearance he was a taut figure, with a flattened nose that gave the impression of a boxer—in which sport (as a recreation) the nose was in fact flattened.

What was quite interesting about Forrestal, for our purposes, was his world view when he became secretary of defense. He was one of the original cold warriors of the Roosevelt cabinet, and indeed of the Truman cabinet as well. Convinced that the Soviets would exploit any perceived weakness on the part of the United States, Forrest was a firm believer that the strongest possible military force was the only deterrent that would influence the Russians. The Soviet threat was central to his thinking and was to govern most of his major efforts as secretary of defense.

Any cabinet official is only as strong as the backing he receives from the president, and in the case of the Truman/Forrestal relationship, there developed some ambivalence as time went on over defense and other issues. It is important to recall that during the first fourteen months of Forrestal's defense tenure, the 1948 election was uppermost in Truman's mind. Truman was a strong president, who made his own decisions and could be adamant with those who wanted to change them. In their differences over the form that unification would take, Forrestal's view in a technical sense had prevailed. Forrestal, however, had done yeoman service in achieving that unification, and Truman was not unmindful of that.

A much larger issue between the two was Truman's views of the United States budget, of which the defense portion was a key element. Truman fixed firm budget ceilings, based on what he felt that the Republican-controlled Congress and the American public would bear. In the vote-gathering environment of the early postwar period, it was better to talk of cutting taxes than of raising the defense budget. Truman effectively employed the Bureau of the Budget, through the director, James E. Webb, to control budget development. Given Forrestal's world view, which caused him to perceive the need for greater defense expenditures, he and Webb naturally played adversary roles.

Another area of difference between Forrestal and Truman was the Palestine question. This was a matter of great sensitivity in American domestic politics. Shortly before the 1946 elections, Truman had pledged American support for the formation of a separate Jewish state. Obviously, the Arabs rejected this notion. Forrestal's personal position was to side with the Arabs for two reasons: he feared the loss of oil from an alienated Arab world, and he believed that a conflict between the Arabs and Jews might cause Soviet intervention. There is some evidence that by the time Israel was established in May 1948, Forrestal had changed his mind or at least was less outspoken about his views. His position, however, caused him to be subjected to many attacks in the press and elsewhere, and in this respect he was obviously not an asset to an underdog presidential candidate.

Another point of difference worth noting concerned the National Security Council and especially its executive secretary. As Forrestal saw it, this official should oversee cabinet departments by assuming responsibility for ensuring implementation of decisions reached in the NSC—not a popular view, one can assume, with most cabinet officers and certainly not with President Truman.[9] Forrestal also had the notion of the NSC functioning as a kind of "super-cabinet" along British lines. Truman himself was cautious with the NSC, especially before the outbreak of the Korean War, guarding his own prerogative as the decision-maker. He also made it clear from the outset that the NSC staff was his staff.

In terms of political philosophy, there could not help but be a considerable difference between Truman and his defense secretary. Forrestal, though a Democrat and perhaps liberal as compared with most of his Wall Street friends, was nonetheless a good deal more conservative on most domestic issues than the president, who was campaigning hard on a Fair Deal program. But there was also a substantial degree of respect between the president and his secretary. Forrestal saw Truman on business matters about once a week during most of his tenure, and although he was not one of Truman's inner circle, he occasionally played poker with his chief.[10]

Forrestal's cabinet colleague, General of the Army George C. Marshall, secretary of state, was in his own right a national hero. Chief of staff of the army during World War II, he had been the most influential American military man in the prosecution of that war in his role as a member of the wartime Joint Chiefs of Staff. This was followed by a frustrating tour as the president's personal ambassador to China during which he attempted unsuccessfully to mediate between the Nationalist and Communist forces. Then, in January 1947, he replaced James Byrnes as secretary of state.

Quite obviously, Marshall would have enormous influence with the president because of his great prestige and his previous service. One would think offhand that Forrestal would have found a powerful ally in a secretary of state who had spent most of his adult life as a military officer. It did not work that way, however, for a couple of reasons, though their relationship was not personally adversarial. First, Marshall leaned over backward as secretary of state to avoid the impression of being a military enthusiast. Second, and more important, was Marshall's chief preoccupation (which in effect was competing with Defense Department programs for the budget dollar) with the European Recovery Program, or the Marshall Plan.

Secretary Forrestal's bureaucratic problems arose more from the organization he headed than from the president or the secretary of state or other government agencies. When he became secretary of defense in September 1947, he took over responsibility for two existing departments and one new one. There are two important matters to emphasize at this point. First, the Departments of Army, Navy, and Air Force were during Forrestal's tenure headed by cabinet-level officials who were regular members of the National Security Council and the cabinet, the same as Forrestal. Second, Forrestal had little to say about the appointment of these secretaries or the military chiefs of the services.[11]

Today none but specialists in the field would be expected to know the names of the service secretaries. In those days, however, they were fairly familiar to the public and, as cabinet-level officials, potentially powerful on the Washington scene. Kenneth C. Royall had been under secretary of war for almost two years and secretary for a couple of months before he was sworn in as the first secretary of the army. Royall's relationship with Forrestal developed in a most constructive way from the secretary of defense's point of view.

John L. Sullivan, the secretary of the navy, had been Forrestal's under secretary until the latter became secretary of defense, and Forrestal had a reasonably close relationship with him. Forrestal's main adversary was the first secretary of the air force, who had formerly been assistant secretary of war for air, W. Stuart Symington. Symington proved a serious problem for Forrestal in the White House and with the Congress. In some ways he was closer to Truman than Forrestal by working through Truman's "palace guard."[12] The adversarial relationship between Forrestal and Symington became the major point of focus in attempts by Forrestal to assert the authority of the new office.

The six military chiefs who served under Forrestal were well-known figures as a result of their exploits in World War II. When they spoke publicly, people listened, and they were a bureaucratic force to be reckoned with in a way that would be unimaginable today. The army chiefs were General of the Army Dwight D.

Eisenhower, who had been Supreme Allied Commander in the European War, followed by his former subordinate and army group commander in Europe, General Omar N. Bradley. The navy and air force chiefs were not quite as well known but they bore important names: Fleet Admiral Chester W. Nimitz, followed by Admiral Louis E. Denfield, and General Carl Spaatz, succeeded by General Hoyt S. Vandenberg.

Forrestal's concerns went, of course, beyond the executive branch to the Congress. From his early days as navy under secretary, he considered congressional relations as one of his most important responsibilities and worked hard at them. As a result, he was acquainted with a large number of congressmen and enjoyed fairly good relations on the Hill during much of his Washington tour. These eroded to some extent in time, as the interservice competition that developed over the defense budget found its way to the congressional supporters of various competing programs. But overall they remained excellent, with the House Armed Services Committee honoring him the day after he left office.

In making this new and uncharted office with its vast responsibilities work, the new secretary was given little assistance. He had no deputy or under secretary, which, given Forrestal's work ethic, meant essentially no vacations during the eighteen months he held that office. He was authorized to have three special assistants and he developed a small professional staff composed of civilians. Two of his special assistants, Wilfred J. McNeil and Marx Leva, came with him from the Navy Department, while the third, John H. Ohly, came from the War Department.

McNeil, who was an admiral in the reserves, was Forrestal's comptroller and remained in that position until 1959, becoming quite a well-known and powerful Pentagon official before he returned to a successful civilian career. Leva, a Harvard Law School graduate, handled legal and legislative matters for the secretary, while Ohly, also a graduate of Harvard Law School, handled matters not covered by the other two special assistants. These included studies on various strategic and international questions and coordination with such agencies as the National Security Council and the National Security Resources Board. Forrestal's staff was extremely loyal to him but, considering the magnitude of his task, also extremely small.

In the month before Forrestal took the oath of office as the first secretary of defense, there occurred two public events that foreshadowed the basic contradiction between President Truman's perception of budgetary constraints on defense expenditures and Forrestal's world view, with its perception of the need for strong military forces. This contradiction was never resolved during Forrestal's tenure and was to cause most of the problems he struggled with during the eighteen months he held the office.[13]

On August 20, 1947, Truman held a news conference at which the gist of his preliminary remarks was that he, not Congress, was responsible for the great reduction in budgetary outlays that had occurred since the big wartime budgets.[14] It was quite clear that Truman perceived federal budget reduction as a major issue in the presidential election then only a little over a year away.

About a week later, James Forrestal addressed the American Legion in convention at New York's Madison Square Garden. To carry out American international policy, which included world stability, Forrestal said, United States military power must "be kept vigorous, modern, and capable of swift mobilization."[15] Obviously the American forces, now barely recovering from the demobilization, were not going to achieve such goals with reduced defense budgets.

The management problems that this budget versus world view dichotomy were to bring Forrestal lay, of course, in the future, and his initial ideas on his management role could not take them fully into account. The role he depicted for himself in his first press conference sounded modest indeed. A newspaper account of the conference quoted Forrestal as saying, "The Departments of the Army, Navy, and Air Force would remain as autonomous as possible." The day before he took office, Forrestal wrote to the three service department heads, "It will be the usual practice of the Secretary of Defense to consult the War Council before taking action on matters of major importance."[16]

The first major project with which Forrestal became involved was seeing the fiscal year 1949 budget through its final stages. This did not represent a true departmental budget (it was too late in the budget cycle for that) but was rather an amalgamation of three separate budgets. The secretary did attempt to gain as much control as possible, although there are few references to the 1949 budget in his diaries that fall. There is, however, recorded a meeting with his assistant McNeil and with Major General Alfred W. Gruenther, director of the Joint staff (the staff of the Joint Chiefs of Staff). Gruenther reported some unhappiness on the part of the army and air force over the navy's share of the budget, which they considered disproportionate to the navy's tasks.[17]

There was also a memorandum that fall from Forrestal to the service secretaries, advising that no recommendations or reports concerning legislation would be forwarded to the Bureau of the Budget or Congress unless they had been coordinated among the three departments. Failing such coordination, the secretaries were to send the documents to the secretary of defense for resolution.[18] A small start at unification, but a beginning. Not relying entirely on directives, Forrestal started that fall the practice of bringing together every three or four months the high-ranking military and civilian officials of the National Military Establishment and related agencies for a buffet supper and "team talk."

During the course of the fall, the president appointed an Air Policy Commission (frequently called the Finletter Commission after its chairman, Thomas K. Finletter) to look into national aviation policy. The report, which was published on January 1, 1948, became a source of support for the air force in its ensuing budget battles, but its weak analytical structure reduced it to more of a propaganda document than a tightly reasoned piece of work. It was, however, a useful instrument for the air force in supporting its case.

Since the commission had looked primarily into air power, its recommendations were slanted in that direction, with only lip service paid to the army and navy. Its conclusions were quite straightforward: "In our opinion this Military Establishment must be built around the air arm. Of course an adequate Navy and Ground Force must be maintained. But it is the Air Force and naval aviation on which we must rely. Our military security must be based on air power." Later, when dealing with specifics, it said: "We have concluded that the minimum force necessary at the present time is an Air Force . . . organized into 70 combat groups."[19]

The implication of the seventy-group program was that the overall forces—army, navy, air—would be unbalanced. Since there were tight budgetary limitations, an air program of this magnitude would reduce navy and especially army forces to a subsidiary role. If the forces were to be kept in balance, either the air force program would have to be reduced or a considerable increase would have to be secured in the overall budget. Since many threats might occur below the threshold of nuclear war, there was something to be said for Forrestal's strongly held views that the United States should provide balanced forces.

One of the most telling arguments on behalf of a balanced force was offered at a briefing by General Gruenther about a month after the Finletter Commission report was made public. The occasion was a formal review of the strategic situation before the president.[20] Gruenther's presentation concerned the available U.S. military strength, compared with actual and potential military commitments by the United States. Except for the occupation troops in Germany and Japan, which were not organized, trained, or equipped for combat, the United States could count on less than three divisions of army and marines for emergency employment. Gruenther pointed out the potentially explosive points around the world where such troops (and many more) might be required—Greece, Italy, Korea, and Palestine.

Neither the briefing nor the earlier Finletter report had any immediate effect on the fiscal year 1949 defense budget of $11 billion that the president had submitted in January. Events were soon to occur, however, that would call for an increase and result in interservice competition for a large share of that increase.

On February 24, 1948, less than a week after Gruenther's briefing, the communist coup in Czechoslovakia took place, ending what had been considered a model democratic state since its establishment at the end of World War I. The shock throughout the Western World was profound. The coup aroused a sense of alarm that was to continue throughout the spring and, combined with another event, bring on what became known as the March Crisis.

The other event was a message in early March from General Lucius D. Clay, the United States commander in Berlin, to army intelligence, which received wide distribution. He stated: "For many months, based on logical analysis, I have felt and held that war was unlikely for at least ten years. Within the last few weeks, I have felt a subtle change in Soviet attitude which I cannot define, but which now gives me a feeling that it may come with dramatic suddenness."[21]

In the sense of a growing crisis, which portended an upward revision of the budget, and with the service cleavages that the balanced-unbalanced force concepts exposed, Forrestal decided to get the Joint Chiefs together for an extraordinary session. He was by now conscious of his lack of power to compel cohesion and knew that changes would have to be made to increase the defense secretary's powers.[22] Such changes would, however, take a long time to achieve. In an attempt to solve the immediate problem, Forrestal called the military leaders together at the navy base at Key West, Florida, for a meeting that lasted from 11 to 14 March 1948. Its purpose was to get some agreement on roles and missions of the services. Forrestal let it be known in a press conference that the differences would be settled even if he had to impose a decision.[23]

The secretary reported to the president on Monday, March 15, on the results of the conference—not great results but some progress: strategic air power reserved to the air force; the navy not to be denied use of the A-bomb and to proceed with development of an 80,000-ton carrier; marines limited to four divisions; support for resumption of the draft to meet the army's immediate needs; and agreement that the president should seek a supplemental appropriation for the armed forces in view of the world situation.[24]

Forrestal found the president in the mood for some degree of rearmament. Truman indicated to Forrestal that he was going to deliver a message to Congress in two days supportive of selective service and Universal Military Training (which was still being talked about). He had already scheduled a Saint Patrick's Day address in New York in which he would further develop this theme.[25] The message to Congress turned out to be a forceful one in which the Soviet Union was identified as the nation blocking peace. The president had three major recommendations: enactment of the Marshall Plan, still being considered by Congress; adoption of Universal Military Training; and temporary reenactment of the draft.[26] But there was no specific program for rearmament. This did not come until a Forrestal presentation to the Senate Armed Services Committee on March 25. The course of resolving the size and distribution of the supplemental program is highly revealing in regard to the problem Forrestal faced with the services.

Early in March Forrestal had asked Robert Cutler, president of the Old Colony Trust Company of Boston, and a wartime army brigadier general as well as a Pentagon hand, to help develop the presentation of a supplemental to the fiscal year 1949 defense budget. In his initial meeting with Cutler, Forrestal spoke of the troubled world situation, his lack of real power as secretary of defense, and the need for balanced forces as contrasted with full reliance on air power alone. Finally, he indicated that the president was thinking of a $3 billion supplemental, whereas the services totaled it up at about three times that figure. To preserve any semblance of a balanced force was going to be a real fight.[27]

Forrestal's testimony before the Senate Armed Services Committee was presented on March 25.[28] After a depiction of the world situation, he went on to recommend an increase in military strength of about 350,000 personnel, of which over 70 percent would go to land forces. Forrestal also stressed the need for balanced forces to meet the commitments that had been outlined by Gruenther in his White House briefing the previous month.

During the course of Forrestal's presentation, several specific questions were put to him by the senators, with the answers to be provided later. Cutler's task at this point was to obtain from the three services the facts needed for Forrestal's response. The central problem in giving specific answers was that the president had authorized a supplemental request of no more than $3 billion, and Forrestal had supported that request. But to obtain the seventy groups that the air force was demanding would unbalance the forces if they were restricted to that level of funding overall.

When Cutler tried to write a draft reply to the Senate that addressed this problem, he ran into difficulties with the air force. Symington took the position that the Senate already had enough information, so why send any more?[29] Cutler insisted that there should be a reply and this led to a confrontation with Symington.

Forrestal did eventually sign the draft reply without air force concurrence, but first he had a long and revealing conversation with Cutler. "Shall I tell the President that Stu (Symington) is undercutting my authority and say that either Symington or I must go?" he asked Cutler. "Shall I put it up to Truman right now?"[30] In the end he did not, at least, not for the moment.

The struggle over the amount of the supplemental and its distribution continued. The problem was joined in many forums: executive-Congress; White House-Pentagon; and secretary-Joint

Chiefs. In all this, Symington maintained his position that seventy air groups were necessary. In a more guarded way, the other services also made it clear that they had requested more than was included in the Forrestal program.

That Forrestal felt Symington's statements that spring on the seventy groups, as well as the air secretary's lukewarm support for Universal Military Training and the draft, were disloyal seems fairly clear. It also, however, seems clear that he felt he would not have the president's backing if he asked for Symington's resignation.[31]

While the struggle went on in public, Forrestal attempted to work out the problem himself with the Joint Chiefs. The climax came in a meeting between Forrestal and the Joint Chiefs on April 19. They were able to come to an agreement on a $3.5 billion supplemental, about a half billion over the Truman ceiling. This would raise the air force from fifty-five to sixty-six groups and provide a slight increase in army strength.

At this point Truman, with strong support from James Webb and the Bureau of the Budget, advised Forrestal that the upper limit he, Truman, would authorize him to present to Congress was a supplemental of $3.1 billion, and, even so, that it was to be understood the services would not actually spend all the funds. In the end, Congress appropriated a total of $13.8 billion, including the supplemental.[32] The president elected not to spend all the funds, however, and the air force program ended up at fifty-nine groups.

On May 13 there was a meeting in the White House at which the president provided preliminary guidance for preparation of the fiscal year 1950 budget. Reading from a memorandum to the assembled group,[33] the president reviewed events leading up to the fiscal year 1949 supplemental and then went on to say that he did not want to "create a military structure which would require in excess of approximately $15 billion for the next fiscal year." "In September," he continued, "I want to have a review of the whole situation to see if administratively we should not place a ceiling on our program at less than we contemplated in this supplemental. . . . If any one present has any questions or misgivings concerning the program I have outlined, make your views known now—for once this program goes forward officially, it will be the administration program—and I expect every member of the Administration to support it fully, both in public and in private."[34]

During June and July, the cold war heated up, with the issue being access to West Berlin. At the end of March General Clay had been informed by a Russian official that a new system of entering or leaving the Russian Zone (which had to be crossed to gain land access to West Berlin) would be instituted the following day. The Soviets thus were asserting the right to judge who and what would be allowed into West Berlin. In a couple of days the Russians had relaxed the announced restrictions, but now in June they were started in earnest.

On June 18, 1948, the Western occupying powers began a program of currency reform that in effect would reconstitute the West Germany economy. That same day the Soviets retaliated by stopping all surface traffic in and out of the western sector of Berlin. This was a challenge at the most tenuous point for the West, as it was deep in the Soviet occupation zone. The United States and its allies announced that they intended to stay in Berlin and countered the Soviet move with a massive airlift. The first operational battle of the cold war was on. The president also authorized the placing of B-29s in the British Isles and augmenting those already in Germany.[35] The Berlin airlift was successful beyond expectations and in the end the Russians backed down. This occurred after Forrestal's tenure, however, and the blockade was in the background during the remainder of his tour as secretary of defense.

Meanwhile, after his experiences of the spring, Forrestal had the fiscal year 1950 defense budget very much on his mind and he provided some early guidance—in person in mid-June and by memorandum on July 19.[36] Further, in what he knew would be another climate of divergent service opinions, he was interested in getting some direct military advice outside of the JCS channel. An earlier attempt to have some senior military person detailed to his office was abandoned, and now he was asking the chiefs for their ideas on how he could secure this help. The outcome was the appointment of a board of three high-ranking "budget deputies," headed by General Joseph T. McNarney (air force) and reporting to the Joint Chiefs. The group began their deliberations in mid-August.[37]

About the time of the July memorandum, Forrestal was at it again with an old adversary, Air Force Secretary Symington.[38] The occasion was a speech by Symington before five hundred aviation engineers in Los Angeles on July 17. The speech Symington was originally planning to give had been subjected to many changes by Forrestal's staff, with the cleared version wired to Symington in Los Angeles. He did not like the altered version, however, and spoke "off the cuff," attacking "ax-grinders" who contended that large air appropriations might unbalance the three services. Air power, said Symington, should not be in balance with the army and navy but with the power of potential enemies—a fairly obvious attack on the secretary of defense's policies and programs.[39]

After reading of the speech the following day in the *New York Times*, Forrestal sent a message to Symington asking for an explanation and stating that the speech, if the account was accurate, was "an act of official disobedience and personal disloyalty." That same day Forrestal discussed the matter with the president and indicated that he might have to ask for Symington's resignation. Apparently either Symington offered a satisfactory explanation of the speech or Forrestal felt he did not have a strong enough hand with the president to force his resignation. In any case the diaries have an entry a few days later that reports a meeting between the president, Symington, and Forrestal, in which the latter indicated that the air secretary had reported "extenuating circumstances." That ended the matter, but it must have been clear to Forrestal that there was more to come unless the authority of his office was strengthened or there was a change in administrations.

By the summer of 1948 it was evident that there were deep differences between the air force and the navy concerning the control and use of the atomic bomb.[40] This issue had been addressed at the Key West conference but not actually settled, especially when translated into specific hardware items such as the flush-deck carrier to which the navy aspired in order to be able to launch aircraft capable of delivering atomic weapons. Such an expensive carrier system was bound to come in conflict with the ambitious air force seventy-group program—not over doctrine, although it was couched in those terms, but over budgetary resources.

In early August 1948, in an attempt to define the issues between the navy and the air force with respect to atomic delivery, Forrestal requested the former air force chief of staff, retired General Carl Spaatz, and retired Admiral John Towers to recommend decisions that should be made in light of the air force-navy differences on strategic warfare. They responded with a memorandum dated August 18.[41] Their response was not as far-ranging as Forrestal's questions, but there was agreement that the navy should be capable of delivering atomic weapons and that no sharp line could be drawn between strategies and tactical bombing. Disagreement centered on who should control the atomic weapons—the service employing them, as the navy felt, or the air force, as Spaatz felt.

With this paper in hand and the fiscal year 1950 budget development period at hand, Forrestal went to Newport to meet with the Joint Chiefs. The conference, which was held at the Naval War College from 20 to 22 August,[42] did not come to grips with issues as fundamental as those at Key West, but some progress was made. The key decisions included operational control of the atomic weapon to be given temporarily to the air force; each service in the field of its primary mission (in the case of strategic bombing, the air force) to have exclusive responsibility for planning and programming, though in the execution of any mission, the navy as well as air force would be used;[43] establishment of a Weapons System Evaluation Group, probably to be under the control of the Joint Chiefs (established the following October); a small military group to be added to the secretary of defense's office for closer contact with the services; a Western European Headquarters to be established beyond the Rhine.[44]

On July 16 James Webb in a memorandum to the secretary of defense had set forth the presidential ceiling of $14.4 billion and other matters of guidance, thus initiating action on the fiscal year 1950 defense budget.[45] The following day Forrestal requested two sets of data from the Joint Chiefs: the forces that in their judgment should be maintained during the fiscal year; and the forces that could be maintained in view of the ceiling of $14.4 billion. On August 16 Forrestal received the estimates of the first set of data, which totaled the staggering sum of $30 billion. The McNarney Board was then given the problem of reducing this figure.

The backdrop of events from this point until early November was the presidential election campaign, in which President Truman played the role of underdog to the Republican candidate, Thomas Dewey. The campaign was fought largely on domestic issues, since the perceived international tensions that had surrounded the March

Crisis had largely disappeared—not withstanding the Berlin Airlift, which continued. Thus the defense budget was not a campaign issue and Truman had every intention of holding firm on his ceiling.

By the third week in September, the McNarney Board met with Forrestal to obtain some guidance, which he provided. He wanted them to determine the military and security implications of living within the $14.4 billion budget and to ascertain the minimum additional budget "which would achieve an acceptable degree of risk to our security."[46]

On October 5 Forrestal discussed the budget ceiling with Truman, indicating that at the $14.4 billion level the Mediterranean could not be held. Forrestal felt that something in the order of $18.5 billion would be required if the Mediterranean were to be kept open. Always cagey on defense budget issues, Truman told Forrestal not to disclose the preparation of the increased budget but rather to hold it in reserve lest it be interpreted as a step toward preparation for war.[47] The commander-in-chief was deeply involved in the election campaign, which was soon to swing his way, and wanted no public discussion of increased defense expenditures.

The following day Forrestal informed the Joint Chiefs that he expected a definite recommendation from them on the allocation of funds within the $14.4 billion ceiling. He wanted this matter cleared up before they considered a higher ceiling.[48] On October 7 they replied that they were unable to agree on any program within the limit of $14.4 billion. In a memorandum to the chiefs, Forrestal, reacting to their nonresponsiveness, said, "The results of your work" in setting forth the forces that could be maintained within the ceiling "have been inadequate . . . it would appear that our efforts have degenerated into a competition for dollars. . . . You are hereby instructed to reconvene for the purpose of giving further consideration" to this problem.[49]

On October 10 Forrestal met with Secretary Marshall, who had just returned from Europe. The Joint Chiefs, as well as Generals McNarney and Gruenther, were in attendance. Marshall's central theme was the importance of furnishing military equipment to the Western European nations. Bradley, the army chief, wondered if it would not also be desirable to improve the U.S. force posture so as to give tangible proof that we would come to the assistance of the

Europeans if necessary. Marshall agreed, but the immediate problem, as he saw it, was to provide "intensive and immediate aid."
Gruenther came away from the session with the impression that
though Marshall might be sympathetic to the chief's budget problems, he was not going to come to their or Forrestal's support at that
time by providing any rationale for a budgetary increase.[50]

On October 15 Forrestal met again on the budget problem with
the Joint Chiefs. He took a new approach—and was at the peak of
his managerial skills on that day.[51] He noted that the McNarney
Board had worked the $30 billion figure down to $23.6 billion, a
figure he considered to be maximum. Now he wanted the Joint
Chiefs to agree on a division of the $14.4 billion and to come up with
an agreement on an "intermediate" program of around $17.5 or $18
billion. He wanted to be able to point out what could be achieved in
war-fighting ability at the two levels. By this approach, he hoped to
convince the president and Congress that the lower level simply
could not do the job. The intermediate level, although it would not
include everything that was wanted, would do a credible job. By
using this approach, he felt the JCS would gain in stature and avoid
being looked upon as a group that put service interest above national interest.

Although the public's attention that fall was largely taken up
with the presidential campaign, Forrestal himself focused on the
international situation. On October 21 he breakfasted with General
Clay, who was back on a trip from Germany to report on the Berlin
blockade and other matters. Forrestal suggested to Clay that he
speak bluntly to the president and point out, as he had to Forrestal,
that "any policy which contemplates withdrawal from Germany
means withdrawal from Europe and in the long run the beginning of
the third world war."[52]

On the positive side there was at this point considerable progress toward establishment of the North Atlantic Treaty Organization. This had been helped along by the Vandenberg Resolution of
the previous June, which in effect called for the commitment of U.S.
military strength to a regional alliance.[53] On the other side of the
world, the collapse of Nationalist China seemed more and more
unavoidable and there appeared to be nothing that could be done
about it by Washington.

With all these matters on his mind, Forrestal made another attempt to enlist the support of the secretary of state in his efforts to get presidential approval of a higher ceiling for the defense budget—this time by way of a formal letter. Forrestal put three questions to Marshall: 1) "Has there been an improvement in the international picture which would warrant a substantial reduction in the military force we had planned to have in being by the end of the current fiscal year?" (The $14.4 billion ceiling for fiscal year 1950 would require a considerable reduction in personnel that the services would have by June 30, 1949). 2) "Has the situation worsened since last spring and should we, therefore, be considering an augmentation of the forces we were planning at that time?" 3) "Is the situation about the same—that is, neither better nor worse?"[54]

Marshall's answer was evasive; in fact, he answered only the third question. Yes, Marshall said, the situation was about the same, and the important task was to rearm Western Europe. No help there for Forrestal from the senior soldier-statesman.

By early November Forrestal had his response from the Joint Chiefs on how to divide the $14.4 billion. The army and air force sided together and Forrestal ended up in between.

The major domestic political event of that fall was, of course, Harry Truman's upset victory over Thomas Dewey. Forrestal sent a telegram off immediately to his chief: "My congratulations on a gallant fight and a splendid victory."[55] The splendid victory placed Forrestal in a difficult personal position. A Dewey victory would have permitted him to make a graceful exit along with the remainder of the Truman cabinet, or perhaps even be retained for a time as the defense secretary who had avoided the political campaign. Now, however, the problem was different and Truman would have to weigh Forrestal's assets and liabilities. Also to be considered were the pressures of his chief campaign fund-raiser, Louis Arthur Johnson of West Virginia, who wanted to be secretary of defense.[56]

By mid-November the chiefs had accepted the division of funds as set by Forrestal within the ceiling of $14.4 billion (army 4.8 billion, navy 4.6 billion, an force 5 billion) and this budget was submitted to the president.[57] Subsequently, this figure was reduced to $14.2 billion by the Bureau of the Budget. This amount provided for a forty-eight-group air force, in contrast to the supplement the previous spring, which provided for a sixty-six group. Along with the budget under the president's ceiling, Forrestal forwarded an intermediate budget of $16.9 billion that provided for a fifty-nine-group air force. The course of this intermediate budget deserves attention at this point.

Forrestal set off on a whirlwind tour of Western Europe during the second week in November. Upon his return there was waiting a memorandum from his assistant McNeil regarding the intermediate budget and related matters. During Forrestal's absence, McNeil and James Webb, budget director, had some discussions on the intermediate budget. Webb felt that Forrestal had gone over his head by discussing this concept with Truman in a preliminary way, since this discussion would lead to a formal presentation of the intermediate budget at a later time. The department, Webb felt, was undermining the federal budget process. Continuing, the author of the memorandum had this to say: "I think it is of more than passing interest that many of the comments Webb made about you . . . had to have their origin in someone in the Military Establishment. I suspicioned that they had come from Mr. Symington, because they spent the previous evening together. My suspicions as to the source and basis of some of his comments were confirmed by a telephone call from Symington to Webb while I was there and which I couldn't help overhearing."[58]

With the assistance of the McNarney Board, the Joint Chiefs had agreed on the allocation of the intermediate budget among the services (army $5.575 billion, navy $5.375 billion, air force $5.950 billion) and Forrestal was ready to defend this figure to the president. The day for presenting the intermediate budget to Truman, for which Forrestal had been preparing for months, came on December 9, 1948. In attendance with Forrestal were the secretaries, the Joint Chiefs, McNeil, Gruenther, Webb, and Sidney Souers, executive secretary of the National Security Council.

Considering the long buildup for this meeting, it was rather brief, less than one hour. The president listened politely to all that the defense contingent had to say. In the end he said, "Thanks, boys, I used to be a judge in Kansas City and found a couple of bottles of bourbon. Let's have a drink."[59] That was the end of the intermediate budget. The economic arguments of Webb and the Council of Economic Advisers[60] won, and the ceiling stood. When

President Truman sent the budget to Congress on January 10, 1949, it was for $14.2 billion (exclusive of stockpiling).

If Forrestal was less than successful in securing the kind of defense budget he thought necessary, he was quite successful in securing reforms in the defense organization, although these did not come to fruition until he had been out of office some four months. Shortly after he became secretary of defense, the Hoover Commission on Organization of the Executive Branch of the Government was established.[61] Since the National Military Establishment was so new, it was decided that the commission would not include the defense organization in its inquiries. By the following May, however, enough controversy had been stirred up by the new organization for a task force headed by Ferdinand Eberstadt to be established by the commission to survey the National Military Establishment.

During October 1948 Forrestal appeared before the task force and gave his views, which he already had discussed with the president.[62] He believed that the secretary needed greater powers, which could be achieved in part by removing the word *general* from the description of his authorities. He also felt that there should be an under secretary and that the Joint Chiefs should have a chairman. He was uncertain whether the service secretaries should be downgraded.

The task force was understandably subjected to a variety of views, some controversial, such as a proposal to place naval aviation under the air force. The president himself in March 1949, the month after the Hoover Commission made its report, resurrected some of his earlier thinking by proposing a JCS chairman who would replace the Joint Chiefs as the principal military adviser to the president and the secretary. All this was still unsettled during Forrestal's final months in office.[63]

In early 1949, with his future tenure as secretary uncertain,[64] Forrestal was faced with a reopening of the seventy-group controversy. This time it came in the form of the secretary of the air force's first annual report. About that time Forrestal suggested to Truman that he tell the civilian and military heads of the services to keep their differences within the department or resign. Forrestal even had drafted some remarks the president could use which included a reference to loyalty to the president and his "alter ego," the secretary of defense.[65] The meeting was never held, but Truman did reiterate at a press conference that he felt forty-eight air force groups were adequate.

In early 1949 Forrestal was beginning to show signs of fatigue. He had been working hard in Washington since the summer of 1940. The interservice battling, the lack of clarity as to his own authority, and the president's failure to back him were all beginning to take their toll. If all these problems were not enough, he now had to contend with broadsides from the newscasters, Walter Winchell and Drew Pearson, indicating that his resignation was in the offing and also making some personal allegations concerning an income tax return of Forrestal's and other matters.

As Forrestal's fatigue increased, he was less and less able to make decisions. On January 21 Eisenhower returned to duty at Forrestal's request to become a kind of de facto chairman of the Joint Chiefs. This helped somewhat, although Ike himself was tired and had other preoccupations.

The president became aware in late 1948 of a number of nervous habits that Forrestal had acquired, as well as of Forrestal's belief that he was being followed. Truman ordered the Secret Service chief to look into the matter, and although there was no basis to the belief, a number of disturbing symptoms were discovered which indicated that Forrestal was suffering from "a total psychotic breakdown . . . characterized by suicidal features."[66]

Toward the end of January 1949, according to Louis Johnson, Forrestal's successor, Johnson was asked by Forrestal and the president to take over the defense post about May 1. There is other evidence that suggests that Forrestal considered his planned resignation less definite than Johnson later remembered it.[67]

On March 1, 1949, Forrestal was summoned to the White House and the president requested his resignation. It was a shattering experience for the still ambitious Forrestal, who somehow had by now convinced himself that he had failed as secretary of defense. The following day there was duly exchanged a pair of letters, one beginning, "My dear Mr. President" and the other, "Dear Jim." At a news conference on March 3, the president announced Forrestal's resignation and the selection of Louis Johnson as his successor. There was a spate of news articles concerning the event, most of them highly favorable to Forrestal.

On March 28 Johnson was sworn in at a ceremony in the Pentagon courtyard. Following the ceremony, the former secretary went to the White House and there, to his surprise, were assembled many high officials of government, including the cabinet and the Joint Chiefs. The president awarded him the Distinguished Service Medal—Forrestal was unable to respond. The following day, in an unusual ceremony for Washington, the House Armed Services Committee met to honor him. Directly from the meeting, the exhausted Forrestal went to the airport, where he was seen off by his loyal staff on a trip to Hobe Sound, Florida, to be a guest of Robert Lovett.

Unfortunately, his departure from office had come too late (or perhaps too early) and he was seized with a severe depression. He was, as many later said, a casualty of the cold war. On April 2 he was returned to Bethesda Naval Hospital and placed under psychiatric care in the VIP suite on the sixteenth floor of the hospital. By May he seemed to be improving and was given a bit more freedom. When last seen, he was copying from an anthology of poetry in the early morning hours of May 22. About 3:00 A.M. he walked across the hall to a small diet kitchen, opened a window, and fell to his death. The poem he had been copying just before was a translation of Sophocles' "Chorus from Ajax":

> Worn by the waste of time—
> Comfortless, nameless, hopeless, save
> In the dark prospect of the yawning grave.

The years between early 1946 and early 1949 were characterized by a steadily deteriorating relationship between the United States and the Soviet Union. One only has to recall a few of the events to regain a sense of the times: Stalin's speech of early 1946 and the tougher diplomatic approach assumed by the United States in that period; the Truman Doctrine speech of March 1947; the European Recovery Program; the Containment Policy; the March Crisis of 1948; the Berlin Blockade; and the founding of NATO. In that short span of time, the United States went on the offensive diplomatically. One would have thought that it would also have been a period of intense defense preparations and high defense budgets to support such an increasingly aggressive foreign policy. Such, however, was not the case.

The size of the defense efforts was conditioned more by events at home than by the international situation. There had been the pell-mell demobilization ending in the spring of 1947 that left the United States forces in a state where they could have conducted only the most minor combat operations. Attention was focused by the president not so much on their condition as on the pressing need to reconvert the economy of the nation to peacetime and the attendant demands of all sectors—business, labor, agriculture. Among the public there was a strong desire to return to normalcy, whatever that might be. To the president, the most important objective was to balance the budget. Above all, continually in the background from 1947 on was the prospect of the upcoming presidential election and the president's perception of what the public wanted.

It was in this situation that the first secretary of defense, holding a strong view of the communist menace, attempted to rebuild American military forces for the future. To do so, he had a weakly federated National Military Establishment, which he had helped mold, in charge of three military services who considered themselves autonomous and who had their own individual views on military strategy and the amount of resources it would take them to carry it out.

In the White House there was a president who had his own ideas on defense matters. Skeptical of the military and their claims on the budget that he was trying to balance, wary of the new National Security Council, lest it usurp his powers, Truman wielded his control over strategy and military requirements by controlling the defense budget. In this he had a dogged ally in James Webb, director of the Bureau of the Budget.

The chief device employed was a ceiling for the defense budget, established by the president after consultation with the secretary of the treasury and the budget director. The ceiling varied in level, the best known one being the $15 billion ceiling for fiscal 1950 established by Truman in a meeting with defense officials and others on May 13, 1948. The underlying assumption of the ceiling was that there was a fixed limit to what the country could spend for defense.

This assumption seems not to have been proved, nor was it challenged by Forrestal in economic terms. He did challenge it indirectly in the course of the fiscal 1949 supplemental and in the development of the fiscal 1950 budget. But the challenge never arose in the economic terms employed by the president. The president's ceiling was based more on perceived political realities than on purely economic considerations. Apparently he did not, especially in preparing for the 1948 election campaign, wish to go before the public and ask for increased defense expenditures that would presumably result in increased taxes.

Forrestal tried on several occasions to enlist the support of the secretary of state in his efforts to convince the president that higher defense budgets were required. Marshall was at the height of his prestige and highly regarded by the president. But, however sympathetic Marshall may have been to Forrestal's problems, he was not willing to come to his assistance. The secretary of state was well aware of Truman's tight budgetary views. Within that budget Marshall had his own priority, and not a small item at that—the Marshall Plan. To the secretary of state, the most effective way of dealing with the Soviet threat was to help Western Europe get on its feet, economically and militarily. He did not want this program disrupted by other claimants.

Forrestal enjoyed a good relationship with Congress, by and large, yet there were limitations there as to how far he could go in achieving his objective of a larger defense budget. Forrestal was extremely loyal to the president and defended Truman's budget before congressional committees, as best he could. On many occasions, Truman reiterated the need for the defense officials to speak publicly with one voice on the budget. The reason for this is fairly clear: as long as he could keep his military experts in line, Congress was not in a position to challenge his defense budget. On this, Truman succeeded with Forrestal, but he was not successful with the services—especially Symington and the air force.

Forrestal's major problems during his eighteen-month tenure as defense secretary came mainly from within the National Military Establishment. These were occasioned by honest differences concerning strategic concepts; the scramble for budgetary resources within the President's tight budgetary ceiling; and the organizational autonomy retained by the services under the 1947 act. These differences were to continue long after Forrestal's time, but it is interesting to see how he, as the first secretary of defense, attempted to deal with them.

Forrestal's strategic notion of balanced forces brought him into conflict with the air force. It was not that the service had any objection in theory to such a notion, but with only so many resources, the seventy-group air force appeared to be the answer. Whatever the merit of the Finletter Commission or the Brewster Board reports, they did support the air force position. This position also fitted in nicely with public perceptions of an atomic war striking at the heart of the Soviet Union, which was without its own atomic power to retaliate at that time. Forrestal made his best case for balanced forces in congressional testimony. The debate, not resolved in Forrestal's time, was in different terms to reach its peak in the 1950s.

The main forum for the interservice competition was in the budget development process. When the services' requirements were aggregated at $30 billion—twice the president's ceiling for fiscal year 1950—Forrestal clearly had a serious problem on his hands. Try as he might in person or by memorandum, he was unable to get the Joint Chiefs to agree on the distribution of the $14.4 billion limit set by the president.

At this point he introduced a new approach in his meetings with the Joint Chiefs—the notion of an intermediate budget. Their aggregated requests (by this point, with the assistance of the McNarney Board, at $23.6 billion) would be the maximum, the president's ceiling the minimum, and now something in between they would be able to brief the president on. He appealed to their public responsibility: it was their job to agree on a budget and not to look like a group who put service interests above the national interest.

On October 5, 1948, Forrestal explained to Truman what he was doing and received a rather cautious response. To a degree, his approach to the Joint Chiefs worked. With divergencies between air force and army on one side and navy on the other, the $14.4 billion pie was cut, with Forrestal taking an in-between position. There was also developed a $16.9 billion intermediate budget that was presented to the president on December 9, 1948. Truman listened and thanked them and that was the end of the intermediate budget. The meeting was merely a formality and Forrestal's rational approach had failed: the president's ceiling stood.

On organizational reform Forrestal was more successful, although he did not live to see the changes made. It seems clear that within months after taking office he knew the secretary needed more power. The year 1948 confirmed this at every step—in particular, his confrontations with Air Secretary Symington. At year's end, his report as secretary outlined a number of organizational reforms needed to strengthen his hand. Many of these and others found their way into 1949 amendments that were passed several months after his suicide.[68]

Forrestal's contributions were many during his relatively brief tour as secretary of defense but were generally unfinished when he left office. He achieved a modest degree of success in getting the services to think through the problem of roles and missions at the Key West and Newport conferences. He secured the first integrated defense budget, however inadequate it may have been. He made and secured decisions on a whole range of programs that were the first steps toward solving the problems of the military in the postwar world. These were problems involving such questions as conscription, reserve forces, research and development, how to build a shield in Europe against the Soviets, and many others. But Forrestal's biggest contribution was to lay the foundation for what in subsequent years became the Department of Defense.[69]

2

Eisenhower, Wilson, McElroy, and Budgets

With the inauguration of Dwight David Eisenhower in 1953, the country acquired a president who perceived himself as an expert in matters of national security. When he took office, he had definite ideas on strategic policy, defense budgets, and the kind of secretary of defense he wanted to work with. His two major promises during the 1952 campaign had been to end the Korean War, which had been stalemated for over a year, and to reduce the budget. There was a direct relationship between the two, since ending the war, which he did within six months of taking office, was necessary before the budget could be reduced. But this was not enough. To reduce the overall budget to the degree he felt necessary—from $74 billion in the fiscal year he took office to $70 billion the next year and to $60 billion the following—would mean further paring of the defense budget.[1] This, in turn, required a close look at the kind of strategy the United States was going to pursue in the post-Korean War period.

Eisenhower's conservative economic views were central to his thinking on all issues, including national security. These views were genuine and of long standing. To Eisenhower, the United States economy was like the source of a mother's milk—tender and soft and not to be abused.[2]

As for his strategic concepts on assuming office, he has set them forth for us in his memoirs. They may be summarized as follows: to rely on deterrence and rule out preventive war; to stress the role of nuclear technology and to reduce reliance on U.S. conventional forces; to place heavy reliance on allied land forces around the Soviet periphery; to stress economic strength, achieved especially through reduced defense budgets; and to be prepared to continue the struggle with the USSR over decades.

Given Eisenhower's strategic views and the domestic and international constraints he perceived, his problem was how to blend those views into a credible strategy that could be implemented at a relatively low cost and be sold to both the American public and America's allies. To accomplish this objective, the president used organizational means, careful selection of key political appointees, his large experience in handling bureaucracies, and his great rapport with the American people. The personalities of his lieutenants were important, as was the process of strategic policymaking he oversaw: the interrelationships of the decision-makers' departments, and agencies responsible for U.S. national security.

At the apex of the defense and foreign policy organization, Eisenhower established a refurbished National Security Council. Originally the NSC was created by Congress as a small advisory body over which the president was to preside. Under Truman the council had been rather loosely structured. Eisenhower transformed this loose framework into a highly structured system.

Soon after taking office, Eisenhower appointed Robert Cutler as special assistant for national security affairs. The president wanted continuous policy planning by a board functioning as the "planning arm" of the NSC. He also wanted wider representation in the NSC, including the secretary of the treasury and the budget director. Eisenhower viewed the council as a corporate body—that is, the members not only represented their departments but could give advice in their own right. Procedures were also to be established so that meetings would follow a standard pattern, including an advance agenda and circulation of policy papers to be considered.[3]

The substructure that Cutler developed to support the council included two boards. For input, there was established a Planning Board (known as the NSC "Senior Staff" under Truman), which Cutler chaired and whose members (at the assistant secretary level) came from departments represented on the council. The functions of the board, which was in fact an interagency committee, were to draw up the agenda for each council meeting and to put in final form policy papers for council consideration. On the output side, there was created the Operations Coordinating Board (OCB), initially chaired by the under secretary of state. It also was an interagency committee, but at the under secretary level. Its function was to implement presidential policy decisions by transmitting them to the proper departments and to supply the president with progress reports.

Not all defense matters came to the president through the NSC. If a defense issue did not involve the formulation, revision, or clarification of an NSC policy, then it was not part of the NSC system. These matters were handled by the staff secretary (who was also the defense liaison officer) directly with the president. The procedures might involve informal briefings by Brigadier General Andrew J. Goodpaster on operational or intelligence matters or meetings with cabinet-level officials and others, which Goodpaster normally attended. Apparently the number of such meetings on defense-related matters was rather substantial. At least one well-placed observer, who was present at nearly all the National Security Council meetings during the last twenty-seven months of Eisenhower's administration, felt that the informal office meetings were much more important than the council sessions. In his words: "As a matter of fact, I think the Boss regarded both the Cabinet and the National Security Council meetings as debating societies. . . . His real decisions were in the Oval Room, with a small select group."[4]

This latter point sheds a rather different light on the conventional critique of the Eisenhower National Security Council system, the most quoted source of which is the report of Senator Jackson's Subcommittee on National Policy Machinery.[5] Jackson's subcommittee felt that the Eisenhower NSC was too large a group with too crowded an agenda and that its procedures were too stylized. What the subcommittee overlooked was that Eisenhower was, in most instances, using the NSC meetings as a coordinating device and as a forum to announce decisions rather than a body to make them.

To help accomplish his budgetary and strategic objectives Eisenhower selected his key appointees with great care. His selection of John Foster Dulles as his secretary of state was not inevitable, but neither was it surprising. Dulles had campaigned and worked long and hard for the office, and his talents for such a position were not inconsiderable. He had spent most of his life as a highly successful Wall Street lawyer, specializing in international cases. In 1944 he became presidential candidate Dewey's chief adviser on foreign policy. This role inaugurated for him an association with government that was to continue for the remainder of his life. At the United Nations San Francisco Conference in 1945, he became directly involved in diplomatic practice. By the late 1940s, he was the unofficial foreign policy spokesman for the Republican party. Dewey's defeat in 1948 cost Dulles the job of secretary of state at that time, but the Truman administration, in efforts at a bipartisan foreign policy, had employed him extensively. Perhaps his most important assignment for Truman was as chief United States negotiator of the Japanese peace treaty in 1951.

The relationship between Eisenhower and his new secretary of state had not been close before the 1952 election. There seems to be a general consensus among observers at cabinet and NSC meetings that, in the early days of the administration, Dulles was cautious in his dealings with the president. As time went on, the relationship altered, and by 1954 it had become a close one. As Sherman Adams points out, Dulles was the only cabinet-level official who routinely used his right of direct access to the president's office. Apparently many of these visits came late in the day and led into philosophical discussions, once business had been disposed of.[6]

The president's "chief of staff," Sherman Adams, felt that Dulles was the most successful of the cabinet-level officers in selling his point of view to the others, even where there was disagreement on basic policy. This was no doubt due in part to his powers of persuasion but also in part to a proclivity to stay out of what he considered to be others' areas of competence. Nowhere is this better illustrated than in what Dulles regarded as the purely military area.[7] No doubt the military background and reputation of the president were basic reasons for this. Whatever the reason, this lack of involvement is significant, since military force played such a large part in his policies, writings, and speeches when he was secretary of state.

Another cabinet officer with considerable influence was the secretary of the treasury, George Magoffin Humphrey. The United States Treasury is a powerful institution, at the center of domestic and international struggles concerning financial, fiscal, and tax policies. It would take a relatively weak man to underplay the role of secretary of the treasury, considering the large domestic and international clientele who have a stake in his approaches and policies. With the advent of the Eisenhower administration, the importance of the job became even more evident. The Republican campaign had stressed and promised balanced budgets, debt and tax reductions, and fiscal and monetary checks on inflation.

Humphrey arrived in Washington with a "passion for domestic economy and dispassion toward foreign affairs." He was, in keeping with his business background, highly conservative on economic issues. He seems to have been extremely vigorous in NSC sessions, into which he frequently interjected short talks on checking deficits. Many of those who had an opportunity to observe him remarked on his personal charm, warmth, and vitality. Of great value to him in cabinet meetings were his debating skill, aggressive manner, and conviction, which permitted him to overwhelm most of his colleagues.[8]

Charles E. Wilson, Eisenhower's choice for secretary of defense, was suggested to the president by Lucius Clay. Wilson was the highly successful president of General Motors who, in his own field, exhibited a powerful and confident personality. Bluff and colorful in manner, he was prone to making highly quotable statements of a type not designed to enhance his relations with Congress. When he arrived at the Pentagon, his insight into foreign affairs or strategic issues was negligible, and he did not seem to gain much sophistication as time went on.

Wilson, in the view of many observers, was inclined to overtalk situations with the president and to bring to Eisenhower too many internal problems of the Defense Department. Apparently his presentations were also frequently so rambling that the president became impatient. As time went on, "Engine Charlie," as he was known, declined in influence with the president, while the other two powerful men in the cabinet, Dulles and Humphrey, greatly increased their influence.[9]

Operating at the interface of the military and the higher political authority is the chairman of the Joint Chiefs of Staff. His effectiveness is highly dependent on his relationships with the secretary of defense and the president. Admiral Arthur Radford, whom the president-elect had given Wilson an opportunity to evaluate during the Korean trip, was Wilson's choice for chairman. Radford subsequently gained great influence with the secretary of defense and became highly regarded by President Eisenhower.[10]

Radford's predecessor, Omar Bradley, although a political spokesman for the Truman administration, had generally maintained a position of neutrality on matters of interservice conflict. Radford, however, was another sort of person. When he had been vice chief of naval operations during the interservice controversies of the late 1940s, he had been a ruthless partisan and outstanding bureaucratic infighter. These talents he brought with him to the chairman's job. Far from assuming a position of neutrality, Radford took positions on written documents and during NSC meetings and other discussions. Since he normally represented the military in meetings with the president, the NSC, and the secretary of defense, he was in a position to wield considerable power. Articulate, personable, and in sympathy with the president's outlook on budgetary and strategic questions, he was someone to be reckoned with in the 1950s. He had a close rapport with Secretary Dulles, overshadowed Secretary Wilson on strategic matters, and had the confidence of the president.[11]

Matthew B. Ridgway, Eisenhower's successor at SHAPE, was the president's choice for army chief of staff. Ridgway, fifty-eight years old, was well known, especially for his command of the Eighth Army in Korea and as MacArthur's successor in Japan. Since the Korean War had only recently ended when Ridgway assumed office, one of his pressing planning problems concerned army manpower in the future. The peacetime army had always been small, although larger before the Korean War than before World War II. But Ridgway understood the situation in 1952 to be different from that of the pre-Korean period. First, he saw an increasingly sophisticated Soviet military threat. Second, he saw constantly increasing U.S. military commitments to other countries. Finally, he did not agree that heavy reliance on a nuclear weapons capability was adequate to meet the threat; he took the long-standing army position that the man on the ground, the foot soldier, was the decisive element.

Eisenhower's selection for air force chief of staff, Nathan F. Twining, began his new role with a distinct advantage over the other service chiefs, since that service's strategic concepts, which stressed the central importance of the strategic deterrent, were highly congenial to the new administration. Before Twining's arrival, there had been a heated dispute between the outgoing air force chief, Hoyt Vandenberg, and the new administration—not over strategic concepts but whether the old Truman goal of 143 air force wings by fiscal year 1955 or the new Eisenhower goal of 120 wings would be

sufficient. Eisenhower had prevailed, but the dispute possibly accelerated Twining's assumption of his new position about six weeks
before the other chiefs.

Admiral Robert B. Carney was Eisenhower's selection to be
chief of naval operations. The navy's strategic concepts lay somewhere between those of the army and those of the air force and were
based upon two principles: control of the sea commensurate with
needs; and the ability to deny its use to unfriendly or inimical nations.

Eisenhower was convinced that the Defense Department
needed some reorganizing and greater central control.[12] In his first
year in office he signed Reorganization Plan Six, which, after some
opposition in Congress, became effective on June 30, 1953. Two
parts of the plan are worth noting. Within the Defense Department,
the number of assistant secretaries was increased threefold, at the
expense of separate boards and agencies such as the Munitions
Board and the Research and Development Board. This change provided a clearer channel between the secretary of defense and his
department as well as a potential for better central control. The
expectation was that the secretary could also exercise greater control
of the department's budgetary and administrative activities. The
reorganization also improved the cohesiveness of the JCS staff and
strengthened the position of the chairman. Prior to the reorganization, the staff did not have a director, nor were appointments to the
staff cleared by the chairman. It is easy to imagine the difficulties
this caused the chairman, sitting in the same building with highly
integrated, powerful service staffs who would fill "their" vacancies
on his staff. Eisenhower, in *Mandate for Change*, stated that his
objective had been to divorce "the thinking and the outlook of the
members of the Joint Staff from those of the parent services and to
center their entire effort on national planning for the over-all common defense."

By July 1953 the president felt the time had come to take a new
look at the U.S. strategic policy.[13] He initiated this policy in a meeting with the new service chiefs. Since the Korean Armistice was
about to be signed, the president wanted to develop a defense
posture that could be continued indefinitely. He wanted the new
chiefs, before they were caught up in the details of their offices, to
produce a single paper on overall defense policy. This paper was the

first step in what subsequently became known as the New Look, which the president later defined as "first, a reallocation of resources among the five categories of forces, and second, the placing of greater emphasis than formerly on the deterrent and destructive power of improved nuclear weapons, better means of delivery, and effective air-defense units."[14]

The chiefs were able to agree on a basic paper of strategic premises and guidelines, but translating these generalities into the specifics for the fiscal year 1955 defense budget was another matter. After some deliberation, the Joint Chiefs decided that no substantial changes should be made in the defense budget, which totaled $42 billion, since there were no changes in the perceived threat or in alliance commitments and no new guidance on the employment of nuclear weapons.

Defense Secretary Charles Wilson presented this problem to the NSC on October 13, 1953.[15] The reaction of Secretary Humphrey, who had expected a defense budget of $36 billion, and Budget Director Joseph M. Dodge was what one source called "horrified."[16] It fell to Chairman Radford to defend the Joint Chiefs' premises, and he centered his discussion on the nature of presidential guidance for employment of nuclear weapons. His message, which was to have significant results, was that if the use of nuclear weapons from the outset of a conflict was accepted as a planning premise, then a less costly force structure could be developed.

This led to a subsequent NSC session on October 29 at which the president approved NSC-162/2, which became the policy basis of the New Look.[17] This paper picked up Radford's suggestion of October 13 which placed maximum reliance on nuclear weapons from the outset of a conflict. Radford's remarks had been entirely his own, that is to say, neither the army nor the navy agreed with the new NSC policy on nuclear war. Nevertheless, Secretary Wilson, with Radford's help, was able to get qualified agreement from Ridgway and Carney and to use the new policy to get the defense budget down to a level acceptable to Eisenhower and Humphrey.

Throughout the fall and winter, high-level administration spokesmen engaged in the task of selling the New Look to the public. The president's primary public pronouncements on the subject came in his messages to Congress: State of the Union, Budget, and that accompanying the Economic Report. Of all the speeches made to explain the new defense policy, however, only John Foster Dulles's "massive retaliation" speech made to the Council on Foreign Relations on January 12, 1954, is now remembered.[18] This speech, which surely represented one of the high points in the rhetoric of the cold war, caused such an uproar that Dulles published an article in the April 1954 issue of *Foreign Affairs* stressing that there were wider options than nuclear weapons. By fall the immediate flurry of criticism and clarification brought on by the speech subsided. Still, there ensued over a period of many years a rather large volume of analyses and writing critical of U.S. defense policy. Some writers concentrated on alternative deterrence strategies, whereas others focused on the notion of limited war.[19]

The congressional examination of the New Look occurred in connection with the hearings on the 1955 defense budget. These, however, offered no challenge to the concept and almost none to the particulars. The administration's image of unanimity on the Eisenhower strategy remained intact during the hearings, except on the part of army chief Ridgway, and his misgivings about the administration's lack of emphasis on land forces were more implied than actual. Floor debate was more active in the Senate than in the House, but in neither case was it systematic or informed. With the clearing of the defense appropriation, Eisenhower had achieved his own strategic policy.[20]

During President Eisenhower's second administration, he was under considerable pressure from critics of his defense strategy; however, his skillful employment permitted him to retain his strategic innovation intact until the end of his administration. Events connected with the development of the fiscal years 1959 and 1960 defense budgets are most illustrative of his handling of the problem. But first, it will be useful to recall the changing context in which Eisenhower was forced to operate in the years after he secured his New Look strategy.

This was a more turbulent period for Eisenhower than his earlier years as president. Salient domestic events included his lopsided victory in the 1956 election; a serious recession in 1957–1958, and a landslide victory for the Democrats in the 1958 congressional elections. Among the major external events were Soviet technological successes in the field of missiles (especially the orbiting of Sputnik);

Khrushchev's attempt to exploit the Soviet technological image by creating a crisis over Berlin; crises in Hungary, Poland, the Middle East, and the Straits of Formosa. In no case did the president modify his strategic policy, despite pressure from limited war proponents on the one hand and from the nuclear superiority enthusiasts on the other.[21]

There was considerable continuity in the individuals who shaped the first and second Eisenhower administrations. John Foster Dulles continued as secretary of state until cancer immobilized him in the early months of 1959. Throughout his term as secretary, the problem of Soviet intentions remained central in his thinking. Yet there were changes in his outlook over time: he came to manifest a less critical attitude toward neutrals and perhaps some disenchantment with massive retaliation as a concept, at least in the terms in which he originally articulated it. His rapport with the president, already great by 1955, never waned. Nor did his penchant for employing unfortunate phrases. An article in *Life* magazine, based on an interview with him, added "going to the brink" and "brinkmanship" to the cold war vocabulary. Perhaps this was his way of simplifying complex issues so as to build public support for administration policies.

Treasury Secretary Humphrey remained irrepressible and fiscally conservative to the day of his departure from the administration in July 1957. John Eisenhower remembers one of his parting shots in the NSC this way: "I realize we have to spend $38 billion on defense right now, but if we keep it up year after year, we're going to have real trouble."

Robert B. Anderson, Humphrey's successor at the Treasury, had served previously as both secretary of the navy and deputy defense secretary. Still a relatively young man, he was a lawyer and estate manager in Texas before entering government. Although apparently somewhat more flexible than Humphrey, he was equally conservative in his economic philosophy. He was not as ebullient as his predecessor, but he was both tenacious in argument and adroit in negotiations. Although not part of the president's bridge-playing or quail-shooting coterie, there is no question of the high esteem in which Eisenhower held him. In his memoirs, Eisenhower mentions Anderson as a potential vice-presidential candidate and secretary of state. He was definitely a major force for conservative economic policy during the second administration.

Charles Wilson's tour as secretary of defense lasted almost five years, though he never developed any real rapport with the president. His penchant for the colorful but politically disastrous phrase continued as a liability. Wilson was strong on management ability and weak on strategic understanding. Another of his characteristics was a tendency to involve the president in Pentagon business. This is easy to understand, considering Wilson's role as business manager of the defense establishment. Out of the mainstream of the strategic dialogue and yet making budgetary decisions that could have considerable impact on strategic capabilities, Wilson's only alternatives were to turn to the president or to be wholly dependent on the chairman of the Joint Chiefs.

Wilson's successor, Neil Hosler McElroy, arrived in the office at a difficult time, being sworn in less than a week after Sputnik's launch and just in time for the final efforts on the fiscal year 1959 defense budget. McElroy apparently was surprised at being selected for the job and accepted it on the basis that he would serve no more than two years. His previous career, most recently as president of Procter and Gamble, had been concerned with the promotion and sale of soap and thus he had far less background relevant to defense activities than had Wilson as president of General Motors. Like Wilson, he could be regarded as a functionalist in his approach to the secretary's role. He did have one distinct advantage over Wilson: his public personality. As he himself put it: "I think maybe I was a little more accustomed to dealing with the public than Charley was."[22]

Like Wilson, McElroy relied on his subordinates to carry out the president's policies. He also felt that he could instill in the service chiefs a sense of being good businessmen. In neither case was his judgment correct. There was a jingle that went the rounds in the Pentagon in those days: "Nothing is ever complete, neither victory nor defeat." When a service received an adverse decision, it did not, like a subordinate agency in Procter and Gamble, simply carry it out. It used its many-faceted apparatus to attempt to get the decision changed. As for being good businessmen, that was all right if it did not interfere with a service chief's professional views. After all, his role was the apogee of military professionalism; he was not in the profit-and-loss business.

McElroy's arrival with Sputnik forced him into a number of significant hardware decisions at the outset. He projected a good image in making these decisions. As time went on, however, he gave the appearance of vacillation, and his image in his second year was less impressive. In any case, two years is too short a period for a defense secretary, especially one without a defense background, to become truly effective. His role was essentially the same as Wilson's; only the outward personalities were different.

The summer of 1957 brought the retirement of Admiral Arthur Radford. For four years as chairman of the Joint Chiefs he had been an able advocate of the administration's position on defense matters. Highly effective and respected by the president, Dulles, Humphrey, and Wilson, he had the tough job of working routinely with the service chiefs. Only one of these did Radford consider cooperative, and that was Nathan Twining, who succeeded him as chairman.

Twining's approach as chairman was apparently somewhat less partisan than Radford's had been. Admiral Arleigh Burke had absolute confidence that Twining, in representing the chiefs, would tell the entire story. As air force chief, however, Twining had been an advocate of the massive retaliation concept and was unlikely either to change that view or to favor any attempts at a new strategic appraisal. Although his basic professional interests were in strategic bombardment, he seemed to appreciate more than Radford the efforts of the other services. He remained, however, highly loyal to Eisenhower and his strategic policies. Many years after his retirement he wrote a rather curious book in which he gave the Eisenhower defense efforts high marks, except for "a tendency to allow a gradual erosion of U.S. military posture through partial accommodation to... pressure groups who were working for unilateral disarmament, the abolition of nuclear weapons, and the denial of the medium of space for military operations."[23]

General Thomas Dresser White was Twining's successor as chief of staff of the air force. He had been Twining's vice chief for the preceding four years, so there was no break in the continuity of air force leadership. There were senior air force generals—in particu-

lar, General Otto Weyland, head of the Tactical Air Command—
who believed in the possibility of local nonatomic war, but they
were not in power in the air force. Normally those in power would
state that if a local need developed, the Strategic Air Command
could handle it without lessening its general war capabilities. The
White House and air force continued in harmony on overall
priorities. From about 1956 on, however, they began to draw apart
on how much strategic capability was enough. The administration,
with an eye on the budget, decided on sufficiency. The air force
wanted to maintain a counterforce strategy, which, in the light of
increasing Soviet strategic capabilities, would have been expensive
indeed.

General Ridgway's position as army chief of staff had become
untenable by 1955 because of his opposition to the reduced role of
the army under Eisenhower's strategy. The clear front-runner for
the Ridgway appointment was General Maxwell Davenport Taylor,
then Far East commander. Taylor was an impressive-looking officer,
smooth, and a good speaker, with the reputation of being something
of an intellectual. He had risen in reputation within his service in
the latter part of World War II and, as these things sometimes
happen, the conventional wisdom in the army seemed to point to
his eventual appointment as chief of staff.

Before making the appointment, however, the commander-in-
chief wanted to talk with Taylor. Since the army was the main
problem for the president in attempting to maintain his strategic
consensus in 1955, this was an important appointment. The president was quite direct in letting Taylor know what assurances he
wanted from him before Taylor would be appointed chief of staff.[24]
First, Taylor must "understand and wholeheartedly accept that his
primary responsibility related to his joint duties." Second, he must
hold views on strategic doctrine "which are in accord with those of
the President." Since it would be necessary for the new army chief
to express his opinion and convictions openly when called upon,
such agreement in advance was essential. "Loyalty in spirit as well
as in letter was necessary." Taylor indicated understanding and acceptance of the president's views.

Robert Carney's tour as chief of naval operations lasted approximately the same two years as Ridgway's term as army chief of staff.
His critique of the New Look had been considerably more muted

than Ridgway's, but he had problems in his working relationships. One official close to the scene felt that Navy Secretary Thomas was the prime mover in Carney's not being appointed for another two-year term.[25]

Unlike Taylor, Admiral Arleigh Burke's appointment to replace Carney apparently came as a genuine surprise. Burke, who was frequently referred to as a "maverick," was relatively junior, being still a two-star admiral when selected as CNO over ninety admirals senior to him. In his preappointment interviews in May 1955, both the secretary and under secretary of the navy alluded to differences of opinion between Carney and themselves. Subsequently, Burke met with the secretary of defense and the president. Wilson treated him to a homily, the main point of which was the need for greater cooperation between the military and civilian leadership.[26] The president stressed what many other similar appointees had heard: the need for teamwork once a decision had been made. His other point, also a recurring one, was the importance of JCS corporate activities—and the desirability of delegating service responsibilities to the vice chiefs.

The Eisenhower approach to managing national security matters remained essentially the same throughout his term of office. The NSC forum provided an opportunity for a fairly large number of officials to gain an idea of the president's thinking on defense issues. As the 1950s wore on, however, the defense policy process was characterized by an increasingly rebellious Pentagon and a Congress restive in matters of strategic policy.

Since the budget was the focal point of the controversy, it will be useful to recapitulate service reservations about the funding of their particular programs in the late 1950s. Army reservations were four: 1) modernization of the existing army inventory would require $14 billion over a five-year period; the administration was providing less than half of that; 2) the military manpower required to support army needs worldwide, especially an adequate limited war capability, was 925,000; the administration was providing for 870,000, and a similar shortfall existed in army reserve forces; 3) the army surface-to-air missile program, Nike Hercules, was not being adequately funded (This was designed to cope with the potential enemy bomber threat to the United States and areas overseas that were of strategic concern); and 4) the administration would provide only marginal research funds to support the army's proposed antimissile missile, the Nike Zeus. The army wanted enough funds for intensive research, which, if successful, would lead to early production of the weapon.

The navy, for its part, had three major reservations: 1) there were inadequate funds for sustaining the fleet at what the navy perceived to be the minimum level of somewhat over 850 ships; the future was particularly troublesome, in view of insufficient money to build ships, especially carriers; 2) there was also inadequate money for procuring Polaris submarines, which the navy felt should take over a major part of the strategic missile mission; and 3) there were insufficient funds for the antisubmarine program, which the navy felt was moving too slowly.

The air force, which held the favored position in the proposed budget,[27] was less critical than the other services, but it also had some reservations: 1) the aircraft of the strategic bomber force were not being modernized rapidly enough; 2) the Bomarc air defense missile was not being sufficiently funded; and 3) some in the air force felt the strategic missile program was not progressing rapidly enough.

Since funds were seen as inadequate, each service judged that more could be obtained under the overall budget ceiling only by curtailing certain programs of the other services. For example, the army felt that the air force strategic retaliatory force was excessive in size. The navy agreed with this but also felt the army did not need the increased manpower they wanted over the budget allocation. The air force, not wanting any encroachments on its own portion of the budget, agreed with the navy about army strength but also resisted the navy's Polaris program. There were many other areas of mutual concern, such as the army's feeling that the air force was providing inadequate strategic air mobility to them, but the foregoing sets the stage for the struggles over the fiscal year 1959 and 1960 defense budgets.

Preparation of the 1957 budget in 1955 had been characterized by the air force's attempts to accelerate the modernization of its forces, which was partially successful. The next year was the year of an economy mood brought about by George Humphrey's most famous press conference, in which he made reference to a depression that would "curl your hair." Although it did not start that way, preparation of the fiscal year 1959 budget became the year of Sputnik. In July and August 1957, the economy mood of the previous year was still predominant. The president met with Wilson and his deputy, Donald Quarles, in July to go over the guidelines for the 1959 budget. One of the key issues was manpower, and Wilson hoped to reduce the military from 2.8 to 2.5 million.[28] The president generally agreed with the figure, although he was not certain how the cuts should be allocated among the services.

Wilson, by now highly sensitive to Congress and the military bureaucracy, thought the president should meet with leaders in both agencies to discuss the new program. As far as Congress was concerned, Eisenhower felt that for the moment letters would do. In the case of the Joint Chiefs of Staff, the president thought it much too early for him to discuss specific manpower decisions. "The chiefs," he said, "would know that I was being purely arbitrary" in making a decision of this type at such an early date. Further, it was too early to release specifics. He turned out to be correct, because in less than three months the Soviets had orbited Sputnik.

Obviously, Sputnik affected the defense budget. The economy mood of the previous year was now something of an embarrassment, particularly to Congress. The president, however, was not one to overreact, especially when it came to defense spending.[29] On October 9, less than a week after Sputnik, Neil McElroy was sworn in as Wilson's replacement, as previously planned. After the ceremony, the president met with the Pentagon leaders to talk about what attitude to maintain a view of the Sputnik situation.[30] He reminded everyone that separating U.S. military missile effort from the U.S. scientific effort, which was designed to lead to an orbiting, had been intentional. When the military began to say, as some recently had, that certain of their missiles could have placed a satellite in orbit before the Russians, they tended to give the impression of a race, which he felt was wrong. He wanted the Pentagon leaders to avoid making comments on this matter whenever possible. It would probably have been impossible, however, for the services not to have viewed the developing public and congressional concern as a favorable climate for increased emphasis on larger defense budgets.

On October 30 McElroy met with the president on the defense budget. The defense secretary felt that after he had briefed the president on the budget, the service secretaries and chiefs should have an opportunity to meet with Eisenhower in order to bring out deficiencies as they saw them.[31] The president again stated his views on the responsibility of the top defense officials to consider the broader aspects of the budget. "If the budget is too high," he maintained, "inflation occurs, which in effect cuts down the value of the dollar, so that nothing is gained and the process is self-defeating." As far as military manpower was concerned, it was Eisenhower's aim to come down from 2.8 to 2.5 million and still have a stronger force. Such innovations as the army's Pentomic Division would assist in accomplishing this objective. His goal was to find a stable budget ceiling at which the defense budget could be kept, barring inflation or adverse developments. The president noted that "last year although the Chiefs accepted a certain figure, they so organized their programs as to initiate a large amount of work which would cost much more to carry on this year."

On November 22 the president met with McElroy in his office immediately following a cabinet meeting, in order to discuss some points concerning the military budget. He wanted to approach all budget decisions not on the basis of public pressure but rather on the real need for the item in question.[32] He stated that defense requirements were relative to the Soviet Union's posture. Since "Soviet ICBM's would not over-match our bomber power in the next few years," the United States defense pace should be based on good sense and a calm reading of the objective situation vis-à-vis the USSR.

The focus of defense budget sessions in December 1957, two months after Sputnik, was different from that in previous years. The problem for the administration was to convey a public image of understanding the new threat and moving to meet it, without departing significantly from the budgetary constraints that had previously been in effect.

On January 9, 1958, Eisenhower's State of the Union message conveyed the impression that a large expansion in defense efforts was in the making. In it he declared: "Every part of our military establishment must and will be equipped to do its defensive job with the most modern weapons and methods." The budget message of January 13, however, emphasized expenditures for defense but seemed to indicate a more orderly approach, similar to that exhibited in the meetings previously discussed. Eisenhower did request a supplemental appropriation to the 1958 budget of $1.3 billion in spending authority, and a further increase of $2.5 billion in fiscal 1959 over fiscal 1958, to be applied principally to strategic programs. In other areas, especially tactical forces, there were to be decreases in modernization efforts. The emphasis was on missiles, bombers, and nuclear weapons. That spring there were two more supplemental requests for fiscal 1959, one in April for $1.45 billion and one in June for $0.6 billion. The air force was the principal beneficiary of these increases, but they still did not receive as much as air force leaders had hoped for.

Congressional questioning of the administration was wide-ranging and generally critical. There was no disagreement on the matter of strengthening the strategic forces; the issue, rather, was by how much. Appropriations were increased over the administration's request in the case of Polaris and two air force missile programs. There was less agreement on improving limited war capabilities, although some additional money over that requested by the president was voted for army modernization, airlift capacity, and army and marine corps personnel strength. In the end Congress voted the administration $8 billion more than the president's total requests.

The fiscal year 1959 budget was developed in circumstances just the reverse of the economy mood of the previous year because of what some perceived as an extraordinary change in the world situation. Nevertheless, to the president, holding down the defense budget was more important than yielding to the external context or any rational argumentation designed to change the substance of strategic policy in reaction to that context.

While the post-Sputnik budget and strategy meetings were being held, the president was busy with another approach, designed to give him better control over the defense policy and budgetary processes. To Eisenhower the organization of the Defense Department seemed to leave something to be desired. The public and Congress also were uneasy about the frequent, sometimes daily, accounts of duplication and overlap among the military services. Under the impetus of Sputnik, all these apprehensions came together in a general agreement that the Defense Department needed further reorganization. Typical of these feelings was a remark made by John McCloy in a meeting with the president in early November 1957.[33] McCloy felt that there was clearly a need for a reorganization of the Defense Department. Interservice rivalry had now reached the point, he said, where it was "spreading to industries and universities" affiliated with particular services. Eisenhower agreed and articulated some of the organizational proposals he had in mind, such as taking the services out of operational command and integrating the Joint Chiefs of Staff.

In the same month, the Rockefeller Committee on Governmental Organization forwarded to the president its recommendations for organizational changes in the Pentagon. Also, in the Pentagon itself, Secretary McElroy had set up a distinguished advisory group on organizational matters, headed by Charles A. Coolidge. As a result of these efforts, the president became involved and spent many hours working on the details of reorganization plans. On one occasion, in January 1958, he met with the Coolidge group in the Pentagon.[34] McElroy opened the discussion with the question of whether the chairman should be given more power, and whether the members of the JCS should be separated from their service assignment as chief of staff.[35] Radford, retired and a member of the group, thought the chairman needed no additional powers, since his real power came from his rapport with the secretary of defense. Omar Bradley agreed with Radford's conclusion. He felt, however, that the chairman's power derived from his leadership and personal involvement with the chiefs.

At this point, the president, who thought the participants were too eager to support the status quo, interjected some thoughts of his own. He felt the public criticism of the department could not be ignored. Further, he felt that the group was talking about details rather than basic issues. He did not doubt that broad plans and estimates could be worked out harmoniously. When the issues involved specifics of men and money, however, it was hard to get an agreement that was satisfactory to everyone. Eisenhower said the defense secretary should take the stand that the primary duty of the chiefs was their JCS role. "Their greatest task was to work corporately in support of the President and Secretary of Defense." As for the service secretaries, the president felt they "should not be interested in matters of strategic planning." All in all, McElroy's group, Eisenhower thought, was concentrating on "details rather than basic issues." He was determined not to gloss over the issues.

The president was well aware of the spectrum of problems he

would face in Congress in connection with his reorganization ideas. For example, there would be those trying to prod him into premature action, that is, to cause him to announce his proposals before he had developed in the Pentagon enough of a consensus to guarantee the military's subsequent support of the proposals before Congress. To secure that kind of bureaucratic consensus would take time.

On April 3, 1958, President Eisenhower submitted a special message to Congress that contained his proposals for reorganization of the Defense Department. These included actions in two categories: those he would take as president; and legislative actions that he was requesting of Congress. In the first category were establishing unified commands in the field under the secretary of defense, who would operate them through the JCS; strengthening the authority of the secretary of defense over the budget; and eliminating the committee system employed by the Joint staff, thus making it a truly operational staff. Legislative actions recommended included repealing any statutory authority that vested responsibility for military operations in any official other than the secretary of defense; changing the existing law to make it clear that each military chief could delegate major responsibilities to his vice chief; making appropriations for the Department of Defense in such a way as to provide the secretary with greater authority and flexibility; and eliminating the existing provisions for separate administration of the military departments, and other similar restraints on the authority of the secretary of defense.

The Pentagon consensus on the president's proposals had not been completely achieved by the time of his message to Congress. Less than a week after the message Eisenhower met with Secretary of the Navy Gates and Chief of Naval Operations Burke, who had some apprehensions. Though they themselves completely accepted the concept of unified strategic planning, including placing all activities under control of the secretary of defense, they were concerned about others who felt differently,[36] especially the naval staff in the Pentagon, where there was a great deal of "emotionalism and apprehension" over the reorganization. They also mentioned their "apprehensions over what might be done under some future president." In particular, they did not like that part of the proposal that eliminated the provision for the services to be "separately administered."

The discussion apparently did not clear up all Burke's misgivings or relieve the pressures on him from within the navy. Later, when he testified before the Senate Armed Services Committee, he opposed increasing the powers of the defense secretary and downgrading the status of the service secretaries. Twining subsequently discussed Burke's testimony with the president.[37] He indicated that McElroy had read all Burke's testimony on defense reorganization. McElroy, Twining said, felt that Burke had done well, but he had not gone "down the line" as some of the others had done.

The president followed up his message by submitting to Congress on April 16 a draft reorganization bill. The bill left out one important part of the message: the provision that gave the secretary of defense authority and flexibility in handling military appropriations. This proposal had upset Congress enough that it seemed best to delete it in the interest of the overall reorganization project. The president's commitment to the remainder of the legislation, however, was so great that he wrote directly to influential citizens all over the country, asking them to contact the Congress in support of the proposed legislation.

The day before he was to testify before the House Committee on Defense Reorganization, McElroy called on the president. He wanted to understand Eisenhower's thinking on how far the chiefs could go in their testimony.[38] The president indicated that if anyone were to oppose his proposal gratuitously, then that official "should be out." If a chief of staff, in responding to a committee question regarding his personal view, were to oppose some feature of the president's proposal, there would be no action against him, providing he could subsequently loyally and faithfully execute the president's decisions. One reason for his interest in the president's views, McElroy indicated, was his understanding that Chairman Carl Vinson planned to ask for assurances that officers who testified against the proposal would not be penalized. On second thought, McElroy felt, he probably would not accept Vinson's question in those terms, since it was "inconsistent with the dignity of his office."

The struggle with Congress over the reorganization went on throughout the spring and early summer, but in the end the president got almost all he wanted. There were two points in the final bill that bothered him. First, Congress had sixty days in which to vote down any presidential proposal to transfer, merge, reassign, or abolish a "major combatant function." The other provision was one he referred to as "legalized insubordination."[39] It permitted any member of the Joint Chiefs to define what constituted a "major function" and therefore to put before the congressional forum any proposed change by the president. It also gave the secretaries and chiefs the right to go directly to the Congress with any recommendations they deemed proper. In effect, then, the Reorganization Act of 1958 retained the separate military departments and, with them, sufficient alternative viewpoints for Congress to retain whatever meaningful control it still had in national security matters.

In his memoirs, Dwight Eisenhower expresses himself strongly with regard to his intent to get a balanced budget in fiscal year 1960: "I planned to let the Congress know that if it materially added to the budget, I would respond with a veto, and that if the veto were overridden, I would propose a tax increase to cover the increase in spending, and if necessary call a special session for the purpose. In preparing the budget, the giant military demands gave us, as usual, the gigantic headaches. No major item budgeted in each of the Armed Services was approved for inclusion unless the question 'why' was answered to my satisfaction."[40]

After six years in office, and with the Congress heavily controlled by the Democrats, Eisenhower was well aware of the need for carefully thought-out legislative tactics. Apropos of this, an informal body of rules had been developed by this point to guide executive leaders appearing before congressional committees. These were designed to convey the impression of a united administration and to prevent executive personnel from providing gratuitous information to Congress. No testimony was allowed on matters under consideration by the administration but not yet resolved or released, how particular decisions had been reached by the administration, and specific advice that had been given to the president.[41]

In late November 1958 McElroy, Twining, Maurice Stans (the director of the budget), and about eight staff members from the White House and Defense Department briefed the president on the status of the defense budget for fiscal 1960.[42] McElroy covered what he considered to be the key decisions, which were, in the main, force modernization issues. When the issue of navy carriers was reached, a protracted discussion ensued. Twining, in supporting the carrier program, pointed out their use in cold war situations, while admitting their limitations in general war. At that point Gordon Gray, then special assistant for national security affairs, interjected a comment on behalf of the absent Dulles. The secretary of state felt that the carriers recently used in Lebanon and Taiwan had been vital to those situations. He also felt that as long as the United States retained the deterrent, the major threat was not general war but local aggression. He therefore felt that budget decisions should not be made that would "cripple" capabilities for local wars. In Lebanon the United States had employed four carriers, and in Taiwan, five.

The president had some reservations. He did not visualize any battle for the surface of the sea. He then launched into a discussion of fiscal soundness, concluding that without it the nation had no defense. Eventually he deferred for another year the decision of whether to build a second nuclear carrier.

Discussion of other hardware items was followed by comments on the overall defense budget. The president emphasized that defense was the key to a balanced budget, and unless the budget was balanced, "procurement of defense systems will avail nothing." McElroy defended his proposals by highlighting the risk already taken—for example, the downgrading of continental defense.

Budget Director Stans agreed that the Defense Department had made substantial reductions, but he felt more reductions were needed. There were still "exotic and duplicatory programs" included in the budget. Stans felt he "could not recommend approval of the budget as presented by the Defense Department." His recommendation was either to use $40 billion as a ceiling or to make up a new budget. McElroy again defended the budget on the basis of conscious risks already taken. In the end, McElroy was asked to look over the budget again with a view toward further reductions. The NSC meeting at which this matter was to be taken up was set back to December 6.

On December 3 a stag dinner was held at the White House for this group and other individuals to discuss economic matters.[43] Following the dinner the guests moved to the White House library, where the president asked each of the military chiefs to express his views. Army Chief Taylor questioned the division of funds among the services as failing to take into account army modernization needs. He felt it was outside of his responsibility to deal with the broad issue of a sound economy. The president contested this point, stating that the industrial base and the economy had military significance. Chief of Naval Operations Burke stated that if the competition between the United States and the Soviet Union required additional taxes they should be made available. Air Force Chief White felt that the reorganization of the Defense Department would result, over time, in savings by eliminating duplication. Twining said the United States had the big deterrent and forces enough to meet limited aggression of the Korean or Lebanese type. He also felt it was important to act decisively when a crisis occurred. However, adding Twining, if three or four crises happened simultaneously, the United States would be in a major war.

The following day McElroy referred the revised defense budget to the Joint Chiefs for the first time. In the two days remaining before the NSC meeting of December 6, the chiefs were unable to agree on the budget. It was presented at that meeting, therefore, only with the endorsement of Chairman Twining. For the upcoming congressional hearings, McElroy felt the need for some kind of written endorsement by the chiefs of the 1960 defense budget. He finally received a qualified endorsement in the form of a memorandum to him. The qualification was that each chief had "reservations with respect to the funding of their respective service programs."[44]

The public presentation of the fiscal 1960 budget began with the State of the Union message on January 9, 1959. The president used his personal prestige in the message: "The defense budget for the coming year has been planned on the basis of these principles and considerations. Over these many months I have personally participated in its development." Less than a week later, he met with the congressional leaders to attempt to gain support for the budget. He also wrote hundreds of people to elicit their support in persuading Congress to adhere to the balanced budget he had developed.

By 1959 the climate was right for Congress to try to intervene more fully in defense matters. Technology was in a state of flux, raising many technical and strategic questions, and few people seemed certain of the answers. The goals of the services were sufficiently far apart so that it was not difficult to find points of conflict between services or between a service and the administration. The political climate caused by the congressional election just passed and the presidential one on the horizon also encouraged Congress to take on the administration. Finally, the top civilian leadership in the

Pentagon was relatively new and inexperienced, whereas the opposite was true of congressional leaders interested in defense matters.[45]

Although congressional hearings and floor debates on the fiscal 1960 budget covered a multitude of issues, they focused particularly on three areas: the manner in which the executive branch had developed the defense budget; the adequacy of the defense budget; and the adequacy of United States limited war capabilities. In these hearings there was an obvious attempt in Congress to exploit differences within the administration, especially among the services. Of particular interest to Congress were the reservations expressed by the chiefs in their memorandum to McElroy—essentially the reservations previously recapitulated by the services.

This part did not go unnoticed in the White House. In early February Chairman Twining met with the president to cover a number of defense matters.[46] Twining mentioned that during the House hearings Congress had exhibited some sensitivity toward their prerogatives of raising and maintaining armies. The problem arose over the manpower of the army, marines, and reserves. The secretary of defense had been grilled extensively concerning the increment of strength that many in Congress thought should be added to the administration's program. The conversation then turned to the motives of individual congressmen in interfering with the administration's force structure program. The president was not overly concerned with the immediate problem and felt he could handle the matter of military strength.

Final action took place in both houses on August 4. The bill was about $20 million less than the administration's request. There were many internal changes, but none was dramatic. Both the president's strategic policy and his budgetary ceiling, by whatever name, remained intact.

An examination of the congressional phase of the fiscal 1960 defense budget shows that participation by Congress was piecemeal. Issues were examined without any particular attempt to relate them to each other or to the defense budget as a whole. There appears to have been little examination of the underlying rationale of the defense budget or any kind of systematic approach to reviewing it. Considering Eisenhower's determination to balance his budget, his skill in managing the budgetary process, the public's confidence in his military judgment, and the relatively short time and limited resources available to Congress for examining the defense budget, perhaps the outcome is not surprising. What Congress provided was rhetoric and some headlines; their effect on defense policy or budget was negligible, although differences between the services were now in the open in a more detailed way than heretofore.[47]

Any study of the secretary of defense during the Eisenhower period quickly becomes a study of Eisenhower himself. Of all the modern presidents, he intruded most into the policy functions of the defense secretary. Wilson and McElroy were, in effect, the business managers of the Pentagon, playing little part in strategic or policy questions.

Eisenhower came to office with the strategic innovation in mind he wanted to accomplish and he achieved it by 1954. Eisenhower's New Look was not a return to the Truman strategy of the pre-Korean War period; too much had changed for this to be possible. For example, on the international scene, the Soviet Union, the perceived adversary, was growing increasingly stronger, both militarily and economically. Eisenhower felt that the United States should continue to provide leadership to the non-Communist world. He rejected, however, the idea that military strength to support that leadership should be based on balanced forces. Instead he felt it should depend on the strategic deterrent.

Eisenhower perceived the nation's strength and security to be based on a fine balance between its economy and its military capabilities. There would be no more Koreas, where the adversary could initiate war by proxy in any number of places around the world. Such actions would be deterred by serving notice that the United States would not become involved in a series of debilitating and expensive military engagements but rather would respond selectively with nuclear power. Eisenhower made it clear that he had no intention of becoming involved in conventional wars, and he did not.

Eisenhower's role as the primary force in sustaining his strategic policy, which came under various forms of attack, is quite evident. His aggressiveness, confidence, and success in handling his adversaries, especially the service chiefs, come through quite clearly in

the records of the many meetings in his office. It is evident that the
president dominated the defense budget process. Basically, the
technique he employed was to set a budget ceiling—usually called
by another name, such as a "target." He attempted to get the service chiefs to take what he called the broader outlook, that is, to
accept his perceptions of the limitations of the economy. In part he
succeeded in this: not, however, by getting them to accept their
own budget ceilings but rather in getting them to accept the overall
budget ceiling.

It is interesting to note the way in which Eisenhower employed
organizational procedures to retain the primacy of his role in defense matters. Specifically, he operated separate organizational
channels for strategic policy and for the defense budget. For policy,
he dealt directly with the chairman of the Joint Chiefs of Staff, who
in turn dealt with the service chiefs. For the budget, he dealt with
the secretary of defense, whose budget channel then went directly
to the services, the chairman not being involved routinely.

Defense Secretaries Wilson and McElroy were both
functionalists. Neither had great rapport with the president. Their
roles were to manage the Pentagon and to keep the lid on the
defense budget. Neither secretary had a sophisticated understanding of strategic policy, which is perhaps one reason Eisenhower
chose them for the job. There is no evidence that Wilson had any
great influence in developing the strategic rationale for the New
Look, or that McElroy ever got far afield from the defense budget or
hardware debates. The two had different personalities, but they
played the same role: defense secretaries who had relatively little
influence on developing defense policy. Probably this outcome was
inevitable for a number of reasons: Eisenhower's strong interest and
prestige in strategic matters; the personalities and backgrounds of
Wilson and McElroy; and, in McElroy's case, the relatively short
period of time he was the defense secretary.[48]

Although the Joint Chiefs are collectively responsible, by law,
for providing military advice to the secretary of defense, the National
Security Council, and the president, a strong chairman can easily in-
sert himself between the service chiefs and higher political authority.
This was particularly true of Admiral Radford, operating under ideal
conditions because of his rapport with the president and Wilson.
Perhaps the best example of this influence was his October 1953 talk

in the NSC on the need for a decision on planning for early use of atomic weapons if defense budget economies were to be achieved. Radford was talking for himself, but to the NSC audience he appeared to be talking for the Joint Chiefs of Staff. In addition to his rapport with his superiors, Radford had two specific advantages: his strategic and economic views were in harmony with those of the president, and he worked for a functionalist defense secretary who had little strategic understanding. It is true that Radford, as chairman, was at a disadvantage in having no real role in the budgetary process. He made up for that, however, by his influence with Wilson, so in fact he sometimes played an unofficial role in developing the defense budget. Radford's influence as chairman, although shaped by the circumstances of the time, could easily be repeated by different combinations of major actors and circumstances. The potential is there at any time.

In sum, contrary to the conventional picture of him as a passive president, Eisenhower was a skilled practitioner of bureaucratic politics who dominated and frequently manipulated a powerful set of political and military appointees. In managing the strategic policy and defense budget processes, he was personally involved and remarkably effective.

3

McNamara
and Vietnam

On January 20, 1961, John F. Kennedy, the thirty-fifth president of the United States, set forth his vision in his inaugural address. It was vigorous, activist, and optimistic. In view of what happened later in Vietnam, it is worth recalling one passage in particular: "Let every nation know, whether it wishes us well or ill, that we shall pay any price, bear any burden, meet any hardship, support any friend, oppose any foe, to assure the success of liberty."

Kennedy had campaigned long and hard on the inadequacies of Eisenhower's defense and foreign policies. It was, therefore, to be expected that a more aggressive foreign policy and a larger alloca- tion of resources to defense would be forthcoming. The rhetoric of the inaugural address gave support to these expectations.

Since the orbiting of Sputnik in October 1957 the world had witnessed an increasingly aggressive Soviet posture. The Berlin crisis had been allowed to subside temporarily in early 1961, but it was not yet over. During the very month of the inaugural, Khrushchev made his famous speech on wars of national liberation in which he stated that the United States had not intervened in Vietnam because aid would come from the Soviet Union and else- where and this could lead to a world war.[1]

In the months following Kennedy's inauguration, there came along in fairly rapid succession: the Bay of Pigs fiasco in April, for which Kennedy correctly assumed responsibility; the encounter with Khrushchev at Vienna in June at which the Soviets virtually delivered an ultimatum on Berlin; and the erection of the Berlin

Wall in August. These events hardly constituted a reassuring start in foreign policy for the new administration.

Meanwhile the campaign promise to improve the United States defense posture was being met in both conventional and nuclear forces. It turned out, however, that Kennedy's allegations of a "missile gap" were without foundation. One unusual action was a reserve force call-up in connection with the Berlin crisis. This was to have a significant effect on the decision-makers' perceptions of how to fight the Vietnam War—a point that we will return to subsequently. Throughout the Kennedy administration, the Vietnam commitment grew from less than 1,000 American advisers at the start to 16,500 advisers and support forces by the time of the assassination. This period was also the high point of the counterinsurgency notion.

One of Kennedy's major foreign policy accomplishments was the treaty with the Soviet Union ending nuclear tests in the atmosphere. There had been an uninspected moratorium for several years that Kennedy inherited. This was ended by the Soviet Union in August 1961 when the Russians resumed atmospheric testing; subsequently the United States also did. Finally, a Test Ban Treaty ending atmospheric tests was achieved in the summer of 1963. The Joint Chiefs of Staff concurred but not without conditions: underground testing would be continued, readiness to resume atmospheric testing on short notice would be retained, ability to detect tests would be improved, and nuclear laboratories would be maintained. Still, it was no mean feat to get the Joint Chiefs to support the limited test-ban agreement.

The major foreign policy event of the Kennedy years was, no doubt, the Cuban missile crisis of October 1962. The story has been amply, but probably not yet fully, told; in the context of the times it was a major event on the international scene. On the Communist side, it probably led to Khrushschev's eventual ouster and a widening of the Sino-Soviet rift. On the part of the United States, it was a triumph and probably accelerated U.S. interventionist tendencies, in keeping with the rhetoric of the Kennedy inaugural address.

The domestic scene was somewhat less turbulent than that under the Johnson administration, but in some respects it foreshadowed what was to come. In general, Kennedy was content to move slowly in bringing about domestic reforms. He perceived that his most important objective was to resume a high state of economic growth, keeping in mind the problem of price stability and an improved balance of payments position.[2]

One major domestic crisis that did erupt during the Kennedy period was the race question. In 1962 occurred James Meredith's admission to the University of Mississippi as its first black student—a breakthrough that required the deployment of 20,000 federal troops. It was, however, during the first six months of the following year that the race problem clearly became a national issue. Probably the appearance on television of "Bull" Connor and his police dogs in Birmingham did more than anything else to cause this to be perceived as a white as well as a black problem.

When Lyndon Johnson became president, he inherited a mixed situation. Our international posture had been shaky in the early Kennedy years but had shown some important improvements. A significant exception was Vietnam, into which the United States was slowly sinking. On the domestic front, the Kennedy promise had yet to be fulfilled in matters of social welfare, and the race question was becoming increasingly tense. The major international event with which Johnson had to contend was the Ameican involvement in Vietnam, especially after the intervention of the American ground forces beginning in 1965.[3]

The nuclear question remained central to the international concerns of Johnson, as it had for every president since Truman. In October 1964 the Chinese exploded their first nuclear device, thus giving added impetus to Soviet-American negotiations over nuclear matters. The major successes of the Johnson administration in this regard were the Nonproliferation Treaty, signed on July 1, 1968, and the announcement on the same day of the agreement to hold strategic arms limitation talks (SALT). These talks did not transpire until the next administration because of the Soviet invasion of Czechoslovakia in the following month and the lame duck nature of the Johnson administration thereafter.

The nuclear issue also remained a significant one on the NATO agenda, as it had since the second Eisenhower administration. Basically the question was how to give the Europeans a feeling of greater participation in the nuclear strategy that was vital for their defense. There were legal and congressional inhibitions that had prevented both Eisenhower and Kennedy from solving the problem. What

Johnson inherited was the notion of a multilateral force that would be a NATO-controlled seaborne-missile force manned by nationals of various NATO countries. For a variety of reasons—in particular President Charles de Gaulle's opposition and pressure on the West German leadership—the idea never came to fruition. What finally developed was the NATO Nuclear Planning Group. This stemmed from a proposal in the spring of 1965 made by Secretary of Defense Robert McNamara, the intent of which was to provide a forum for NATO countries to study nuclear questions vital to their defense. The first meeting was held in Washington in the spring of 1967 and the arrangement subsequently proved to be successful.

There were of course other issues within the alliance, perhaps the most notable being the "equitable sharing of defense burdens." In 1967 the Johnson administration was able to negotiate an agreement that linked security and monetary policy. This was by no means the end of this issue, but it provided a temporary easement.

It was in the domestic area—the Great Society—that Johnson intended to make his greatest mark. Early in his administration he was able to shift efforts toward domestic priorities. During his honeymoon period with Congress, he was remarkably successful. Within half a year Congress passed numerous bills, including minimum wage increases, more liberal social security benefits, a housing bill, and a farm bill. Johnson's efforts continued throughout his administration and resulted in a remarkable body of revolutionary legislation pertaining to poverty, education, civil rights, and medical services.

There had developed meanwhile serious fissures in American society. The race problem accelerated, moving from the South to northern cities, where especially serious riots occurred in the summer of 1967. The peak occurred in April 1968 after the assassination of Martin Luther King, Jr. Many American cities were involved, most spectacularly Washington, D.C., with fires not many blocks from the White House.

There were other problems for the president besides race—in particular, a growing antiwar sentiment that increased in stridency as the war dragged on. There was also that remarkable phenomenon, which started in Berkeley in 1964, of dissident white affluent youth. Nurtured in affluence, yet questioning the material values of their parents and the relevance of their universities, they merged with the antiwar movement, reaching their apogee in the Kent State shootings of May 1970—long after Johnson had left the presidency.

For the Johnson administration, the international and domestic context merged in one great spasm in the early months of 1968. In January the U.S.S. *Pueblo*, on an intelligence-gathering mission, was seized by the North Koreans. A few days later the watershed event of the Second Indo-Chinese War occurred—the Communist Tet Offensive. To a people who had been told that they were winning, news of this stunning offensive was staggering. Not only the youth and antiwar movement but now even the establishment, at least in part, sent the president a message: get out of Vietnam. On March 31, 1968, President Johnson announced to a nationwide television audience that he would not seek his party's nomination for reelection.

The foregoing, then, is the international and domestic context that circumscribed the tenure of Robert Strange McNamara as the eighth secretary of defense—from January 1961 until the end of February 1968.

As was evident throughout his campaign, John F. Kennedy had a keen interest in foreign and defense policy. Like all presidents, he had his own views on how these interrelated policies should be managed and the kind of persons he wanted to be his chief advisers. Kennedy had offered Robert Lovett the post of either secretary of state or secretary of defense, but he declined them both. Lovett, however, subsequently recommended Robert McNamara for the defense post and supported Dean Rusk to head State.

There were differences in the manner in which the president dealt with the two departments. Kennedy had not known either of the two men before. In the course of accepting the job at Defense, McNamara had insisted on selecting his own assistants. In fact he presented a letter to Kennedy for his signature that would put this arrangement in writing. Kennedy laughed and put the letter in his pocket, but he agreed to the arrangement.[4] Rusk was not as fortunate, and many of his assistants were selected by the White House.

There was, however, a more important point of difference in Kennedy's handling of the two departments, as told by W. W. Rostow: "Administratively, Rusk's problem was vastly more complex than McNamara's because Kennedy was determined to deal intimately with foreign affairs and to reshape foreign policy, piece by piece. McNamara's reorganization of the Pentagon and of the American force structure was, perhaps, even more radical than Kennedy's innovations in foreign policy, but Kennedy did not monitor that reorganization in the way he engaged in foreign policy."[5]

As for the White House organization to deal with national security affairs, Kennedy also had his own ideas. He held the conventional, but somewhat incorrect, view of how Eisenhower had managed his NSC system. Kennedy disliked the formal NSC structure that Eisenhower had created and dismantled it. He placed considerable reliance on his special assistant for national security affairs, McGeorge Bundy. It was Bundy's job to see that the president was presented with all the options on important security issues. Kennedy made it clear that Bundy was not to interfere in the normal interactions of the secretaries of state and defense with the president.[6] As it turned out, it worked that way in the Defense Department, but in State it was well known that Bundy frequently was in touch with persons well down in the hierarchy.

Comparatively unknown when President Kennedy selected him as secretary of defense, Robert McNamara had been president of the Ford Motor Company about a month when Sargent Shriver approached him about a cabinet post on behalf of the president-elect.

McNamara was born in San Francisco in 1916 and graduated from the University of California at Berkeley in 1937. He received a Master of Business Administration degree at Harvard in 1939 and the following year joined the faculty there, specializing in the application of statistical analysis to management problems. During World War II he served as a commissioned officer in the Army Air Corps, working as a staff officer in statistical control. After the war he and nine other statistical control experts hired themselves out to the Ford Motor Company. He rose rapidly in the firm, and when he was elected its president in 1960, he was the first to hold that office who was not a member of the Ford family.

Although he obviously had enormous ability and drive in order to succeed as he did at Ford, in certain respects he was not typical of the automobile industry. Eschewing the usual habitats of automobile executives, such as Grosse Pointe Shores, he preferred to live in the college community of Ann Arbor near the University of

Michigan. Here his relaxation was more that of a college professor—discussion, books, symphonies—than of the relentlessly driving automobile executive that he was. These avocations were to stand him in good stead in the social life of Kennedy's Washington.

When McNamara went to Washington to see Kennedy after the Shriver visit, the two hit it off well, and he was offered the post of secretary of defense. As his deputy, McNamara chose Roswell L. Gilpatric, a New York lawyer and Pentagon hand during the Truman administration.[7] Gilpatric assumed that his own prior experience would give him an early advantage over McNamara, but this proved erroneous, as McNamara was a quick study and soon got a fix on the management and organization of the Defense Department.[8]

There seems to be a general consensus on many of McNamara's personal characteristics: intelligent, able, decisive, self-confident, hard-driving, puritanical, and free of cynicism are terms used most frequently by his associates in describing him. He was most comfortable in dealing with a problem when he could view it in terms of figures, and he required, when possible, that papers submitted to him employ such a format. The rimless glasses and slicked-down hair helped give him a stern and formidable look, but he could be as engaging a person as anyone in Washington.

Others of McNamara's characteristics set forth by those who knew him best are perhaps less desirable in a secretary of defense. He was apparently incapable of compromising on issues—in this sense he was not a political animal, a disadvantage in the Washington jungle. He was an emotional person, but only occasionally did this come through in his public appearances. Once he made his mind up on subordinates' being "good" or "no good," that was the way it remained. The "no goods" were rarely fired; they were simply ignored.

As it turned out later, the characteristic that caused him the greatest problem was his lack of a sophisticated world view. Detroit had not provided one and, therefore, he absorbed the view of Kennedy and some of his associates—and that was the outlook of the 1940s or 1950s. To describe it in a shorthand way, he perceived a Communist monolith, with Asia in the same category as Europe as far as the need to contain the Communist threat was concerned.

McNamara approached his new duties in the same activist spirit he had displayed at Ford. This comes through quite clearly in his approach to management. As McNamara stated it: "The direction of the Department of Defense demands not only a strong, responsible civilian control, but a Secretary's role that consists of active, imaginative and decisive leadership of the establishment at large, and not the passive practice of simply refereeing the disputes of traditional and partisan factions."[9]

With his deputy secretary, of which he was to have three,[10] McNamara followed the tradition that had been set by Marshall in 1950, allowing the deputy to be a true alter ego. He accepted their decisions and backed them up when this was required. In effect, he doubled his decision-making capability.

McNamara's relationships with the Joint Chiefs of Staff were complex and covered a fairly wide spectrum. When he became secretary, General Lyman Lemnitzer, who had been appointed by President Eisenhower the previous October, was chairman. Lemnitzer was highly regarded by Eisenhower but apparently did not develop any great rapport with either McNamara or President Kennedy. Whatever chance there was for such a relationship, the Bay of Pigs fiasco a few months into the new administration no doubt finished it.[11] One result of the Bay of Pigs was the return of Maxwell Taylor to government service, first to conduct an inquest into the military operation and thereafter to become a presidential adviser. Taylor fitted in well with the Kennedys and McNamara and in October 1962 returned to the active list and became chairman of the Joint Chiefs. He had a close relationship with McNamara and was in a position to be the most powerful chairman since Radford's tenure in the first Eisenhower administration.

The chairman with the longest tenure under McNamara was army General Earle G. ("Bus") Wheeler. Appointed in early July 1964, he was closely involved in the decisions concerning United States troop intervention in Vietnam and the subsequent escalation of that effort. The success of Wheeler, a West Point graduate of 1932, was based on his superb skills as a staff officer. Gentlemanly, urbane, and highly articulate, he understood the Washington bureaucracy better perhaps than any active duty officer at that time.

As for the other members of the Joint Chiefs, there were no less than nine military service chiefs during McNamara's period as secretary. Army chiefs of staff were Generals George H. Decker, Earle G. Wheeler (before he became chairman), and Harold K.

Johnson. The last named served during the critical decision-making period concerning the war in Vietnam. Johnson was a survivor of the Bataan death march and subsequent imprisonment in Japanese war camps. He gradually returned to the mainstream of the army and received his big opportunity when he was named army deputy chief of staff for operations. A year later, when Wheeler was made chairman, Johnson was selected by McNamara over many generals senior to him to be chief of staff. A deeply religious man and one inclined toward introspection, Johnson, like the other service chiefs, saw little of the president or the White House during the McNamara years. Presidents Kennedy and Johnson preferred to deal with the chairman rather than the chiefs as a group.

There were four chiefs of naval operations during the McNamara years. Admiral Arleigh A. Burke, a brief holdover from the Eisenhower period, was followed by Admiral George W. Anderson. Between Anderson and McNamara there was a good deal of abrasion. In part this was based on Anderson's dislike of McNamara's active management, which could be interpreted as an infringement on service prerogatives. This came to a head in their well-known confrontation during blockade operations resulting from the Cuban missile crisis. Apparently McNamara sought operational details that Anderson felt went beyond the defense secretary's role. In any case, McNamara declined Anderson's reappointment to a second term as chief of naval operations, and on Gilpatric's recommendation the president appointed him ambassador to Portugal.

The naval chief during the Vietnam escalation was Admiral David L. McDonald, a naval aviator, who had served in Supreme Allied Headquarters near Paris and subsequently commanded the Sixth Fleet in the Mediterranean. A smooth person, McDonald was able to adjust to the frustrations of working with McNamara and his staff. His successor, Admiral Thomas H. Moorer, also a naval aviator, served only briefly during McNamara's tenure and subsequently became Nixon's chairman after Wheeler's retirement in 1970.

There were three air force chiefs during the period. General Thomas White was a brief holdover from the Eisenhower period. He was replaced by his vice chief and former commander of the Strategic Air Command, General Curtis E. LeMay. LeMay's tour lasted from the end of June 1961 through January 1965. Relations between the cigar-smoking former bomber commander and the defense secretary were not good. McNamara was reluctant to have LeMay's tour extended beyond the summer of 1963. The president, however, did not want to take the political risks that might be involved in what could be interpreted as a premature retirement for LeMay. As another consideration, Kennedy was always interested in keeping the military happy, whereas McNamara was not especially concerned about that factor.

The air chief during the Vietnam escalation was General John P. McConnell. A classmate of Wheeler's, McConnell was, like Westmoreland later, the first captain of the cadet corps at West Point. He too had lengthy service in the Strategic Air Command.

As had his predecessor, Thomas Gates, McNamara met routinely with the Joint Chiefs. Following the format that Gates had established, the secretary and his deputy met with the Joint Chiefs in their own meeting room, the so-called Tank. There was an advance agenda for the meeting. However, one former chief of staff told me he could not recall anything definite coming out of the meetings and he never came away with the sense that there had been any real discussion. "The meetings were," he said, "a cosmetic."[12]

Another forum, in which the secretary and the senior military came together, was apparently more productive, at least for a while. In addition to the chiefs, the service secretaries and the assistant secretaries of defense also attended a weekly meeting with McNamara. Although General Johnson felt these were more substantive than the Tank meetings, he likened them to a classroom situation in which McNamara played the role of teacher. There was, he indicated, no true give-and-take in the discussion.

Some senior military men have described two McNamaras. On a one-to-one basis, he frequently came across as warm, responsive, and understanding. With a group of people he became increasingly authoritative. One service chief felt this was essentially a defense mechanism to prevent the bureaucracy from finding "a crack in his armor."[13]

Whatever his personal characteristics, McNamara and the two presidents he served did not want the entire array of Joint Chiefs to meet with the president any more than was absolutely necessary, and so such meetings became a rare event. In a 1965 meeting with

President Johnson some disagreement on strategy arose between the army chief of staff and the marine commandant. McNamara became highly irritated and told Chairman Wheeler that he did not want to see that kind of session again.[14] What developed then was that Wheeler, like his predecessor Taylor, represented the Joint Chiefs in presidential forums. By statute the Joint Chiefs are advisers to both the secretary of defense and the president. Failure to carry through the intent of that statute, for whatever reason, was to have some rather profound consequences on the conduct of the Vietnam War.[15]

Wheeler was never considered quite as much the administration's man by the chiefs as Taylor had been. For one thing, he refrained from bringing to McNamara, when possible, splits on issues between the services and emphasized issues where the services spoke with a united voice. Prior to Wheeler's becoming chairman, the chiefs perceived that McNamara was using the splits against them.[16] Whatever the long-run tactical advantage of this procedure to the services, there are potential dangers in not carrying certain divergencies forward to the highest levels.[17]

Secretary McNamara's principal colleague in the development of United States security policy, in the broad meaning of that term, was of course the secretary of state, Dean Rusk. Rusk, a Rhodes scholar, joined the faculty of Mills College in California following graduation. He was an associate professor of government and dean of the faculty when he went on active duty in the army in 1940, having held a commission in the reserves since his cadet colonel days at Davidson College in North Carolina. The war eventually took him to the headquarters of the China, Burma, India theatre in New Delhi. The quality of the cables written by him brought Rusk to the attention of officials in General Marshall's command post in Washington, the Operations Division (OPD) of the War Department General Staff, and he found himself ordered there in 1944.

Here Rusk joined a remarkable group of young officers in the Strategy and Policy group headed by Brigadier General George A. ("Abe") Lincoln, which included among others Colonel Charles H. ("Tick") Bonesteel, and Lieutenant Colonel Andrew J. Goodpaster. Association with this group and with Marshall himself eventually led Rusk to the State Department, where by 1950 he was assistant secretary of state for far eastern affairs. In 1952 he became president of the Rockefeller Foundation, a prestigious and powerful post. During the course of his eight years with the foundation, he became fairly well known to the Democratic establishment and in April 1960 published an article in *Foreign Affairs* concerning the president and the conduct of foreign policy.

Shortly after his appointment as secretary of state, Rusk and McNamara met together and agreed on what was the proper relationship between the Defense and State departments. Thereafter there was a close rapport between the two of them. McNamara supported the conventional understanding that defense policy is derived from foreign policy. Still, if one goes back over some of McNamara's pronouncements in the 1960s, such as those concerning NATO or nuclear strategy, there is a curious component in what comes through as original foreign policy statements. Take, for example, McNamara's annual posture statements, first published in February 1963 (in support of the fiscal year 1964 defense budget). The first part of the statements are from 25 to 50 percent foreign policy—basically written in the Pentagon. State had the opportunity to comment, but it is well known that the person who writes the first draft is in charge of the situation.

Quiet and introspective by nature, Rusk had a personality that contrasted in many respects with that of the brisk, confident defense secretary, who could astonish audiences with his total and precise recall of facts and figures. Nevertheless the two seemed to work well together. They differed considerably in the way that they dealt with the president. McNamara would caucus his own people in advance of meeting with the president and come up with an agreed position. On the other hand, the Rusk team might raise diverse opinions in discussion with the president. Obviously, in most cases the Defense Department's position was somewhat clearer to the president and accordingly somewhat more appealing. Still, the approach did permit Kennedy a greater hand in foreign affairs than in the business of the Pentagon, which is apparently the way he wanted it.

In his relations with Congress, McNamara found the going fairly difficult, especially during his later years in office. Not experienced in the Washington method of operation, he found it difficult to go along with political views that suggested solutions at variance with rational solutions to defense problems. At the outset his deputy, Roswell Gilpatric, was of considerable assistance in working out a *modus vivendi* with congressional groups.

In his early years in Washington, McNamara's testimony before congressional committees literally dazzled them. The facts and figures poured out in a torrent and with great assurance. Never had a secretary of defense been as much on top of the issues or his job as McNamara. Congressional committee chairmen congratulated him on his performance. As time went on, decisions had to be made on important issues and McNamara made them: base closings; hardware decisions, such as the TFX, the B-70, and nuclear carriers; plans for reorganizing the reserves and their call-up in 1961; strategic policy decisions; and Vietnam. Confrontations with Congress over such issues took an enormous amount of McNamara's time and energy. Inevitably, the nature of the issues was bound to erode his position with the Congress. At the worst point, five congressional investigations on such issues were under way simultaneously.

The sources of McNamara's problems with Congress lay not only in varying views on the issues but also in the military. As the senior officers gradually recovered from the initial McNamara onslaught on the Pentagon, they began to feed their frustrations to their various constituencies in Congress. This, combined with pressures from certain local powers in congressional districts, built up a multiplicity of forces opposing McNamara's programs. After all, every base closing affects some congressional district, every hardware decision favors one firm located in one state over one located in another. McNamara handled himself well through all this, but it took its toll. Seven years is a long time to be secretary of defense.

When Lyndon Johnson succeeded to the presidency, he kept Kennedy's principal national security and foreign policy advisers. Johnson was greatly impressed with McNamara's performance as secretary of defense. In fact, he was so impressed by McNamara that he drew him into many problems not directly related to defense matters as a kind of high-level troubleshooter. In time, however, Johnson and McNamara drew apart on the war.

Rusk's survival was not due as much to Johnson's being impressed with his qualifications as to his appreciation of Rusk's good treatment of Johnson the vice president, at a time when other Ken-

nedy cabinet officials were ignoring him.[18] McGeorge Bundy stayed
on as special assistant for national security affairs until the end of
1965, when he was replaced by Walt Rostow.

Johnson retained the same informal approach to policymaking as
Kennedy had used. He did, however, introduce one innovation in
early 1964 that he retained until the end of his administration—the
Tuesday luncheon group, or Tuesday Cabinet, as it was sometimes
called. At first the meetings were irregular, but as the Vietnam crisis
deepened the sessions were held weekly, even though the forum
discussed many topics not related to Vietnam. The members attending regularly, in addition to the president, were the secretary of
defense, the secretary of state, the special assistant, and the press
secretary. Occasionally others, including the vice president, were
invited to a session. Since the Vietnam War was normally discussed
and decisions taken relating to the war, there were two curious
omissions from this group who did not become regular attenders
until the fall of 1966, the Joint Chiefs chairman and the director of
the CIA.

The forum was apparently collegial in nature, following a prepared agenda, but there was no publication of the proceedings,
except in the form of implementing presidential decisions by the
official concerned.[19] The forum has sometimes been criticized for
being isolated and living in a world of its own, but those involved
felt it was an effective way of doing business without everyone in
Washington knowing the details of how each decision was made and
the positions taken by various officials.[20]

There were, of course, many other forums than the Tuesday
lunch, both more and less formal, at which decisions on a great
variety of matters, including Vietnam, were made by the president.
The National Security Council, at least from 1966 on, became much
more formalized and systematic under Johnson than it had been
under Kennedy, with meetings being held on an average of slightly
more than once a month during the entire Johnson period. Unlike
the Tuesday lunch, however, NSC meetings during the last three
years of the Johnson presidency were concerned more with an-
ticipating problems than with treating current ones.[21]

Of all the writings on McNamara's tenure in the Department of
Defense, the vast majority stress his management approach.[22] It

was thus that he made his major impact on defense decision-making. Moreover, certain aspects of this management approach were his major legacy to the Defense Department. McNamara was interested in more than simply efficient management. He wanted to achieve more effective top-management control of resource allocations by being able to cut across the services horizontally on such issues as force structure and competing weapons systems. To place his tour in the Pentagon in proper perspective, certain aspects of McNamara's management apparatus should be highlighted here.

Prior to McNamara's appointment, a Pentagon study examined what the Eisenhower-sponsored 1958 Defense Reorganization Act authorized the secretary of defense to do that he was not already doing.[23] Thomas Gates, McNamara's immediate predecessor, was impressed by the study and recommended it to McNamara. In essence, the study pointed up the fact that the secretary's authority under the act was extensive and had not yet been exploited. McNamara himself decided that no further legislation was needed but that management changes were. As he put it: "From the beginning in January 1961, it seemed to me that the principal problem in efficient management of the Department's resources was not the lack of management authority. The National Security Act provides the Secretary of Defense a full measure of power. The problem was rather the absence of the essential management tools needed to make sound decisions on the really crucial issues of national security."[24]

The primary management tools that McNamara initiated were the Planning-Programming-Budgeting System (PPBS) and systems analysis. PPBS was installed by Charles J. Hitch, an economist who had been with RAND and had, in 1961, coauthored with Roland N. McKean *The Economics of Defense in the Nuclear Age.* Systems analysis was developed as a technique within the department under the supervision of Alain G. Enthoven, who joined the Defense Department in 1960 as an operations research analyst. When Hitch was made assistant secretary (comptroller) at the beginning of the new administration, Enthoven became his deputy, focusing specifically on systems analysis. Subsequently, in 1965 he became an assistant secretary himself, when the Systems Analysis Office was raised to that level.

PPBS provided both an information base and a control device linking together long-range planning and shorter-range budgeting through programs financed over a five-year period.[25] Although Hitch wanted to take eighteen months to install the new system, McNamara decided to do it in six months, so that it could be used in developing the fiscal year 1963 budget—the first budget for which the new administration was fully responsible.

The planning phase was one that had previously existed but with a somewhat different thrust. The basic military input was the Joint Strategic Objectives Plan (JSOP) developed by the Joint Chiefs of Staff. The first volume was a joint document that viewed the strategic threat to the United States in the context of its worldwide commitments. The second volume, which recommended force levels to meet the world situation, tended to be less of a joint document. Since force levels eventually determined each service's future, there was a strong tendency for this document to reflect the needs as seen by each service and hence in aggregate to set forth unrealistic requirements.

The new emphasis introduced into the planning phase by McNamara was to require military-economic studies, which compared alternative ways of accomplishing national security objectives based upon cost-effectiveness. These studies (which were prepared in Enthoven's office, rather than as part of the JSOP) were in reality the basis for the remainder of the PPBS cycle. The instruments for implementing the studies were called Draft Presidential Memoranda (DPM) and were issued for each of the Defense Department's nine mission and functional areas into which the defense budget was divided.[26] The DPMs then were based on an analysis that cut across the services and affected the way they carried out their roles and missions.

The programming phase was the bridge between planning and budgeting and began with the secretary's receiving the JSOP and the DPMs. Actually the planning and programming phases are somewhat difficult to separate analytically. Programming is, however, more specific than planning and determines the resources needed to reach specific objectives. It was, moreover, the key phase in the entire process. The major programming document was known as the Five-Year Defense Program (FYDP).[27] After reviewing the JSOP and the DPM, the secretary provided guidance to the services for proposing changes to the FYDP through their use of program change requests (PCRs).[28]

Upon receipt of PCRs, the Systems Analysis Office again played a key roll. Having previously prepared the Draft Presidential Memoranda, the office now analyzed the service recommendations for changes in the FYDP.[29] The task at this point was to determine the issues, assumptions, and cost alternatives and to suggest the questions for the secretary to ask the service proposing a particular change.

Meanwhile, the Joint Chiefs were also reviewing the Draft Presidential Memoranda and providing their own recommendations. During each summer McNamara, aided by the Systems Analysis Office and other staff members, made decisions on the JCS and service proposals and toward the end of August issued DPMs as the basis for the final budgeting. This stage, which usually culminated in presidential decisions in late December, was not without controversy. In this respect it was more than merely figuring the cost of the first year of the five-year program. In a sense, however, the controversy during the final budget phase had been preempted by the programming state (which had its own share of controversy) that preceded it.

Systems analysis was in effect the instrument by which data were compared as a means of determining the cost of various options. It also provided the means for judging the logic of the many proposals (sometimes conflicting) that came from the department, including the services. These proposals might involve such matters as forces, hardware decisions, or training.

This, then, in rather general terms, was the McNamara mangement approach. Probably nothing in the McNamara period caused more debate within the Department of Defense and the Congress than his management apparatus. This was especially true of Systems Analysis, manned by the so-called Whiz-Kids who allegedly paid little attention to the professional military. The system had its supporters as well as detractors[30] and its successes as well as its failures. The best known of the latter probably was the TFX or F-111, as it eventually became known.

The best case in support of the McNamara management is made

in Enthoven and Smith's book. As they see it, defense policymaking was improved in two broad ways. First, strategy, force requirements, and costs were brought together in a single analysis, rather than as a result of negotiations among the services that led to an arbitrary allocation of resources. The second area of improvement lay in providing the secretary with an independent, mainly civilian, analytical staff. This approach was necessary since McNamara had decided to play an active role rather than merely judging between competing military claimants.

There is little question that McNamara's management system permitted him to take the initiative from the services. For example, the Draft Presidential Memoranda were a way of setting forth the assumptions and thus for all practical purposes defining the solution. There is little question either that this system established an increasingly adversarial relationship between the secretary's office and the Joint Chiefs and the services, and eventually also with elements of the Congress.

Critics of the McNamara management and especially of systems analysis were many. One of the more frequent criticisms concerned with the downgrading of military professionalism. In effect, it was alleged, decisions were being made by civilians on military questions without proper consultation with the professional military.[31] Another criticism is that much of the analysis was designed to support decisions already made or preconceived solutions. Perhaps this is not too surprising. Defense decisions are, after all, highly political in nature. The most rational solution to a problem is frequently foreclosed by a call from the White House,[32] or from an influential congressman, or even by a previous career commitment on the part of some official in the Pentagon.

The tendency to take a strictly rational view of PPBS and systems analysis raises a related point. My brief summary of the system only indicates how it was supposed to operate. In actual practice, there were many slippages. For example, in many instances Program Change Requests were not negotiated until after the budgetary cycle was completed rather than before the final phase of the cycle.

Although McNamara's major impact was in the area of defense decision-making, he was also responsible for establishing certain defense agencies of a functional nature. During the Eisenhower period, the Defense Atomic Support Agency and the Defense Communcations Agency reported to the secretary through the Joint Chiefs of Staff. McNamara himself established the Defense Intelligence Agency, also reporting through the Joint Chiefs, and two other agencies reporting directly to him: the Defense Supply Agency and the Defense Contract Audit Agency. The above agencies were in keeping with the single-manager concept, by which technical activities were consolidated under a single head rather than being distributed throughout the services. In the case of Defense Intelligence Agency, one could argue that intelligence is not all that technical and that some pluralism is healthy.

In retrospect, McNamara's management approach was a major innovation. It was bound to be a source of bureaucratic friction, since power flowed from the military to the secretary. This in time was also bound to cause confrontations with Congress. McNamara's major accomplishment was no mean feat: for the first time, the secretary of defense gained control of the Pentagon. Whether he was able to retain this control as the Vietnam War became the major concern, we will see. The early PPBS was primitive, but it was later refined and retained and was perhaps McNamara's major legacy to the Department of Defense. Systems analysis survived in a different way, not as an all-powerful office but as an analytical mode of thought throughout the Pentagon in both the service staffs and the Joint Chiefs of Staff.

Before the outbreak of the Korean War, two National Security Council papers set the terms for the overall United States objectives with respect to Indo-China that were intended to offset what later became known as the "domino principle."[33] Indo-China was important because it was the only area in which a large European army (French) was in conflict with Communists (Viet Minh). The key operative paragraphs were:

It is important to United States security interests that all practicable measures be taken to prevent further communist expansion in Southeast Asia. Indo-China is a key area of Southeast Asia and is under immediate threat.

The neighboring countries of Thailand and Burma could be expected to fall under Communist domination if Indo-China were controlled by a Communist-dominated government. The balance of Southeast Asia would then be in grave hazard.

The outbreak of the Korean War in 1950, and particularly the Chinese intervention that fall, had the effect on United States policymakers of making the French struggle in Indo-China appear as part of a worldwide struggle to contain communism. At this point the People's Republic of China rather than the Soviet Union was perceived as the principal source of the Communist threat to Southeast Asia.[34]

By the time Dien Bien Phu fell in May 1954, the United States was paying 80 percent of the cost of the French effort in Indo-China. In October 1954 President Eisenhower informed Premier Diem (who became chief of state the following October) that henceforth U.S. aid would be given directly to his government rather than through the French. In a few months a Military Assistance Group was on the ground to take over from the French the training of South Vietnamese armed forces.

During the Eisenhower years, the commitment of advisers was not large, never reaching 1,000. However, as the Viet Cong insurgent activity, which surfaced by 1957, began to reach serious proportions in 1959, so too did the U.S. objectives change: not only were the South Vietnamese to be assisted in building up their forces to assure internal security, but they were to be encouraged to plan their defense against external aggression. This was the situation when Kennedy took office in January 1961.

In the early days of the new administration, Laos and Berlin were considered greater problems than Vietnam. Then in April 1961 came a crisis in Laos and the Bay of Pigs in Cuba. Although the latter episode was not directly connected with Vietnam, it became connected in Washington perceptions of the United States-USSR struggle for prestige of which Vietnam was another part. On April 20, shortly after the Bay of Pigs episode, Kennedy asked Roswell Gilpatric to appraise the situation in Vietnam and to recommend actions to prevent Communist control of South Vietnam.

The report's recommendations were limited and included a modest increase in the Military Advisory Group. This Kennedy approved. At the same time, the situation in Laos was becoming less favorable to the United States. In view, then, of what was perceived as a steadily deteriorating situation in Southeast Asia, the president in May dispatched Vice President Johnson to meet with Diem. The outcome of his visit was a new presidential program for South

Vietnam, announced in May and designed to strengthen the Diem government, as well as to improve its popular support in that country and in the United States. This was a major decision on Kennedy's part to hold in Vietnam. Important military changes included increasing the aid program, increasing the regular South Vietnamese forces to 200,000 and providing United States Special Forces to train these forces. An unannounced decision was also made to study the possible commitment of U.S. forces at some time in the future.

In October 1961 the famous Taylor-Rostow investigation of the increasingly shaky situation in South Vietnam took place. Following Taylor's recommendations, President Kennedy sent additional advisers, equipment, and support, including helicopter units. He did not, however, approve the introduction of a U.S. military task force that Taylor had also recommended. The Taylor mission was a definite benchmark in the escalation of the war and involved the second major decision on Kennedy's part—committing the United States to stay the course in Vietnam.

In the early days of the administration, McNamara had not been deeply involved in the South Vietnam question. In the fall of 1961, however, he became increasingly involved and in December he attended the first of many meetings on Vietnam in Honolulu,[35] while en route home from a NATO Ministerial Meeting in Paris, where the chief concern was the Berlin Wall and negotiation problems with the Soviet Union. The military had many questions to ask McNamara about equipment for the South Vietnamese, about the overall policy on assistance, and so forth. McNamara's responses were positive. "We are," he said, "going to the uttermost limits of policy."[36]

When he returned to Washington, McNamara reported to Kennedy and Rusk. At this point, the defense secretary assumed a major supervisory role with respect to American actions in Vietnam. He in fact became the "action officer" on Vietnam for the president. From this point on no one in the State Department was in a position to vie with him for this role, even if he wished to.

Early in 1962 McNamara was off again to Honolulu for a couple of conferences on progress in South Vietnam. The situation "seems to be stabilized," but it would be "a long and hard struggle." At the same time Robert Kennedy in Saigon was assuring the South

Vietnamese government that "United States troops would stay in South Vietnam until Communist aggression was defeated."[37]

By spring the official outlook concerning progress had become more optimistic and by summer almost euphoric. On July 23 the fourteen-nation neutralization declaration on Laos was signed.[38] On the same day at a conference in Honolulu Secretary McNamara, noting that "tremendous progress" had been made, directed development of a plan for building up the South Vietnamese armed forces and phasing out the American role.[39] He assumed this could be accomplished in approximately three years, or by the end of 1965.[40]

This optimism continued into the following spring, with the United States headquarters in Saigon predicting the possibility of a military victory that year. McNamara was writing memoranda to his assistant secretary for international security affairs[41] directing that 1,000 troops be removed by the end of the year and requesting that estimates on military aid to South Vietnam beginning in fiscal year 1965 be reduced. It was not the last time during the long Vietnam affair that official optimism was soon laid to rest.

In May there occurred a series of riots in Hue. Police handling of these set off disputes between the Buddhists and the government. The harsh manner in which the government reacted caused increased concern in Washington over the viability of the Diem regime as summer came on.

In late September McNamara, accompanied by Maxwell Taylor, went to Vietnam to assess the situation. Their report to the president, though it considered the political situation "deeply serious," was still optimistic about the prosecution of the war. Then in November in rapid succession came the assassinations of Diem and Kennedy and a new evaluation of the situation. McNamara was back in Vietnam in December and now his report to the new president took on a new tone: "The situation is very disturbing. Current trends, unless reversed in the next two or three months, will lead to a neutralization at best and more likely to a communist-controlled state."[42] In March McNamara in Honolulu agreed with the military that United States support should be increased.

In early 1964 it would still have been possible to reassess the American role in Vietnam. Johnson was a new president, and a changed political situation in Vietnam in the wake of the Diem assassination would have made a reevaluation of the United States role a real option. But 1964 was an election year in America and Johnson had assumed the Kennedy mantle. In addition, he believed in the American effort, perhaps more than Kennedy had. In any case, the reassessment did not take place.[43]

Whatever ambiguity there may have been in the degree of commitment of the United States up to this point, none was left after publication of National Security Action Memorandum (NSAM) 288 in March 1964: "We seek an independent non-Communist South Vietnam. We do not require that it serve as a Western base or as a member of a Western alliance. South Vietnam must be free, however, to accept outside assistance as required to maintain its security. This assistance should be able to take the form not only of economic and social measures but also police and military help to root out and control insurgent elements."[44]

The same spring McNamara, on another of his many visits to South Vietnam, met with the incoming and outgoing commanders, Generals William Westmoreland and Paul Harkins. "Paul," asked McNamara, "how long do you think it will take to wind up this war?" Harkins responded, "Oh, I think we can change the tide in about six months." Westmoreland said he found this exchange incredible.[45]

In part as a result of McNamara's trip, his report, which was not encouraging, moved President Johnson to ask Ambassador Henry Cabot Lodge and Westmoreland to meet with his principal Washington advisers in Honolulu, but the conference brought about no change in objectives. At this point the Republican Convention was only a few weeks away and Johnson was not interested in setting up any barn-sized targets. He even resurrected a letter from President Eisenhower to Diem in 1954, implying that the letter set forth the basic American position.

During the early afternoon of August 4, 1964, the United States destroyers *Maddox* and *C. Turner Joy* were apparently subjected to an attack by some torpedo boats of the North Vietnamese navy. The *Maddox* had been similarly attacked two days earlier. The precise nature of the destroyers' mission and the exact location of the attack with respect to the coastline of North Vietnam have been subjects of controversy ever since. On the night of August 4, President Johnson informed the nation of the second attack, indicating that air action was in progress against North Vietnamese gunboats and supporting facilities and that he would seek a congressional resolution making it clear that the United States was united in its efforts in Southeast Asia.

Subsequently, in his request to Congress for a resolution Johnson linked the objectives of his administration in Southeast Asia with those of Eisenhower and Kennedy. On August 10, Congress passed Public Law 88–409, the so-called Tonkin Gulf Resolution, by a margin of 502 to 2 votes. The resolution declared that Congress supported the determination of the president to take all necessary measures to prevent further aggression and added: "The U.S. regards as vital to its national interest and to world peace the maintenance of national peace and security in Southeast Asia." The United States, furthermore, was prepared "to take all necessary steps, including the use of armed forces, to assist any member or protocol state of the Southeast Asia collective defense treaty."

In the middle of August Westmoreland (by now the American commander in Vietnam) sent a message to Washington in which he suggested that consideration be given to improving the military posture in South Vietnam and he advocated sending some quick-reaction marine forces to Da Nang and an army brigade to Ton Son Nhut airfield near Saigon. Maxwell Taylor, now ambassador to South Vietnam, was not interested at the moment in this sort of commitment, and with the presidential campaign under way, the proposal got nowhere for the time being.

In mid-September, a message came from Secretary of State Rusk to the ambassador that expressed the full commitment of the United States to the security of South Vietnam in stronger terms than heretofore. In that same month Saigon formed its third government since Diem—an unhappy situation for the United States, which was looking for some stability in Saigon. In November, Lyndon Johnson overwhelmingly defeated his opponent, Barry Goldwater, for reelection. Johnson's campaign theme with respect to Vietnam was for a peaceful solution. Events were to work out differently.

Beginning in the late fall of 1964, events moved rapidly in Vietnam: two days before the United States election the enemy attacked the American base at Bien Hoa; and on Christmas they attacked the Brinks officers' hotel in downtown Saigon. By this time, with the election over, the president was considering his options. In late January, McGeorge Bundy was dispatched to Saigon to look over the situation. Then came a benchmark event that set in motion a series of actions from which there was no turning back. On the afternoon of February 6, 1965 (Washington time) there occurred the Pleiku incident, in which United States barracks and helicopters were subjected to surprise fire from the Viet Cong, resulting in a substantial number of casualties. After receiving recommendations by phone from Taylor and Bundy in Saigon, Johnson decided to respond by aerial attack on North Vietnam. Senator Mike Mansfield urged negotiation rather than military action, but the president was cool toward the idea.

In the next month marine ground units were dispatched to the Da Nang area as security for the air base, from which by now U.S. aircraft were conducting missions in South as well as North Vietnam. Apparently, at this point there was no systematic consideration of the introduction of ground troops by Washington. It is doubtful, however, that anyone with military experience missed the important threshold being crossed. If combat organizations were introduced, it would be a long time before they could be removed from a situation such as existed in Vietnam at that time.

The announced rationale for the initial deployments of U.S. ground units was for the security of American bases and installations in South Vietnam. These were bases whose aircraft were primarily involved in Rolling Thunder, the bombing of North Vietnam. By the time most of the deployments were under way, however, the rationale had shifted. In the first place, Rolling Thunder was not meeting the expectations of its proponents about bringing Hanoi to negotiations.[46] Further, there was at the same time a deteriorating military situation in South Vietnam. Therefore, by late March the possibility of introducing large numbers of U.S. combat troops into South Vietnam was a real one. Ambassador Taylor was opposed to a commitment of American ground forces at that time, while the Joint Chiefs and Westmoreland were proponents. Taylor came back to Washington to make his case on April 1 at a National Security Council meeting.

Taylor made a successful case against a troop commitment for the present. Westmorcland did get two additional marine battalions, together with some leeway as to how to employ the marines, who heretofore had been restricted to base security missions. Such victory as Taylor achieved was a short-lived one. Events were now

moving rapidly and the military was pushing in concert for a troop
build-up—Westmoreland from Saigon; Admiral U. S. Grant Sharp,
Westmoreland's boss, from Honolulu; and the Joint Chiefs in
Washington.

A key meeting that marked a watershed in the troop build-up
occurred in Hawaii on April 20 with McNamara, Bundy from State,
Joint Chiefs Chairman Earle Wheeler, Sharp, Westmoreland, and
Ambassador Taylor present. Westmoreland gained a commitment
for 40,000 more troops, including an army brigade, the 173rd Airborne. The floodgates were about to open. Meanwhile the situation
continued to get worse for the Vietnam army (ARVN)—an ambush
here, a defeat there, it seemed as though the South Vietnamese
forces were coming unglued.

By late May reports from Vietnam began to take an ominous turn
as word came in of ARVN units melting away in battle. By early
June, plans were under way to send 75,000 troops to Vietnam. By
late June Westmoreland felt the need for major reinforcements, and
McNamara was dispatched to Vietnam to look into the situation.
Events moved rapidly following his return. His report endorsed the
view of sending up to 150,000 troops by the end of 1965 and the
possibility of exceeding 300,000 troops a year hence.

Shortly after McNamara's return, there was a meeting in the
White House at which all officials involved expressed support of
McNamara's recommendations. The climax came on July 28, 1965,
when President Johnson addressed the nation by means of a press
conference concerning the troop reinforcement and redefined
United States objectives in South Vietnam. He declared: "We insist
. . . that the people of South Vietnam shall have the right of choice,
the right to shape their own destiny in free elections in the South, or
throughout all Vietnam under international supervision, and they
shall not have any government imposed upon them by force and
terror so long as we can prevent it." At this point Johnson introduced a new objective: "We intend to convince the Communists
that we cannot be defeated by force of arms or by superior power."
The president was definitely laying United States prestige on the
line.

In his initial recommendations to the president following his
return, McNamara had recommended a call-up of the reserves.
However, the bad taste left by the call-up during the Berlin situa-

tion in 1961 and the desire to avoid a debate with Congress convinced Johnson that he did not want a reserve call-up. The president
wanted his Great Society and the war at the same time—guns and
butter. A congressional debate might well have given some of its
opponents an opportunity to derail the Great Society.

Johnson's decision was to send 175,000 troops for the present,
although in the press conference he used the number 125,000 and
indicated that more would be sent later.[47] Since Johnson's plans
were based on an assumption that the reserves would not be called
up, the base from which to draw manpower for Vietnam was somewhat restricted. Westmoreland at one point had his staff in Saigon
make its own estimate of the highest troop strength the United
States could support in Vietnam without a mobilization. The answer
was a half million men. This, rather than any specific strategic or
tactical plan, was the basis of the manpower goal that the Military
Assistance Command sought. Increase followed increase toward this
goal through the years, each increase being called a "program." The
goal was called by Westmoreland "minimum essential forces,"
rather than the "optimum forces" of 670,000 that he occasionally
requested but that were never seriously considered.

Each of these proposed increases had to be sold to Secretary
McNamara, who early on told Westmoreland not to "worry about
the economy of the country, the availability of forces, or public or
Congressional attitudes." He, Westmoreland, should ask for what
he felt was necessary to achieve his objectives, and McNamara
would do his best to accommodate. After the decision was made and
McNamara was back in Washington, he would pressure the army to
meet the request immediately. With no reserves to call up, this
threw the army into turmoil, in time wrecking the United States
Army in Europe and the army strategic reserve in the United
States.

If the foregoing seems to indicate more preoccupation in
Washington with how many troops were needed and the amount
that could be provided, rather than why they were needed, this is
what the record shows. It is true that some officials outside the
primary command circuit were concerned about what the ground
troops were to do, but these persons played no part in the real
decision-making process. Some allusion was always made to aims as

justification for each troop-increase proposal, but these statements were so general as to be almost meaningless.

Approval of the deployment programs themselves, which are the benchmarks of decision-making in the war, related to size of forces alone; missions were not ruled on at all. Moreover, no set of documents exists elsewhere that deals with the question of precisely what the forces were for or how they were to be used. The original commitment of large-scale ground forces was an emergency measure, and subsequent increases were responses to a changing situation. Basically, the increases were escalatory moves to compensate for enemy increases. The enemy in turn tried to compensate, and so it went, in what seemed for a time to be an endless struggle.[48]

A few months after the president's July decisions and as the American build-up continued, an ominous development occurred. Infiltration of combat units from North Vietnam began to increase. By mid-November there were eight regimental-sized units from the north in South Vietnam. It was in this context that the United States First Air Cavalry Division was committed in the bloody battle that took place in the Ia Drang Valley—the first major U.S. battle of the war. The implication of the North Vietnamese build-up was that they intended to match the American build-up, thus setting the stage for a test of national wills.

Faced with this changed enemy situation, McNamara flew to Saigon from a NATO meeting in Paris. Primary discussion focused on the need for additional troops beyond those already programmed for Vietnam. On his return to Washington, McNamara drafted a memorandum to the president in which he recommended a troop increase by the end of 1966 of 67,000, to a total of 400,000.[49] A number of other items were included in the memorandum, the most important here being the notion of a pause in the bombing of North Vietnam. McNamara gave two reasons for the pause: first, to lay a foundation in the minds of the American people and world opinion for an enlarged war effort; and second, to give the North Vietnamese a face-saving way of beginning negotiations.[50]

President Johnson was fairly skeptical about the value of the pause technique and this skepticism was shared by the military, as well as Secretary Rusk (who eventually felt it might be worth the risk) and Ambassador Henry Cabot Lodge, who had by now replaced Taylor in Saigon. However, McNamara had his bureaucratic allies on the issue, including McGeorge Bundy, the president's national security affairs adviser. Eventually, Johnson approved a bombing pause from Christmas 1965 until the end of January 1966. Nothing much came of it, however, despite a fairly extensive diplomatic campaign to secure some concessions from North Vietnam that might subsequently lead to negotiations.

As President Johnson describes in his memoirs, by late 1965 and early 1966 the American economy began to show troublesome trends.[51] The cost of Vietnam on top of expenditures for domestic programs was bringing on a serious inflation. We cannot puruse that important issue here except to highlight the involvement of the secretary of defense in one aspect of the problem. From mid-1965 until at least mid-1966, the budget planning on Vietnam was held closely by McNamara. The concern was that if Congress faced up to the full implications of Vietnam, the Great Society would lose key congressional support. The true projected costs of the war were concealed for a time through massive dissimulation by the president, McNamara, and Charles Schultze, the budget director. This weighed heavily on McNamara's mind, but he was loyal to the president, who above all wanted to protect his Great Society programs.[52]

Barely had one troop increase been approved in 1966 when another request was on the way from Saigon. In April the president approved a ceiling of 425,000 to be achieved by June 1967. By summer a request for a ceiling of 542,000, to be achieved by the end of 1967, was received in Washington. By this point a new development was intruding on troop projections for South Vietnam. The shaky South Vietnamese economy was undergoing a runaway inflation based on United States expenditures there. Ambassador Lodge wanted to hold down these expenditures and one of the most practical ways to do so was by holding down the number of U.S. troops in the country.

McNamara was off again to Vietnam in October 1966 to survey the situation. With the mid-term elections a month away and a meeting with the heads of the countries who were contributing troops facing Johnson shortly thereafter, the president wanted the best assessment of the increasingly unpopular war that he could get from his defense secretary. This trip was very important in persuading McNamara that the war was a losing proposition.[53] Although he did not openly communicate this feeling, probably out of loyalty to the president, in retrospect it seems clear that doubts he had already harbored were strongly reinforced.

In his report upon his return, the secretary began to question the premises of the United States combat commitment. "I see no way to bring the war to an end soon," he wrote. Despite the high enemy casualties, McNamara felt that there was "no sign of an impending break in enemy morale and it appears that he can more than replace his losses by infiltration from North Vietnam and recruitment in South Vietnam."[54] As for the Rolling Thunder bombing campaign in the north, McNamara felt that it had neither affected infiltration to the south nor cracked morale in the north.

The secretary's recommendations to the president were designed to stabilize the U.S. military posture in a way that could be maintained indefinitely, while at the same time stressing pacification and the improvement of the South Vietnamese armed forces. Specifically he recommended stabilizing U.S. ground forces at 470,000 constructing an infiltration barrier,[55] and stabilizing the Rolling Thunder bombing campaign at the present levels.

Clearly, McNamara had decided to try to bring a halt to the continued expansion of the war effort, reversing the approach of the preceding eighteen months. The military were, to say the least, unenthusiastic. For one thing, the barrier would require resources that would have to come from other programs. McNamara had the month before set up a task force under General Alfred Starbird, notwithstanding the military's reaction. Eventually the barrier was in part completed, using sensors that when activated would trigger a response by aerial bombardment. The arrangement probably did increase casualties among the Vietnamese moving south. It was not the substitute for the bombardment in the north that its proponents had hoped for but the military always knew was unrealistic.

McNamara's recommendations concerning stabilizing ground force strength in the south and Rolling Thunder operations in the north brought into the open a conflict between the Joint Chiefs and the defense secretary over the conduct of the war. On the notion of stabilizing ground forces at 470,000, the chiefs were initially guarded. On the bombing, however, they were straightforward in their written reaction to McNamara's recommendations: "The Joint

Chiefs of Staff do not concur in your recommendation that there should be no increase in level of bombing effort and no modification in areas and targets subject to air attack. . . . To be effective, the air campaign should be conducted with only those minimum constraints necessary to avoid indiscriminate killing of population."[56]

Subsequently, the Joint Chiefs did come in with a higher manpower recommendation, but after much discussion back and forth, McNamara's ceiling of 470,000 held for the time being. Among the more salient reasons that McNamara cited as controlling his (and, in effect, the president's) decision was the need to stabilize the South Vietnamese economy. Most important, this was the first time Washington had denied a field request for additional forces. Obviously, alternatives to continued force increases were on the mind of the secretary.

In a short time the Joint Chiefs of Staff attacked McNamara's premise that the economy of South Vietnam was of overriding importance. Also, pressure from outside the Pentagon was placed on McNamara by some hawkish senators regarding the troop issue and the bombing campaign in the north. Senator John Stennis declared that Westmoreland's troop request should be met, "even if it should require mobilization or partial mobilization."[57]

On March 18, 1967, General Westmoreland submitted by cable his view of force requirements projected through June 30, 1968. He felt that the current ceiling of 470,000 did not "permit sustained operations of the scope and intensity required to avoid an unreasonably protracted war."[58] He held that a force of approximately 560,000 was required, and although a rationale was provided to justify this increase, it was not detailed enough for the kind of questions McNamara would ask.[59]

By mid-April the Joint Chiefs believed that they had sufficient justification from Westmoreland to communicate the request to Secretary McNamara (who had in fact already seen it in its original form). The chiefs strongly recommended that Westmoreland's troop request be approved and also took the opportunity to support increased bombing in North Vietnam as a means of reducing future force requirements.

Later in April Westmoreland returned to the United States to bolster public support for the war effort. In the course of this visit, he addressed both a press convention in New York and a joint session of Congress. Of more importance here, in a meeting attended by the president, Westmoreland, and Chairman Wheeler, McNamara was not present, but his assistant secretary for international security affairs, John McNaughton, was. Westmoreland emphasized the need for the troops he had requested to prevent progress from being slowed down. An important point, he thought, was the ability of the enemy to continue to provide reinforcements from the north. Westmoreland concluded with an estimate: "with a force level of 565,000, the war could well go on for three years"; with a level of 665,000. "it could go on for two years."[60] The president was noncommittal but was concerned about the costs (resources and public opinion) associated with such an increase.

By mid-May McNaughton had prepared a Draft Presidential Memorandum (DPM) on the issue of the troop increase for McNamara. It was a comprehensive document, using analyses prepared that spring by the Systems Analysis Office as well as by the CIA and the State Department. The document described the ground force strategy as a "trap which had ensnared us."

McNaughton also raised the problem of the increasing unpopularity of the war among many diverse sectors of American society. The paper concluded with two important recommendations: 1) that a troop ceiling of 550,000 (this was later revised downward) be set and that the military be advised that there would be no further increases; 2) that bombing in the north be concentrated in the southern part of that country, south of the twentieth parallel.[61]

At the end of May, the chiefs replied to the DPM prepared by McNaughton. As could be expected, they took strong exception. The paper, they said, indicated emergence of an "alarming pattern" that suggested a major realignment of the United States objectives and intentions in Southeast Asia. Among other things, they recommended that the DPM not be forwarded to the president. State's reaction was essentially to support the position set forth by McNaughton.

In the midst of this controversy, McNamara prepared for a trip to Saigon to hear what the military there had to say—or at least discover the tenor of their thoughts, as he already knew what they would say. He himself was thinking of a troop ceiling of somewhere between 485,000 and 500,000, in contrast to Westmoreland's minimum ceiling—at this point, one of 550,000. The Mid-East war that broke out in early June caused a postponement of the trip, but McNamara finally reached Saigon on July 7.

The briefings pretty much followed what McNamara had heard many times before: there was an increasing North Vietnamese presence in the south and the war therefore was becoming more a main-force battle than a guerrilla war. Therefore, an increase in United States combat forces was required. There was no real resolution of the civilian view, as expressed in McNaughton's DPM, and the military view, as presented by Westmoreland. On the final night of his visit, McNamara worked out with Westmoreland a compromise for a new ceiling of 525,000. This was considered close to the highest level that could be sustained without mobilizing the reserves, something the president did not wish to do.[62] In mid-July the president approved the compromise ceiling after meeting with McNamara, Wheeler, and Westmoreland.

The controversy over the bombing was to follow a different and more dramatic course than had the troop-ceiling issue. The Pentagon in the summer of 1967 was split over the bombing issue. The military endorsed a significant expansion of the air campaign in the north. McNamara and many of his key civilian advisers, on the other hand, favored a restricted campaign south of the twentieth parallel. It was an important and divisive issue not only in the Pentagon but also in Congress and in the public realm.

In any case, the issue became public enough and controversial enough for Senator John Stennis of the Preparedness Subcommittee of the Armed Services Committee to announce that he would conduct a probe into the air war in North Vietnam during August 1967.[63] McNamara already had under way a detailed analysis to show that increased escalation of bombardment would not accomplish U.S. objectives. Indeed, he felt that deescalation might well further the possibilities for a negotiated settlement of the war.

Shortly before the hearings began, Congressman Gerald Ford strongly attacked the president's bombing policies as having pulled our punches, thereby preventing our air power from bringing North Vietnam to its knees. McNamara immediately refuted Ford's charges on the basis that the congressman did not understand the real objectives of the bombing—i.e., not to destroy North Vietnam but to restrict men and materiel from coming south.

McNamara began his testimony on August 25. This occasion was the only time that McNamara took a position that, if not contrary to the president's position, probably hedged Johnson's future options. The official relationship between the president and his now dovish secretary of defense was never quite the same again. Nor was McNamara's influence with the president ever to be the same.

McNamara's testimony (which went on all day) had to convince both extremes: those who wanted more bombing, that it would be futile; those who wanted none, that there was a purpose to bombing in certain areas. The air war was not a substitute for the war in the south, as some believed it could be, he stated. Still, he pointed out, it had its objectives: to reduce infiltration to the south; to raise morale of the South Vietnamese people; and to cause the North Vietnamese to pay enough of a price that they would finally conclude that negotiations were preferable.

McNamara's presentation was a remarkable tour de force, but the secretary did not win over the hawks in the Senate or anywhere else. The story on page one of the *New York Times* of September first gave the reactions of the Senate Preparedness Subcommittee. "Senate unit asks Johnson to widen bombing in North." "Scores McNamara on policy of restricted air war in light of military views." "Joint Chiefs supported."

McNamara's August testimony did set the stage for a diplomatic initiative on the part of the president, the so-called San Antonio formula. By challenging the military position on the bombing, McNamara had put the entire issue in a new perspective. Hence when the president proposed to stop the bombing under certain conditions, perhaps leading to negotiation, the public reaction was muted, as compared to what the reaction would have been, had the military position been left unchallenged by the secretary.

The key part of the formula, delivered publicly by the president in San Antonio on September 29, 1967 (and already unsuccessfully proposed to the North Vietnamese privately) read: "The United States is willing to stop all aerial and naval bombardment of North Vietnam when this will lead promptly to productive discussions. We, of course, assume that while discussions proceed, North Vietnam would not take advantage of the bombing cessation or limitation."[64] This relaxed a previous offer somewhat in that it did not require advance action by North Vietnam nor the stopping of all military effort by them: it asked only that effort not be increased.

The initiative led to nothing at the time. It did, however, help to set the stage for the bombing halt that took place the following fall.

Another McNamara initiative came in a discussion with the president on October 31, 1967, followed up by a memorandum the next day. Basically, at this point McNamara felt that continuation of the current course of action in Vietnam was fruitless. Without some new initiatives, he foresaw more of the same—more troop requests, increased bombing requests—without decisive results. The secretary had three recommendations: stabilize the United States effort and announce that there would be no expansion of troop strength beyond that already planned and no expansion of the air effort; call a bombing halt by the end of 1967; and prepare a study of military operations in the south with the objective of giving the South Vietnamese greater responsibility.[65]

Johnson consulted with a large number of persons whose opinions he respected: Dean Rusk, McGeorge Bundy, Walt Rostow, Maxwell Taylor, Abe Fortas, Clark Clifford, and—after recalling them from Vietnam—Ambassador Bunker and General Westmoreland. In varying degrees, there was lack of support for McNamara's recommendations, some advisers disagreeing on all points and some just on the bombing halt. Finally, on December 18, 1967, President Johnson wrote a memorandum for the files giving his own view of the McNamara proposals.[66] In sum: Johnson rejected the bombing halt at that time; rejected the notion of announcing a policy of stabilization, although he saw no need to increase the force level; and agreed with studying ways to get the South Vietnamese to take over more responsibility.

The preceding April McNamara had been tentatively offered the presidency of the World Bank. In a subsequent discussion about the job with the president, there was no direct response from Johnson. In mid-October, the president finally asked McNamara if he was still interested and, upon receiving an affirmative reply, indicated he would help him get the position.[67] Johnson was true to his word and the nomination went to the Bank on November 22. On the twenty-ninth the announcement was made and even Washington, where leaks of cabinet changes are routine, was surprised.

McNamara stayed on until the end of February to help with the fiscal 1969 budget, but his power was gone. True, some important events occurred for him to cope with and he worked to the last day. There was the seizure of the *Pueblo* by the North Koreans on January 23 and then there was Tet 1968.

The Tet Offensive of early 1968 was the high point of military action in the Second Indo-Chinese War. It was a watershed, and afterward nothing was ever quite the same in the war. Although it represented a military defeat for the Viet Cong/North Vietnamese in a technical sense, it was a tremendous psychological victory for them in the United States. In part, this was due to the optimistic expectations that the American people had developed on the basis of the pronouncements of their own civilian and military leaders.

That an enemy attack was staged was not a surprise. What was s surprise was the scope and magnitude of the attack when it came. In the first days of October 1967, General Westmoreland was cabling Washington that the enemy had made some serious decisions. He hypothesized that they were feeling the effects of the attrition strategy and had perhaps decided on a maximum effort over a short period of time.

The bubble broke in the early morning hours of January 30, 1968. As the reports of enemy attacks began to pour into the American headquarters, followed by an even greater number of attacks the following two days, it became evident that an enemy effort of major proportions was under way. Essentially simultaneous attacks (there were understandably some problems in coordination) took place in over one hundred cities and towns, including Saigon, where the American Embassy was briefly under siege. What, the American people wondered, was happening? Were we not supposed to be winning? How could an attack of such proportions be initiated by an enemy we were defeating?

Actually, the Tet Offensive was a tremendous military defeat for the Viet Cong and the North Vietnamese. Nowhere, for very long, could they carve out defensible areas, and there was no general uprising by the South Vietnamese population. The Viet Cong were able to hold on here and there until late February, finally being cleared out of Hué by the twenty-fifth of the month. With that, the tactical aspects of the Tet Offensive had run their course.

Friendly losses were high, about 6,000 killed, but enemy losses were staggering. No one knows for certain, but perhaps they reached 40,000. The Viet Cong had borne the brunt of the action and thereafter had to be replaced increasingly by North Vietnamese.

The South Vietnamese government and forces held and gained enough political strength to achieve their first real mobilization. The American public, however, who was the key to the problem, did not hold. The psychological impact on a nation that thought itself to be winning was too great. It was obvious that popular support for the war no longer existed.[68]

On February 28, 1968, in the East Room of the White House, the president awarded McNamara the Medal of Freedom—the highest American civilian award. McNamara was too moved to respond. The next day, in front of the Pentagon, the president awarded him the highest noncombatant military award—the Distinguished Service Medal. Now McNamara was another casualty of the Vietnam War. Like Forrestal he had stayed too long.

When McNamara became secretary of defense in January 1961, the department was more than thirteen years old and had had seven secretaries. From a loose federal arrangement in the Forrestal days, the control of the secretary had gradually tightened. Eisenhower's 1958 Reorganization Act provided for even greater central control, but the act was basically untapped when McNamara was sworn in.

The highly successful, intelligent, and dynamic new secretary was determined to be an activist in the carrying out of his new role. Although his intellectual interests had developed far beyond managing the Ford Motor Company, nevertheless his business mind-set was that of an accountant. He arrived in office without a world view and so accepted that of the new president and his immediate advisers.

McNamara's imprint as secretary of defense was made through management. He was the watershed secretary and the Pentagon has never been the same since. Through his management approach, he achieved true civilian control of the Pentagon in the early 1960s, the first time since World War II that such control existed below the presidential level. Although much of what he accomplished was subsequently lost, the potential exists for any future holder of the office.

The Planning Programming Budgeting System he initially installed was primitive, but it gave a sense of direction and with subsequent improvements survived. This was a legacy of some importance. On systems analysis, something more must be said. The early unit within the Comptroller's Office did some groundbreaking work. Later, as an independent agency, the office became too large and the work was less well done. Also the adoption of a public adversarial role vis-à-vis the military stretched the office's creditability. In later years, exercise of this role led to the downfall of the office. Systems analysis as a mode of thought was another matter. This has survived throughout the Pentagon, and the analytical approach is a major McNamara legacy.

Much has been made here and by others of McNamara's accountant's approach, his ease with charts and quantification, and his employment of systems analysis. At this point, a note of caution is in order. The driving force in all analysis is the assumptions that lie behind it and in these McNamara was not simply a computer. He relied on intuition and hunches and it is erroneous to assume otherwise. This is not to depreciate the analytical mode but only to stress that the ideal of the management model developed by McNamara is not the way it worked in practice.

In an earlier chapter, the conservative fiscal outlook and tight budgetary controls of Eisenhower were stressed. Early in the McNamara period, the services were advised to state their requirements and were told that if they could justify them, they would be approved, the implication being that there was no budgetary limit. It is true that the defense budget was larger under Kennedy, and even larger under Johnson because of the war. There were, however, upper limits and everyone knew this. The budget under McNamara determined strategic policy as it did under Eisenhower, but it was more liberal from the military's standpoint.

One final management tool of McNamara's that should be highlighted is his use of the International Security Affairs (ISA) Office. McNamara had adopted the Kennedy world view; however, he was not by any means passive about matters of foreign policy. He became, in fact, a principal foreign affairs adviser to the president—a role that Henry Kissinger closed off from the secretary of defense from 1969 until 1977. ISA was McNamara's instrument both in Washington and elsewhere, especially in NATO. In those days, the office reached the peak of its capability and prestige. Not by accident, the agency declined dramatically during the Nixon administration and remained in decline when President Ford was in the White House.

If we leave aside Vietnam, McNamara played a major and successful role in the development of national strategy and defense policy in the first three or four years of his tenure. Although the necessarily brief length of this chapter did not permit me to trace the development of his strategic thinking,[69] he deserves fairly high grades in this regard. He attempted with a high degree of success to make American military power more responsive to U.S. foreign policy and national security objectives. While rejecting a counterforce strategy, he did oversee the development of a U.S. deterrent that could survive a USSR attack and still inflict unacceptable losses on that country. He also strengthened the command and control facilities of our strategic retaliatory forces, thus increasing the flexibility with which they could be employed. The foregoing was accomplished with budgetary constraints in mind, although not to the extent of the previous administration.

McNamara's major failure was the war in Vietnam—not so much in matters of its technical management as in the strategic direction it was permitted to take. Here some comment is in order. First let us recognize that there were major domestic constraints on McNamara, based primarily upon presidential perceptions. The Great Society dominated Johnson's thinking and he wanted no public debate that would jeopardize it. This meant no debate on a reserve call-up and no debate on the budget; hence in the latter case there had to be for a time some concealment of what actual costs would eventually be.

While certain constraints on the conduct of the war were based on genuine concern about possible reactions by the Soviets and Chinese, there was also a need to avoid public debate on that question. Thus when the senior military complained, as they did, about constraints placed on them in the conduct of the war and attributed them to inexperienced civilians, "wielding undue influence in the decision-making process,"[70] they were correct in one way, but not perhaps in the way they meant.

Inexperience there was, but it caused the defense secretary to give the military too much leeway, rather than too little. Henry Brandon recounts having asked McNamara whether he tried to influence military strategy in the field.[71] The essence of McNamara's reply was that he had not, since he did not know enough about it and felt such matters should be left to those in the field. This is in keeping with the long-standing tradition of autonomy for American field commanders during time of war. From June 1965 onward, Westmoreland was in a position to pursue operations within Vietnam pretty much as he wished. The Joint Chiefs were advocates for Westmoreland in Washington as he proceeded with his search and destroy, security, and pacification missions. In time, McNamara became disenchanted with the military approach in Vietnam, but he was reluctant to pay the price of speaking out against the strategy of the ground commander. Westmoreland's autonomy in running the war was fairly complete. Further, lack of any strategic guidance from Washington could also be interpreted by him as approval of the manner in which he was conducting the war. This contrasts with the air war where Washington kept fairly tight controls.

One of the side problems that this autonomy generated was what turned out to be the key variable. American public opinion simply was not considered by those who were actually planning how the war in South Vietnam was fought. This omission had obvious and significant implications that were summed up in an extract from a 1969 speech by Henry Brandon: "Before leaving Saigon on one of my periodic visits to Vietnam late in 1967, I asked the leading civilians and military in charge whether a reduction in the intensity of the war, a reduction of the cost in men and material, would not be worth striving for. I thought it might help to induce a more patient and forbearing attitude towards the war on the part of the American public. . . . Not surprisingly, they all reacted alike. They said it was not their business to include American domestic opinion in their calculations; that was up to President Johnson."[72]

Thus, when Westmoreland writes that there were too many constraints imposed by civilians on his conduct of the war, he may be correct in one sense. From a different perspective, however, one can draw another conclusion: there was not enough civilian participation in terms of asking the big questions about what we were really doing in Vietnam. In part, this was a matter of personality; I find it difficult to believe that Dwight Eisenhower would ever have permitted himself to field an expeditionary force of a half million men in Vietnam without asking the questions that were not asked by

Johnson. In part, it was also the "big war" mentality—let the military run it—in what was a highly political affair indeed. Most of all, it was due to a lack of communication between civilians and military.

McNamara served Presidents Kennedy and Johnson well. He was respected by them and included in the small key groups in which each president liked to do his real decision-making. McNamara was a strong cabinet officer and at the same time a key presidential officer, in the sense that he accurately reflected the president's views to the defense bureaucracy. In this sense, he was intensely loyal to the president. Perhaps he was too loyal—who knows what would have happened had he articulated his misgivings about the war earlier?

What McNamara did not do was to work out a relationship of trust with the military—the ideal example of which is the Stimson-Marshall relationship during World War II. McNamara worked well with Joint Chiefs chairmen Taylor and Wheeler, but more was needed. The JCS as a group did not have enough presidential exposure. One member of the chiefs during that period told me he felt like a spectator of the war rather than one who was involved with decision-making concerning the war. The Joint Chiefs are, after all, the principal military advisers to the president. Of course, they work also for the secretary of defense, but what they should be doing is too important for the secretary to serve as a go-between on major matters. The civilians and military together did not participate adequately with the president on major decisions concerning Vietnam.

4

Laird Winds Down the War

With President Johnson's early withdrawal from the 1968 presidential race it was clear that no matter who the Republican candidate would be, his chances of success were infinitely greater than they would have been against an incumbent president. It was also clear that the Vietnam War would be the major issue of the pre- and post-convention campaigns. As it turned out, Richard Milhous Nixon, who officially announced his candidacy in early February at the start of the New Hampshire primary campaign and who was the front-running Republican candidate from the outset, became the Republican candidate, his opponent becoming Vice President Hubert Horatio Humphrey.

Nixon campaigned on a pledge to end the war, although the details on how this was to be accomplished were vague. Humphrey had the problem of being associated with the Johnson administration's war policies, an image he finally began to change after a speech on September 30 in which he suggested a new initiative toward ending the war. From then on the race between Nixon and Humphrey became dramatically closer, aided by Johnson's announcement, less than a week before election day, of a halt in the bombing of North Vietnam. In the end, however, Nixon prevailed.

Before examining in detail how he went about redeeming his promise to end the war, we must consider briefly the international and domestic contexts of the first Nixon administration as a backdrop for what will follow.

Although not as central to the international political scene as the domestic, Vietnam was nevertheless a key component of the president's world view during the first Nixon administration. Efforts to terminate the war took place on numerous diplomatic fronts, including the Paris Peace Talks inherited from the Johnson administration. From August 1969, when Henry Kissinger had his first meeting with North Vietnamese negotiator Xuan Thuy in Paris, until 1972 the secret talks became the principal negotiating forum.

These talks took the entire first Nixon administration to work out the details of what finally became the Paris agreements of January 1973. The issues concerned troop withdrawal, cease-fire, prisoner release, political settlement, international guarantees, foreign intervention, and reparations. It was against the background of these talks that the unilateral United States withdrawal action called Vietnamization took place.

To set the Vietnam withdrawal and negotiations in a larger foreign policy context the new president in July 1969 enunciated the Guam Doctrine, which has since become known as the Nixon Doctrine. The doctrine was concerned with clarifying United States commitments in the Pacific area in a post-Vietnam environment. Except in the case of aggression by a major nuclear power, future American response to regional aggression against an ally would be limited to furnishing economic and selected military assistance only; the ally being supported would be required to provide the manpower for its own defense.[1]

Preoccupation with Vietnam during the early 1970s did not change America's central foreign policy initiative, NATO, although Europeans at times wondered as they watched United States forces in Europe become in effect a replacement depot for American forces in Vietnam. Nixon sets forth his view of the importance of NATO in the overall American foreign policy context as he perceived it upon assuming office this way: "To the extent that I would have to start somewhere, I felt that I had to put Europe at the top of the list. Only when we had secured our Western Alliance would we be on sufficiently solid footing to begin talks with the Communists. NATO was in disarray, largely because of the failure of the United States to consult adequately with our European allies."[2]

The president's first trip out of the country was to Western Europe in late February 1969. His goal as far as the NATO countries were concerned was to show an increased interest in alliance matters on the part of the new administration. At a time when there was pressure from within Congress to cut American troop strength in Europe, Nixon's interest was important to alliance stability.[3]

Two of the major foreign policy initiatives of the first Nixon administration, however, took place in Asia. The first of these was a combination of actions that eventually became known collectively as the Nixon "shocks" to Japan and that commenced with Nixon's China initiative, which was publicly announced by the president for the first time on July 15, 1971. The revelation came as a great surprise not only to the American public, with whom it was highly popular, but also to the Japanese government, which was deeply disturbed. The brief announcement indicated that talks between Chou En-Lai and Henry Kissinger had resulted in an invitation to the American president to visit China, and that Nixon had accepted. The text stated, "The meeting between the leaders of China and the United States is to seek the normalization of relations between the two countries and also to exchange views on questions of concern to the two sides."

Considering the history of Chinese-Japanese relations, and the proximity of the two Asian countries, it was astonishing to Japanese officials that its close ally America had not informed it in advance of this gambit. Exactly one month later, on August 15, came the second "shock," a United States decision to suspend the convertibility of the dollar into gold and the imposition of a 10 percent surcharge on imports. Although Japan was not singled out specifically, it was obvious that Japan was the primary target of this initiative.[4]

The other foreign policy initiative was the president's China trip itself and its significance as a beginning of normalization of relations between China and the United States. In some respects this was, at least in terms of its future potential, the high point of successful foreign policy initiatives during the entire Nixon administration. The visit itself, which took place in February 1972, received enormous television coverage, and did begin what has been an understandably slow normalization. Side effects of this move included providing the Kremlin leaders with a considerable amount of food for thought and stirring anxiety among certain allies, such as the Taiwanese.

Another major initiative by Nixon during his first administration was the SALT (Strategic Arms Limitation Talks) I Agreement of May 1972 with the USSR. The SALT had begun informally in December

1969, with modest progress in the first year. Basically the positions were that the Soviet Union wanted to agree only on defensive, or antiballistic, missiles (ABM) and the United States wanted to include offensive missiles. By May 1971 progress was adequate to assume that real negotiations would soon begin. In October 1971 there was a joint announcement by the two parties that President Nixon would visit the Soviet Union in the spring of 1972.

It was at the summit meeting in May that Nixon and Soviet Premier Leonid Brezhnev signed the SALT I Agreements. Provisions of the agreements were an ABM treaty that limited each side to two defensive sites, and a five-year interim agreement on offensive missiles that was quantitative in nature and that postponed the qualitative issues to SALT II. The American military was not happy with the interim agreement but that did not deter Nixon or Kissinger.[5]

It was apparent to Nixon in his first term that if he was to win reelection, his campaign pledge to end the Vietnam War would have to be essentially fulfilled by the time of the 1972 election. Early in his first administration Nixon unveiled his plan to end the war, or at least to remove U.S. troops. Termed "Vietnamization," the plan was designed gradually to turn the responsibility for managing the war over to the government of South Vietnam; U.S. troops would be withdrawn on a scheduled basis and in such a manner that the United States would eventually assume only a supporting role.[6]

The plan was designed so that periodic presidential announcements of incremental U.S. troop withdrawals and reports of progress toward self-sufficiency on the part of the South Vietnamese armed forces would mollify a war-weary American public. But the startling revelation of the incursion of U.S. troops into Cambodia on April 30, 1970, a seeming violation of the intent of the Nixon plan, cracked an already crumbling U.S. domestic front.[7] That spring was marked by the Kent State shootings, the disruption of the nation's campuses, and the final public ultimatum to the president to get out of the war.

The administration thus was faced with newly spreading antimilitarism among both new sectors of the public and increasing numbers in the Congress. The impact of such sentiment, left unchecked, was seen as threatening serious inroads into the defense budget and hence undermining U.S. international standing. In fact, as the administration moved along to the final year of its first term it became evident that U.S. forces worldwide had deteriorated to an alarming degree.[8] There was a multiplicity of causes for this condition, primarily stemming from the resource commitment to Vietnam, but it was evident to concerned officials that a post-Vietnam rebuilding of morale, improved training and readiness, and modernized equipment were immediate priorities. With a Congress and public reluctant to commit additional resources, this was an additional imperative to get out of Vietnam as soon as possible.

One important side effect of the antiwar sentiment, especially among the young, was the concept of the all volunteer force. The inequities of the draft and the unpopularity of the war had made popular candidate Nixon's campaign pledge that "once our involvement in the Vietnam War is behind us we should move toward an all volunteer force." Enormous effort and resources were employed during the first Nixon administration to redeem this pledge. As a result, the draft expired by the deadline of June 1973.[9]

Another series of domestic problems of prime importance during the first Nixon administration was related in part to the Vietnam War—problems with the American economy.[10] When Nixon took office in 1969 he inherited an annual inflation rate of almost 5 percent. Increasing unemployment and a legislative nudge by Congress forced Nixon, by the summer of 1970, into steps just short of direct controls in an attempt to find a cure to what has come to be known as "stagflation," that is, increasing unemployment and rising inflation coupled with a slowdown in productivity. Neither this action nor a subsequent attempt at deficit spending to reduce unemployment solved this complex problem. Therefore, commencing in late summer 1971, the administration imposed wage and price controls which went through various phases before being terminated in the spring of 1974. In the end not much of a permanent nature had been accomplished—but then, the effort (such as it was) came from an administration that did not believe in controls to begin with.

With respect to the many domestic issues of importance other than the two key issues of Vietnam and the economy, President Nixon had specific goals relating to problem areas within the American polity. As he himself catalogued them, they were "welfare reform; full prosperity in peacetime; restoring and enhancing the natural environment; improving health care and making it available more fairly to more people; strengthening and renewing state and local government; and a complete reform of the federal government."[11] The 1972 presidential campaign naturally dominated the final year of the first Nixon administration. When the Democratic party chose George McGovern as its candidate, the outcome of the election was all but assumed.[12] McGovern's position on social and welfare issues and defense was perceived as being so far left by the majority of the American electorate, that a Nixon victory was clear even before the campaign was under way.[13]

The defense budget provides one illustration of the sharp difference between the two candidates. At issue was the Nixon fiscal year 1973 defense budget of about $78 billion. McGovern's counterproposal to cut $20 billion from this budget[14] would have reduced all portions of the budget beginning with a cut of about one quarter of the active military strength. Even for a public disenchanted by the military, this position was so extreme that it was never taken seriously.

These then were the chief domestic and foreign policy issues as they developed during the first Nixon administration.

When Nixon assumed the presidency he had definite ideas on the conduct of foreign policy, ideas that were based upon many years of interest in foreign affairs, and eight years of experience as vice president under Eisenhower where he was able to observe the functioning of the White House. As he tells it: "From the outset of my administration, . . . I planned to direct foreign policy from the White House." Therefore he had to choose as secretary of state someone who could manage the State Department and establish good relations with Congress while at the same time be satisfied with being, at least on major items, a merely ceremonial secretary. For this position he chose William P. Rogers, a personal friend and former attorney general during the Eisenhower period.

Since Nixon planned on running foreign policy from the White House, it was quite important who he chose as his assistant for national security affairs. This individual would not only be his immediate adviser on major foreign policy matters but would also be in charge of the National Security Council staff. For this key position he chose Henry Kissinger, who had for many years been Nelson Rockefeller's foreign policy adviser and who was destined to become the most widely known personality of the Nixon years.

So much has been written about Nixon and Kissinger that there is little need to characterize them here. A few words about Kissinger will serve to point up the contrast between him and the secretary of defense.

Henry Alfred Kissinger, a 1938 refugee from Germany, lived in New York City and served in the United States Army during World War II. Afterward, he went to Harvard as an undergraduate, staying on for a Ph.D. which he received in 1954. He subsequently joined the faculty of the Harvard Department of Government, where his chief interests were foreign policy and defense policy. During 1955–1956 he served as director of a Council on Foreign Relations study from which emerged his *Nuclear Weapons and Foreign Policy* in 1957. This was an interesting but somewhat simplistic book concerned with the employment of tactical nuclear weapons in a European context, and he repudiated this analysis in a later book, *The Necessity for Choice*, in 1961. Nevertheless, the subject was timely, and his fame began to spread beyond Harvard. Subsequently he served as special studies director for the Rockefeller Brothers Fund and as a consultant for numerous United States agencies. In November 1968, when Nixon selected him for the White House job, Kissinger was a full professor at Harvard and had published five books and a dozen articles.

Since the new president wanted to centralize foreign policy decision-making in the White House, it was necessary to set up a system which would be responsive to that requirement and attuned to the personalities involved. The essence of the new National Security Council System was a network of interagency committees at the under secretary level, all chaired by Kissinger.[15] These committees were used to require State and Defense to produce for the White House a series of studies entitled National Security Study Memoranda, each of which provided a range of options for the president.[16]

Two of the more important committees for our purposes were the Washington Special Action Group (WSAG) and the Defense Program Review Committee (DPRC), both of which were chaired by Kissinger. The WSAG included senior State, CIA, and Pentagon officials and provided a forum for systematically bringing together all the information needed to make presidential decisions concerning the potential employment of American forces in crisis situations.[17] The DPRC comprised a wider representation of agencies, including State, Defense, the Council of Economic Advisers, and the Office of Management and Budget. This was a forum in which decisions concerning the defense budget could be discussed with a view toward providing advice to the president from a variety of perspectives.[18]

Even from this brief and partial description of the new system, it is evident what a powerful position the new assistant for national security affairs held. To control such an apparatus Kissinger required a fairly large NSC staff. Although this was, theoretically, the president's staff it was in reality Kissinger's; President Nixon withdrew from all but the final stages of the decision-making process.

Of course the various options could be discussed at the NSC meetings themselves. But as time went on, NSC meetings became less and less frequent, being replaced by private meetings between the president and Kissinger. In time also, as assistant for national security affairs, Kissinger began to take his own positions and to thwart the foreign policy bureaucracy by various techniques available to a skilled and powerful manipulator.

Melvin Robert Laird, selected by Nixon to be the tenth secretary of defense, grew up in Wisconsin and received his B.A. from Carleton College in 1942. After wartime service with the navy in the Pacific, during which he was twice wounded, he became involved in Wisconsin state politics as a Republican. In 1952 he was elected to the United States House of Representatives where he was still serving when he was selected by Nixon to be his secretary of defense.

While in the House Laird had extensive experience on the Defense Subcommittee of the Appropriations Committee. His service and interests went well beyond defense matters, as evidenced by his receipt in 1964 of the fifteenth annual Albert Lasker Medical Research Award for doing more than any other public official to promote the nation's health.

In 1962 he wrote *A House Divided: America's Strategy Gap*, a book dealing with vital issues of American foreign policy.[19] Basically a Republican cold-warrior polemic, it does nevertheless present his views on strategic issues and related matters, including his evaluation of military advice.

There was no reason to believe that he would be secretary of defense. His own ambition was to be Speaker of the House. In fact, his own first choice as secretary of defense, as well as Nixon's, was

Senator Henry M. Jackson, who turned down the offer.[20] Nixon once discussed Laird as a vice presidential possibility with Eisenhower who characterized him as "the smartest of the lot, but... too devious." Eisenhower expressed the same doubts to Nixon after Laird's appointment to Defense. Subsequently however, after meeting with Laird, Eisenhower, in talking again with Nixon, grinned and said, "Of course Laird is devious, but for anyone who has to run the Pentagon and get along with Congress, that is a valuable asset."[21]

When he assumed his new office, Melvin Laird's long service in the House gave him in effect his own political base, not only in that body but elsewhere in Washington and in Wisconsin as well. Equally as important as the political base was the political experience of all those years in Washington and his sophisticated insight into how the White House and Pentagon operated. Together, these assets permitted him to play a strong role as secretary when, as was inevitable, he had, on occasion, to assume an adversarial role with the Nixon-Kissinger White House.

Laird perceived his new role both as a manager of resources and, in a broad sense, as a strategist. One of his first actions was to announce the creation of a panel to review the Defense Department, especially in areas of organization, procurement policy, and research and development.

This panel, known subsequently as the Blue Ribbon Defense Panel, or the Fitzhugh Panel (after its chairman), published its report on July 1, 1970. The results of the report were unevenly implemented. The report made a large number of recommendations, of which the vast majority (eventually 92 out of 113) were either implemented or else were largely consonant with existing Defense Department actions. The more fundamental organizational recommendations, such as removing the Joint Chiefs of Staff from the operational chain of command, were either rejected or implemented in a limited sense.[22]

Of perhaps more immediate interest was Laird's personal management philosophy, central to which was his concept of "participatory management." This was an attempt to allow greater latitude for decision-making within each individual service.[23] In keeping with this concept Laird made an active effort to seek military counsel and to involve the services more intimately in budgetary matters—an approach that contrasted sharply with the high degree of centralization prevalent during the McNamara years.[24]

Laird's management approach and other circumstances caused him to handle two Pentagon agencies—the Office of Systems Analysis and International Security Affairs—in quite different ways than they had been used during the McNamara period, when they were important and salient agencies. As employed by McNamara, the Systems Analysis Office formulated defense programs in an adversarial manner to the Joint Chiefs of Staff.[25] No doubt this approach was used by McNamara to help insure civilian control. Understandably, this conception of the Systems Analysis Office also generated considerable ill-will among the chiefs because of the manner in which it operated. Congress, for its part, took advantage of the chiefs' displeasure to criticize the office heavily during the latter part of McNamara's tenure.

When he assumed office, Laird was determined to use Systems Analysis but to use it in a manner different from McNamara. Laird decided to make Systems Analysis function completely in-house as opposed to "public" for two major reasons:[26] first, to improve relations with the JCS in line with his concept of participatory management; second, to keep Defense Department differences under control, in order to develop a "team approach" with the ultimate goal of increased effectiveness. Accordingly, the major function of Systems Analysis was changed from that of initiator of the defense program to a provider of analysis of the service programs. At the same time, Laird demanded that the individual services continue to master systems analysis techniques so that the capabilities of his Systems Analysis Office could be properly used. Under Laird the services thus moved toward a position of initiator of policy. Laird was determined to keep the office in a low profile role and made this concern explicit to all top-level Defense Department officials.

International Security Affairs (ISA), the Pentagon's "state department" and a powerful agency in McNamara's time, was shunted aside by Laird. The new secretary wanted to be "his own ISA."[27] The agency continued to monitor the secretary's interests in foreign policy, but its influence in the national security community was a shadow of its former self. In time an emasculated ISA proved troublesome for the State Department, which previously had relied on the agency as a powerful point of contact with Defense and now had to establish contacts with numerous defense agencies.[28]

As for Laird's strategic concepts, their evolution can best be traced in his annual posture statements. Development of his "Strategy of Realistic Deterrence" is explained in some detail in those messages, and his final report to Congress assesses the strengths, weaknesses, and the implementation of that concept.[29] The strategy was developed to implement the Nixon Doctrine and to develop an international framework in which free nations would support each other "according to their proportionate capabilities, while each bears the major manpower burden for its own defense."[30] The resource goal for the Strategy of Realistic Deterrence in peacetime was a defense budget of no more than 7 percent of the Gross National Product and an active duty military establishment of no more than 2.5 million personnel.

Major operational programs to implement the overall strategy were Vietnamization, the conversion from a conscript force to a volunteer force, arms limitation agreements with the Soviet Union, the development of new political and economic relationships with the Soviet Union and China, and vigorous technological initiatives in strategic and other weapons.

Laird's relationship to President Nixon appears to have been correct but not unusually warm. For one thing, Laird did not trust many of Nixon's White House aides and he made an overt policy decision that all White House contact would come to the Pentagon through designated individuals in his office. This "insurance policy" paid off later, when the Watergate investigation failed to find any involvement of the Defense Department, despite the manifest excesses of the White House group.[31]

Relations with Kissinger, from Laird's point of view, were open but stormy. Kissinger and Laird probably disagreed on about as many things as they agreed on, but there was frequent contact between them. Although it is difficult to determine which of the two was more influential in the defense policy process, some observations may be made. Kissinger was obviously a much closer confidant of the president than was Laird, but on certain specific issues in the defense area, such as Vietnamization, it seems clear that Laird had at least as much influence on policy as did Kissinger.

At times Laird had to employ his political skills to frustrate what he considered Kissinger's interference in the secretary of defense's business.[32] A case in point concerns the Defense Program Review Committee. This committee, chaired by Kissinger, was composed of the deputy secretary of defense, the under secretary of state, the chairman of the Council of Economic Advisers, the Joint Chiefs, and the directors of the Office of Management and Budget and the CIA. The task of the committee was to assess the political, economic, and social consequences that would result from changes in budgetary levels for defense. Since those levels are in constant flux, the committee in effect reviewed defense programs.

According to one well-placed authority, former Chief of Naval Operations Elmo Zumwalt, Laird seldom let the group review his programs. Laird took the position "that as a cabinet member who had been confirmed by the Senate and was responsible to the Congress for his performance, he was entitled to get presidential guidance from the President, and would not accept it from a mere Assistant, however brilliant and capable, who had no administrative authority and was not publicly accountable for his actions."[33] Basically, Laird's technique, as Zumwalt describes it, was to delay the budgeting systems so that the DPRC would play no meaningful part. This technique, Zumwalt goes on to say, "prevented Kissinger from becoming *de facto* Secretary of Defense as he had already become *de facto* Secretary of State."[34]

Nixon describes candidly the competitive relationships between his top security and foreign policy advisers (Rogers, Laird, and Kissinger) and the inevitable clashes. Apparently Kissinger-Rogers clashes were more serious than Kissinger-Laird, and one gets the impression that the Pentagon boss held his own with the White House. The former president recounts the independent tendencies of both Rogers and Laird in occasionally carrying out "sensitive dealings and negotiations without coordinating with the White House."[35] Kissinger is quoted by the Kalbs as reacting to a Laird public statement on Soviet support for North Vietnam with the statement, "Laird forgets he is no longer a Congressman."[36]

In terms of his relationships with the senior military, Laird has, on balance, to be considered a success. He was able to bridge the civil-military gap in a way that McNamara never achieved. When one thinks of the major problems of his tour, a tour in which his position was at times adversarial with the chiefs,[37] the absence of major problems between the secretary and the senior military is remarkable. Laird worked hard at relationships with the Joint Chiefs. His participatory management program, his attendance at their meetings in the Tank, and the low profile mode adopted by Systems Analysis were all part of that campaign.

Laird's relationships with key congressional leaders and his ability to coax his projects through Congress is unique in the history of the institution of secretary of defense. His success was based on his lengthy service on the Hill, his prior friendships there, and his determination to do key liaison work with Congress personally.[38] At the end of his tenure as secretary of defense, he was able to make the unparalleled claim that no major Defense Department budget request had been turned down by the Congress.[39]

Another part of the polity should be mentioned at this point. When one speaks of the "relevant publics" as part of a specific policy process, the larger outside public cannot always be disregarded. This is particularly true regarding issues related to an unpopular war. The growing antimilitary sentiment of the "outside public" was significant, and Laird's perception of the public pulse was far more accurate than other key executive officials formally part of the defense policy process. Many of Laird's subordinates emphasize that he was more attuned to the voices of domestic public opinion than were almost all other high officials in the executive branch of the Nixon administration. Laird was, for example, more conscious of the political reality that the Vietnam conflict was destroying the sociopolitical fabric of the United States than was either Kissinger or Nixon. In addition, Laird did not perceive Congress as "the enemy"[40] as did the president, maintaining instead an open relationship with his former colleagues.

At the same time, as Laird's pronouncements and past writings indicate, he was also attuned to the vital strategic interest of the United States—specifically, the continuing threat posed by a strong Soviet Union. All these considerations serve as the background to Laird's decision to make United States withdrawal from Vietnam his absolute first priority.

Vietnamization was not only the biggest problem the new secretary faced on assuming office but also the one that he monitored closely throughout his tenure, even though, especially in the later years, other problems constantly intruded.

During the Vietnamization program Laird was simultaneously burdened with other significant concerns such as developing the All Volunteer Force, securing an adequate defense budget in a time of disenchantment with the military, rethinking America's nuclear strategy for the post-Vietnam environment; and dealing with arms limitations agreements.

On the first day of the Nixon administration, Kissinger's fledgling White House apparatus sent to the bureaucracy its first National Security Study Memorandum (NSSM 1), which asked twenty-eight questions about the war in Vietnam, including the impact of the war's outcome on other countries in the area, the prospects for improving the South Vietnamese Armed Forces, the effectiveness of the pacification program, and the effects of the bombing on North Vietnam.[41]

The responses, brought together in a document of some 548 pages early in 1969, reflected agreement on some matters among the agencies concerned and substantial differences of opinion on other matters. There was general consensus that the South Vietnamese Armed Forces could not stand alone against both the Viet Cong and the North Vietnamese forces. Also, there was agreement that, though the enemy had suffered reverses, his basic objectives had not changed and that he had sufficient strength to pursue those objectives. Further there was agreement that the enemy was in Paris negotiating not out of weakness but from a realistic view that even though a North Vietnamese military victory was not attainable as long as United States forces remained, a North Vietnamese political victory was entirely possible.

Bureaucratic opinions, however, clashed on several important issues.[42] The condition of the South Vietnamese armed forces was considered more viable by some agencies than others. Gains in the pacification program were considered more fragile by the CIA, for example, than by Military Assistance Command Vietnam and its bureaucratic supporters, i.e., the American Embassy in Saigon, the commander in chief Pacific, and the Joint Chiefs of Staff.

Laird's own appointments were so recent that preparation of the response from the secretary of defense's office fell to second-level officials who had been around for a while. The work was done in

International Security Affairs and the Systems Analysis Office, and both groups, as compared to the military bureaucracy, were decidedly skeptical about the existing situation in Vietnam and pessimistic concerning the future.

As the replies to NSSM 1 were being completed, Secretary Laird was off on his first trip to Vietnam to see for himself. He received the usual tour and briefings and met General Creighton Abrams, the American commander in Vietnam who had replaced General Westmoreland the previous summer. (In the future Abrams was to play a key part in the disengagement in Vietnam as a bureaucratic ally of Laird.) In the course of a Laird-Abrams meeting JCS Chairman Earle Wheeler, who accompanied the secretary, inserted a cautionary note. "You are still not planning," he said, "on turning out a [South Vietnamese] force here that is going to have the capability of standing up to a sizeable attack by the North Vietnamese Forces."[43] It was a prophetic note.

How did the secretary himself feel about the situation upon his return to Washington, and what part did that play in the Vietnamization program? In the words of the president, Laird was enthusiastic about such a program. "Mel Laird had long felt that the United States could 'Vietnamize' the war—that we could train, equip, and inspire the South Vietnamese to fill the gaps left by departing American forces. In March Laired returned from a visit to South Vietnam with an optimistic report about the potential of the South Vietnamese to be trained to defend themselves. It was largely on the basis of Laird's enthusiastic advocacy that we undertook the policy of Vietnamization. This decision was another turning point in my administration's Vietnam strategy."[44]

Some of Laird's associates in the Pentagon project, however, had a somewhat different view. They place emphasis on Laird's perceptions of the American domestic scene, particularly on his sense of the urgency of having most U.S. forces out of Vietnam by November 1972 as a precondition for a Nixon reelection. In any event, it is apparent that during the transition period between the 1968 election and his appointment to office Laird had made his own estimate of the Vietnam situation. He concluded there was no realistic way for the United States to win militarily, and that for better or worse the war must be turned over to the South Vietnamese. Laird's attitude was to hope that the South Vietnamese would prevail,

but if in the end they could not, then at least the United States
had tried its best.[45]

When, that spring, Nixon approved the Vietnamization program, he also placed the secretary of defense in charge. Laird, to
give his direction to the program a personal touch and at the same
time assure his control, established a Vietnam Task Force. Basically
a group of officials from International Security Affairs, the Task
Force also included a representative from the Systems Analysis
Office, and others, as well as Laird's military assistant.[46] For several
years, almost every morning that he was in Washington, Laird met
with this group.

Concurrently with the Vietnamization program there proceeded
apace the dual negotiations in Paris—the formal, ritualized negotiations and Kissinger's secret negotiations, which were the actual
negotiations. Progress in negotiations was much slower than the
unilateral Vietnamization program. As H. R. Haldeman explains it:
"Henry found the North Vietnamese absolutely intractable. They
wouldn't even negotiate. And the reason was clear. No threat, and
no offer, could obscure one great fact known to the world at large.
The American people had turned against the war. The young were
saying they wouldn't fight it. The response to Eugene McCarthy's
Democratic primary campaign in 1968 convinced the North
Vietnamese that it was only a matter of time before the U.S. would
have to pull out, no matter what. So why negotiate?"[47]

Laird himself commented in his first posture statement as secretary on the relationship between Vietnamization and the negotiations: "Vietnamization is both a complement and an alternative to
the Paris talks. By strengthening the capability of the South
Vietnamese to defend themselves . . . we provide an additional in-
centive to Hanoi to negotiate. If, on the other hand, the Paris
negotiations continue to be stalemated, Vietnamization provides the
means for additional American troops to be removed in an orderly
manner without sacrificing our single objective—the right of self-
determination for the people of Vietnam."[48]

Neither in this statement nor in other public pronouncements
did he make clear his feelings that continued United States involvement in Vietnam was an erosion of our capabilities to defend
our vital interests elsewhere. This conviction, plus his perceptions
of the domestic political situation, convinced Laird more and more

as the weeks passed that the time was ripe for the South Vietnamese to go it alone with American material assistance, but not with United States manpower.[49]

There were in fact two approaches to Vietnamization, distinguished only by differences in pace. The withdrawal of American forces could be gradual, provided that American public opinion could be mobilized to support the pace. Alternatively, the pace could be rapid pushing the South Vietnamese toward self-reliance. Laird favored the latter approach.

On the other hand, a political solution through diplomacy, if achievable, could be the most rapid and in the end least costly. During the early period of his administration President Nixon, while espousing Vietnamization, tried energetically to achieve a diplomatic solution. He believed that through a combination of diplomacy and military pressure, the North Vietnamese would be forced into serious negotiations.[50] Part of the military pressure was the secret bombing of North Vietnamese sanctuaries in Cambodia ordered by the new president about two months after assuming office. (Both Secretary Laird and Secretary of State William Rogers opposed this bombing, being fearful of American domestic reaction when it was discovered, but Kissinger's opposite view was espoused by the president.)

In his own mind Nixon "set November 1, 1969—the first anniversary of Johnson's bombing halt—as the deadline for what would in effect be an ultimatum to North Vietnam."[51] Meanwhile he proceeded on his two-track approach. On June 8 at Midway Island in a joint announcement with President Nguyen Van Thieu of South Vietnam, the president announced the immediate removal of 25,000 American troops from Vietnam. The following month, he dispatched a personal letter to Ho Chi Minh which alluded to the November 1 deadline. The reply, dated in late August, shortly before Ho's death, was, as Nixon calls it, "a cold rebuff."

Meanwhile pressures were coming on the president from another direction. The nation's campuses, centers of the antiwar movement, were getting ready to open for the fall term. It was not a coincidence that on September 15 the president announced that another 35,000 American troops would be withdrawn by mid-December. By now, however, there had developed among the antiwar movement a planned national moratorium for October 15, involving voluntary boycott of college classes, along with demonstrations in Washington on the same day.[52] Two days before the moratorium, announcement was made that the president would make a major address on November 3. The following day Nixon received a message from Ho's successor, Pham Van Dong. This time the statement came not by secret letter but by a broadcast to the American people in which the North Vietnamese leader hoped that the demonstrations which he called the "fall offensive" would "succeed splendidly." Thus by mid-October did Richard Nixon know that there would be no early end to the war through negotiation.

The president therefore set about preparation of his November 3 speech with knowledge that it would be highly significant to the future American course in Vietnam. In the preparation of the speech he received conflicting advice. From Rogers and Laird came suggestions to emphasize the hopes for peace, Rogers stressing negotiations and Laird Vietnamization. But Kissinger and some others advocated a hard line.[53]

The outcome was Nixon's appeal to the "silent majority" of Americans to support him in staying the course in Vietnam. It worked. The president had bought more time for both Vietnamization and the negotiations—but realistically he had embraced Vietnamization as the chief hope. From this point on it was Vietnamization that moved ahead while the talks, both formal and secret, were, for all practical purposes, stalemated.

One assumption of Vietnamization was that United States withdrawals would be unilateral—that there would be no comparable North Vietnamese reduction, which meant, if this assumption proved to be true, the South Vietnamese eventually would have to take on both the Viet Cong and North Vietnamese. Withdrawals were to be made on a "cut and try" basis. Periodically General Abrams was to make assessments of the situation, which would provide the basis for the next phase of withdrawal of United States units. In time, however, these assessments, or at least their outcome in terms of announced withdrawals, were influenced more by American domestic considerations than by the actual situation in South Vietnam.

Although the continuing acceptance of more military responsibility by South Vietnamese forces was clearly central, there was a lot more involved in Vietnamization. Another essential element was development of a stronger and more viable political and economic apparatus throughout South Vietnam. How one puts that kind of improvement on a timetable is hard to say, but that was the objective.

The program officially began on July 1, 1969. It was evident from the outset that two critical South Vietnamese problems would determine the eventual outcome: the political leadership and the military leadership. Although most influential Vietnamese had little confidence that either President Thieu or Premier Ky could develop a wide political base, they felt that there was no choice but to retain them. Eventually the Thieu-Ky government became the Thieu government, but the problem remained the same to the end—no broad base of political support.

As for the problem of military leadership, most South Vietnamese despaired that anything could be done to get rid of the incompetent, inefficient, and corrupt among their general officers. Only a handful of generals had the confidence of lower-ranking officers, who in turn felt that the generals were more concerned about their own personal welfare than that of the country.

By the spring of 1970 most observers felt that a point of diminishing returns had been reached in regard to the improvement of the South Vietnamese army (ARVN), except perhaps in the field of logistics. Defensively the army was performing well, but with enormous American fire support. The rampant corruption made any chance of leadership improvement slight; and for the same reason, the possibility of the army's becoming an instrument of social progress was almost nonexistent—a distressing fact in a revolutionary war. By 1970 a high percentage of senior ARVN officers felt that they could hold their own against enemy forces only if significant United States air, artillery, helicopter, and medical support continued. A common concern of this group was that United States withdrawals would be too rapid.

Another aspect of Vietnamization which was of basic importance to the success of the effort was "pacification," a major effort to secure the rural areas. Mounted by the Thieu government, this was in full swing by mid-1969, while the Vietnamization program was under way. The effort had three central features: sustained local security;

an intense effort to destroy the guerrilla infrastructure; and initiatives at land reform and self-help projects for the villages. There was also an attempt at village and hamlet elections that year; it had mixed success.

By mid-1970, under the impulse of Vietnamization, United States and South Vietnamese efforts had actually pushed the Viet Cong out of areas they had controlled, to the point where the Viet Cong were in charge of less than 5 percent of the 12,000 hamlets in South Vietnam (only about 25 percent of the hamlets were contested). For this there were a number of reasons, including the quantity of United States resouces available to government-controlled areas, and a drop in the popularity of the Viet Cong. The South Vietnamese people simply wanted the war to go away, so they could go back to work in their fields.

Most informed persons, however, realized that the gains were fragile and that the Viet Cong infrastructure, although needing rebuilding, remained intact. There was, therefore, considerable uncertainty over the durability of the pacification achievements and the degree to which they could be sustained as the withdrawal of American forces accelerated.

Surveying all this from his Washington command post as best he could, Laird met daily with his Vietnam Task Force. In these one-hour early morning sessions he tried to sort out the issues and spur the bureaucracy, both his own and other's, on to action. Some sessions during the fall of 1969 recalled by one or more interviewees will give the flavor of these sessions.[54]

November 5, 1969
The military did not understand the concept that the residual force would phase out gradually over a relatively short period of time (e.g. 2 years). Mr. Laird indicated he hoped he would be able to give clear guidance on this on Monday after the weekly meeting with the President on Vietnam.

November 13, 1969 [New York Times, November 7, 1979]
Mr. Laird mentioned that he was pleased with the background briefing that Gen. Abrams had given Terrence Smith of the N.Y. Times. He felt it demonstrated that Gen. Abrams understood our objectives and supported them. He also mentioned that the President had read the article and was pleased with it initially. However, by 10 o'clock he had discussed it with Mr. Kissinger and apparently Kissinger had convinced him it was a disaster.

November 18, 1969
Mr. Laird said we would not get any written guidance from the President
on redeployment planning; therefore, he would make whatever assumptions were needed.

December 1, 1969
We very briefly discussed the Phoenix program and its potential for creating
bad publicity for the D.O.D. Mr. Laird said he was concerned over the extent of U.S. participation and wondered if it might be wise for us to try to
extricate ourselves from the program as soon as possible.[55]

   To the fast pace of Vietnamization desired by Laird there was
potential opposition on the part of the Joint Chiefs of Staff. In part
this was due to a perceived need to avoid the appearance of a
military defeat. Laird was acutely aware of this feeling and in time
convinced the service most affected, the army, that it was clearly in
its own interest to be out of Vietnam.[56]
   In general, army and navy withdrawals proceeded at a relatively
straightforward pace. The air force withdrawal was affected by other
considerations. Early in the period the air force did not accept the
comprehensive nature of Vietnamization. Laird had repeatedly to
make clear that the program applied to more than ground combat
operations.[57] This may have been caused in part by an air force
tendency to view its role, though critical, as somewhat more technical than ground operations. Undoubtedly, however, the main cause
of the delay was the South Vietnamese air force's lack of capability.
A whole host of problems, including the training of the South
Vietnamese and the enormous and complex maintenance problems
of a modern air force, can be cited.
   One device Laird employed to stimulate the chiefs' efforts in
Vietnamization was the budget process. This he accomplished in
two ways: by getting them more intimately involved in major
budget matters than they had been under McNamara[58] and by con-
vincing them that the more resources they employed in Vietnam the
less would be available for their worldwide requirements. In general, Laird was much more successful in dealing with the chiefs than
had been his predecessor.[59]
   Laird's chief military ally in the Vietnamization program was not
a member of the Joint Chiefs but the American commander in South
Vietnam, General Creighton W. Abrams. Abrams's support of

Vietnamization was absolutely essential to the success of that effort. Time and again in interviews Laird's associates pointed out the close working relationship between Laird and the field commander. Apparently, Laird convinced Abrams of the political necessity of a fairly rapid withdrawal. Having secured his agreement on withdrawal, Laird was then in a strong position to deal with any opposition the chiefs might raise.[60]

Even beyond the military there were many other officials and agencies for Laird to contend with in the course of carrying out the withdrawal program. At the apex there was the Nixon-Kissinger White House. Here the view was for a somewhat slower withdrawal than Laird had in mind. In the face of North Vietnamese pressure, and in hopes of getting them to negotiate more fruitfully, the president and his assistant wanted to show Hanoi that the withdrawal was not an indication of United States weakness.[61] The pace of withdrawal was also linked in White House eyes with the United States-Soviet relationship, as a kind of bargaining chip.

Secretary of State Rogers seemed to have played little part in Vietnamization and was ignored by Laird. Although Rogers dealt directly with the president, he was out of the NSC mainstream of action. State's Under Secretary Elliot Richardson did, however, relate well with Kissinger. Richardson also had an excellent young adviser on Vietnam, who knew Vietnam from personal experience, and was well tied into the Washington bureaucracy.[62] So Richardson was at least well informed on Vietnamization.

Laird's generally excellent relations with Congress did not prevent some skepticism from certain members of that body, such as Senator William Fulbright, toward Vietnamization. This skepticism, where it existed, was probably due more to previous policy failures in Vietnam than to the program itself. In general, Congress favored the program, although in the early period there had been some difficulties in comprehending the exact nature of the program that Laird had in mind.[63] Laird perceived, however, that this generally favorable atmosphere in Congress had a time constraint[64] and felt that visible progress must be made in order to sustain congressional support. This helped him to decide for a relatively fast-paced withdrawal program—other views held in the White House notwithstanding.

Vietnamization proceeded apace and in February 1970 Laird went again to Vietnam to assess the situation. His briefings and meetings and trips to the field there seemed to give reasons for optimism. A visit to a Catholic hamlet near Saigon where he "pressed the flesh" with a courtyard of flag-waving students assembled for the occasion was followed by a briefing by a Vietnamese division commander, who explained what tigers his force had become. At a departure news conference in Saigon the secretary told reporters that additional withdrawals of Americans could be made because of the "positive progress" he had found in the Vietnamization program.

At the same time, however, in the neighboring country of Cambodia, events were developing that were to lead to a major crisis in the Nixon administration's conduct of the war. As Laird was well aware during his February trip, intelligence indicated a substantial movement by the North Vietnamese of personnel and equipment into both Cambodia and Laos. Then on March 18 an unexpected event occurred—Prince Sihanouk, the Cambodian head of state, who was in Europe at the time, was overthrown by a military coup. General Lon Nol, an anti-Communist, became the new Cambodian head of state.

This destabilizing event was both good and bad from the American point of view. It was beneficial insofar as it brought to power a leader less tolerant of North Vietnamese sanctuaries on his country's border with Vietnam—sanctuaries that the Americans had heretofore harassed only by bombing and occasional small raids based upon political decisions going back to the Johnson days. The detrimental aspect of the coup and its ensuing disruptions was that Cambodian armed forces were already relatively weak and certainly no match for the North Vietnamese. Given the new and, from their point of view, deteriorating situation, the North Vietnamese forces now moved to take over large portions of Cambodia.

Nixon's immediate reaction was to help the Lon Nol government, but Secretaries Rogers and Laird were restraining forces.[65] By the third week in April 1970, however, the situation had deteriorated to the point that Kissinger had the Washington Special Action Group in action, and on April 22 an NSC meeting was held to consider what action was appropriate. By this time, the action being considered went beyond aid to Lon Nol and focused on the enemy sanctuaries, especially two across the Cambodian border from the Third Corps Tactical Zone (the eleven provinces surrounding Saigon).

In the case of one sanctuary, the Parrot's Beak area about thirty-five miles from Saigon, it was felt the South Vietnamese could handle the situation. Concerning the other sanctuary, the Fishhook, about fifty miles north of Saigon, it was felt that American forces would be required. The tactical objectives were clear: to destroy the supply caches and thus disrupt for six months to a year any major attacks planned by the North Vietnamese (thus giving Vietnamization a breathing spell); and to help, in conjunction with an aid program, prevent a Communist takeover of Cambodia. What was less clear was what this would do to the already tenuous domestic political base in America.

Between the NSC meeting on April 22 and April 27 the president and his advisers were absorbed by the problem. Laird and Rogers had serious reservations about an American incursion, about its impact on public opinion in general and on the campuses and on Congress in particular. Since the decision-making forum consisted essentially of those close to the president, especially Kissinger and (at this point) Attorney General John Mitchell, Laird was not intimately involved and certainly not greatly influential in this case.

The president's momentous decision to invade was made on April 27, and the attacks were launched on April 30. Although military successful, they were regarded on the home front as a disaster since by this time there was no domestic support for any expansion of the war, no matter how temporary and no matter how compelling for military reasons. A television presentation by the president, explaining the rationale for the operations, was wholly ineffectual. That spring witnessed the Kent State shootings, the disruption of the nation's campuses, and the final public ultimatum to the president to get out of the war. In the aftermath of the public reaction there was also some reaction among the Washington leaders. In less than a week stories appeared indicating the doubts of Rogers and Laird about the operation and were, of course, denied.[66]

Meanwhile Secretary Laird's Vietnam Task Force continued its meetings. Some samples:

May 7, 1970
Mr. Laird indicated there were many difficult problems ahead and that the Washington Special Action Group was a key problem. He asked Dr. Nutter [assistant secretary for international security affairs] if he had been attending regularly. In some cases when Cambodian issues were discussed he was not permitted to go. Laird would insist in future that Nutter be permitted to attend all meetings.[67]

May 15, 1970
Laird was concerned that the South Vietnamese are wandering all over Cambodia protecting that government while we, in turn, are in SVN protecting the South Vietnamese.

May 27, 1970
Mr. Laird in reading a message he received from Gen. Abrams commented on the approach Abrams takes, which is completely in line with his own view of the situation. In particular he noted Abrams's emphasis on forcing the South Vietnamese to assume more responsibility for combat operations as an excuse to demand that they accept a greater share of the combat burden.

May 28, 1970
Dr. Nutter indicated that Dr. Kissinger, at a WSAG meeting yesterday, had indicated we should consider keeping options open on air support in Cambodia. The president was very concerned that we ensure that a non-Communist government is maintained in Cambodia. Mr. Laird said this was contrary to the president's comments this past Friday and felt that Dr. Kissinger was not reflecting the president's real views.

Mr. Laird indicated he was concerned that Dr. Kissinger simply didn't have a sound knowledge of what tactical air power can do. He wondered what Kissinger's staff did for him on this problem.

It was essential that U.S. casualties are cut back sharply during July. If necessary we ought to do it by edict, but we must demonstrate to the people that U.S. casualty rates were going to go down as soon as the Cambodian operations were completed.

June 10, 1970
We had a big job ahead of us to educate Dr. Kissinger and the president on the limitations of tactical air. The president apparently has been strongly influenced by the 7th Air Force.

Nixon in his memoirs points out that Secretary Laird felt that the Pentagon had been snubbed in the decision-making process concerning the Cambodian operations.[68] There is also an interesting, and apparently authentic, article on Laird's views on decision-making during this period by William Beecher in the *New York Times* of June 13, 1970.[69] Some extracts:

In the fast-moving Cambodian crisis, the formalized machinery of the National Security Council was largely bypassed, and . . . there were frequent direct contacts between White House officials and members of the Joint Chiefs of Staff, with Secretary Laird feeling at times inadequately informed and involved.

Following his [Laird's] talks with military and White House officials, two procedures were changed.

First, the Joint Chiefs were instructed that no military proposal on matters such as the incursion into Cambodia . . . would be forwarded either to Mr. Laird or to other Government departments without first getting an opinion from the Pentagon's International Security Affairs office.

Second, the membership of the top-level Washington Special Action Group, commonly called WSAG, was expanded to include civilian specialists on Vietnam from the Pentagon and the State Department.

One important aspect of the Vietnamization program, the pacification of the rural areas, probably achieved its peak success sometime shortly after the Cambodian incursion. This was an aspect that Laird followed closely through his Vietnam Task Force. In addition to discussing current problems, the morning meetings in the secretary's office heard frequent briefings, sometimes by a brigadier general who led the Task Force itself.

Frequently the briefings went extensively into both pacification achievements and the improvements in the South Vietnamese armed forces. Even though success was measured no longer by the body count of the earlier period, the format was often highly statistical in nature. The new standards, which were the reverse of the buildup period, included troop strength reduction ahead of presidential goals, percentage reduction of United States maneuver battalions, percentage decrease in Americans killed, and increased percentage of Vietnamese air force sorties flown. What it all meant seems problematical. At the time, it sounded as though the Vietnamese were taking over the war, and the military data, such as they were, provided an apparently professional military basis for a political withdrawal.

To be sure, there were misgivings on the part of many officials, especially over the durability of ARVN improvements. Some doubted whether the increased ARVN capability could be maintained as the United States withdrawal schedule continued and increasing burdens were transferred to the Vietnamese.[70] The Communist forces, for their part, seemed convinced that the gains of the other side were transient and the proper approach was to keep a fairly low profile, outlast the United States, and then contend with the South Vietnamese government.

During ARVN operations into Cambodia in the spring of 1970, American strength was about 430,000. By the following February, when ARVN was gearing up for cross-border operations into Laos against the Ho Chi Minh Trail, the figure had decreased to about 300,000. There were, however, other problems more important than military strength. The Senate in December 1970 had, through the appropriations process, prohibited American ground troops from operating outside of Vietnam. Thus although the American forces could provide logistical, air, and firepower support from within Vietnam, advisers were not able to accompany the South Vietnamese forces in forays into Laos.

At first things went well for ARVN on the Laotian operation. They did reach and interdict the North Vietnamese supply trails. At this point Thieu issued an "on to Tchepone" order. It proved to be rhetoric, and poor rhetoric at that, because the North Vietnamese counterattacked and devastated the ARVN. Cut off from their advisers, the South Vietnamese were unable to arrange adequate fire support (a problem they never solved) or resupply. They were able to withdraw, but even though they had severely damaged enemy logistical facilities in the operation, they had appeared ineffectual and disorganized. That ended any grand notions of major ARVN offensives. Henceforth they were to function solely as a defensive force.

As the second year of the Vietnamization program drew to a close in the spring of 1971, American troop strength was about half of what it had been when the program began.[71] By April 1971 the secretary of defense was trying to get the public and the government to look beyond Vietnam. He was, he said, "able to report that U.S.

objectives in Vietnam are rapidly being achieved and that U.S. military involvement . . . is coming to an end,"[72] and it was time to shift the focus to post-Vietnam defense issues. In particular Laird stressed what he called the administration's strategy of "realistic deterrence,"[73] which he described as being based on "the three principles of partnership, strength, and willingness to negotiate." The strategy demanded American allies to do more for their own defense; smaller, but more combat-ready, military forces for the United States; and an acceptance of nuclear parity with the Soviet Union.

Although much of Laird's time was spent considering strategic matters beyond Vietnam, throughout the year of 1971, the war was still uppermost in the public's eye, and consequently also a major preoccupation of the Washington bureaucracy, and Laird himself throughout that year continued to devote much attention to Vietnamization. Although the bringing home of U.S. troops and the shoring up of the South Vietnamese army were the major objectives, there were a large number of collateral issues that concerned the Pentagon, the State Department, Congress, and the White House.

There was the increasingly repressive nature of the Thieu regime itself. This became most salient through press coverage of the South Vietnamese presidential election of October 3 and its preliminaries. The official United States position was not to get involved—probably the only position that could defensibly be taken. Still, the viability of the Thieu regime, on which the success of Vietnamization would eventually depend, was becoming increasingly doubtful.

As 1971 wore on, a deterioration in the American forces also became evident. By the spring of 1971, Vietnam Task Force meetings began to discuss problems of "fragging" (assassination of unpopular junior officers) and drugs. This deterioration of morale was another reason for getting the forces out as early as possible.

Also that spring, the subject of the American prisoners of war held by Hanoi began to take a good deal of the secretary's time. An important psychological issue with the American public, the matter was by then an important part of the negotiations with the North Vietnamese. Some, including Ambassador Bunker, felt it had been made too big an issue and that as a result the North Vietnamese, sensing they had some good leverage, hardened their bargaining position.[74]

Meanwhile, through all these and other issues, the defense secretary continued to contend with the Washington bureaucracy as he proceeded to remove the United States forces from Vietnam. He found the Joint Chiefs still trying to keep as many men in Vietnam for as long as possible, frequently "using logistics problems as an excuse."[75]

Laird also had to contend with an increasingly restive Congress. In the early fall of 1971, the Senate, by a vote of 57 to 33, passed an amendment proposed by Democratic Senator Mike Mansfield calling for an early withdrawal of all United States forces from Vietnam. Secretary Laird, after analyzing the roll call vote, said the "message is clear we have 9 to 12 months to continue major operations including the bombing," but he feared that "the Joint Chiefs are not getting the message."[76] The *New York Times*, commenting on the same amendment in an editorial, stated, "The bankruptcy of Vietnamization is everywhere evident."[77]

Meanwhile interactions with the Kissinger White House apparatus, always wanting a slower rate of withdrawal, continued. One example will suffice. In 1971 the Republic of Korea still had in Vietnam two combat divisions, whose cost was being borne by the American taxpayer. By this time these divisions had passed the peak of their effectiveness, and General Abrams wanted them out as quickly as possible. The former commander and then army chief of staff, General Westmoreland, wanted them to remain and move north to the demilitarized zone. He had an ally in the JCS chairman, Thomas Moorer. Kissinger also wanted the Koreans to remain, as an element of leverage in negotiations. Laird of course wanted them out, if for no other reason than the financial drain. In the end the Laird-Abrams axis prevailed, as it did throughout Vietnamization, and the Korean divisions came out.

Throughout the summer and fall, the problem of how to prepare the South Vietnamese forces to withstand enemy assaults after the bulk of American forces had departed in 1972 was of central concern in Washington.[78] In early November Secretary Laird was off again to Vietnam to see for himself how the South Vietnamese forces were doing. On his return he was optimistic. The South Vietnamese forces "are in a position where they are strong militarily and they can handle the military situation to an extent that I did not think was possible when this program started."[79] A few days later, the *Wall Street Journal* of November 11 carried its own assessment. It was considerably more pessimistic than Laird. But regardless of all opinions, it would be not many months before the South Vietnamese would have an opportunity to prove their mettle.

The North Vietnamese Easter Offensive that began on March 30, 1972, was, in retrospect, the major event of the war during the four-year period from the arrival of the Nixon administration in January 1969 until the signing of the truce in January 1973. For several years beginning in mid-1969, the Viet Cong and North Vietnamese had maintained a fairly low profile during the process of Vietnamization. This approach was apparently based upon the conclusion that main-unit confrontations with American, ARVN, and allied forces were, for the moment at least, losing propositions. Hence there was a return to protracted warfare involving small unit actions. This policy was set forth in the most comprehensive Viet Cong document ever obtained by American intelligence, labeled Resolution Number 9 (July 1969). The underlying assumption was apparently that American patience on the home front for continuing the effort had worn thin, and therefore the best policy was protracted small-scale warfare while the American forces were gradually withdrawn.

By late 1971, however, the North Vietnamese leaders perceived that the situation had changed. First, from their point of view, Vietnamization seemed to be succeeding. If the picture was not as rosy as Nixon and Kissinger were hearing, some degree of success was nevertheless being achieved. Second, this was the time of Nixon's visit to China, soon to be followed by the visit to Moscow which culminated in the SALT I agreements. Time was of the essence for North Vietnam, confronted with what seemed to be a rapprochement between the major powers of East and West. Finally, this was the year of an American presidential election, when they felt, an American administration was the most vulnerable. These events, then, called for new decisions by the North Vietnamese leaders and led to an expansion of the conflict.

Hanoi's 1972 effort was enormous. The resources channeled into the Easter Offensive meant postponing needed economic development and required additional manpower from a society that had already sacrificed heavily during the long war. The offensive was not on the guerrilla pattern of Tet 1968, nor was the manpower that of the Viet Cong, as it had been earlier. Rather, modern weapons such as tanks and self-propelled artillery were involved, as well as surface-to-air and antitank missiles. The manpower sacrificed this time would be North Vietnamese. It was a major gamble.

The operation against South Vietnam consisted of three thrusts, the chief one across the demilitarized zone in the north and the others in the Two and Three Corps areas farther south. There was also some diversionary activity in the Delta. Beginning on March 30, the initial thrust in the north, by the equivalent of four divisions, was successful. Hitting a fairly new and green ARVN division, the North Vietnamese forces rolled through the northern province of Quang Tri and its capital of the same name. Fighting surged back and forth, with some of the early ARVN actions ineptly executed and victimized by South Vietnamese bureaucratic politics. By late spring the impetus of the North Vietnamese advance toward Hue was halted and then rolled back. Quang Tri city was recaptured in September, although the North Vietnamese retained control of large portions of the province, and fighting continued. In fighting in Two and Three Corps, the North Vietnamese made some permanent inroads but failed to capture the provincial capitals of Kontum city and An Loc.

The major factor that stalemated the battle was not primarily the success of Vietnamization but rather decisions made in Washington to apply American power directly to the situation.[80] The president was not greatly surprised when first informed of the North Vietnamese attack. Ever since the previous November, American intelligence had been aware of an enemy step-up in infiltration of North Vietnamese replacements to the south. In fact, the secretary of defense had already made a decision to publicize the expected offensive. But both the timing of the attack (it was later than predicted) and particularly the intensity were unexpected. Shortly, it became evident to the president that the attack was of major proportions and had the objective of knocking the South Vietnamese government out of the war. By April 3 Kissinger had convened his Washington Special Action Group, and by the following day the president had decided to resume bombing of the north, to include the use of B-52s, and to concentrate a large naval task force in the area of the Tonkin Gulf.

As the enemy attack continued to succeed, the president decided that the bombing would have to be brought into the Hanoi-Haiphong area, notwithstanding the fact that "Laird expressed grave concern about the Congressional furor that would follow further escalation of the bombing while Rogers feared that it might endanger the Soviet Summit."[81] The summit was heavy on the president's and Kissinger's minds, and the next several weeks were delicate ones in balancing between operational decisions concerning Southeast Asia and those concerning the Moscow meeting, which was to produce the SALT I agreement the following month.

On May 1 Quang Tri city fell to the Communists, and on the same day a message from General Abrams indicated that "the whole thing may well be lost." On the following day Kissinger was in Paris negotiating with Le Duc Tho, whom he found arrogant and unwilling to negotiate.[82] Clearly the president had some decisions to make which went beyond the Vietnamization program.

The first ten days of May was the critical period, since Hue was potentially vulnerable, and the North Vietnamese seemed ready to move in. Discussion of the mining of Haiphong Harbor and bombing in Hanoi soon became options for presidential consideration, options about which the defense secretary was reluctant. As one well-placed observer put it: "All of Laird's instincts, political and administrative, impelled him to try and temper the vehement Nixon-Kissinger response to the attack across the DMZ. However, with the President taking command personally there was little he could do but remonstrate and worry."[83]

Monday, May 8, the president announced his decision to the NSC that he intended further bombing and intended to mine all entrances to North Vietnamese ports to prevent outside access to them. (Thus the Soviet-supplied North Vietnamese tanks and other vehicles being used in the offensive could no longer count on a continued supply of fuel and other necessary support.) Laird opposed the decision, but the president's mind was made up.[84] That night after briefing the congressional leaders, many of whom, such as Mansfield, were dismayed at the decision, Nixon went on television to announce it to the American people.[85]

This time the public seemed less violently opposed, and in Vietnam the strategy worked. The final attack on Hue never came, and the South Vietnamese forces regrouped, held, and counterattacked. Quang Tri city was recaptured in September, although the North Vietnamese retained control of large portions of that northern province and the fighting dragged on until October, when word came of the impending truce.

For the North Vietnamese, the offensive cost an estimated 50,000 to 75,000 dead. Some 700 of their tanks were destroyed in South Vietnam. Their logistics system, they learned, would have to be improved in order to field and keep up with a modern conventional army. Another lesson concerned the difficulty and perhaps the impossibility of trying to counter American airpower with only conventional forces and an insignificant air force.

For South Vietnam, perhaps 30,000 had been killed. Their army had held, but American support and advisers had been critical. Also, a crippling blow to their position was the continued presence of North Vietnamese forces in South Vietnam. As it turned out, the truce signed several months after the end of the Easter Offensive permitted the North Vietnamese to retain the territory they had gained during their offensive in 1972. Despite their severe losses, therefore, the Hanoi leaders again had gained substantially from what in some senses had been a military disaster. This time, however, the gain was geographical, involving occupied territory, rather than psychological, as had been Tet 1968.

By mid-1972 pacification had regressed considerably from its peak of two years earlier. The key event detrimental to pacification had been the Easter Offensive; for the first time in several years, the Communists were causing wide disruption in rural areas. Largely this resulted from the diversion of ARVN units from pacification programs to meet the North Vietnamese offensive. By the eve of the truce, the government had lost control of perhaps 20 percent of the rural population. This was significant, for in certain areas the government's presence had completely disappeared. The Viet Cong could again recruit, tax, and propagandize in many areas formerly controlled by the Saigon government—and, it might be added, ones that the government claimed still to control. Base areas formerly closed to the Viet Cong were now available, as were infiltration routes. The pacification part of Vietnamization was in a shaky and deteriorating condition.

By October, Vietnamization, except for some massive last-minute deliveries of material, had run its course, and American troop strength was down to about 30,000. It was all up to the negotiators now. The president and Kissinger were directly involved. Nixon in Washington and Kissinger off and on with Le Duc Tho in Paris. There was also the difficult problem of getting Thieu on board. The talks broke off in December, then came the massive "Christmas bombardment" of North Vietnam. Finally, in January, came agreement.

In overall terms, the goals of the participating parties during the last part of the negotiations can be summed up as follows: the United States was looking for a graceful way out, one that would leave the South Vietnamese with a reasonable chance for survival. The North Vietnamese leadership wanted an end to the destruction of their country by American air power and an agreement that would set the stage for eventual unification of the two Vietnams. The Thieu government wanted South Vietnam to survive as an independent nation and the United States to remain a presence in that country as long as possible. The National Liberation Front (or, more correctly, the Provisional Revolutionary Government) wanted to survive as a workable political force in South Vietnam.

In the course of negotiations, there were sometimes eight points being discussed, sometimes seven, sometimes nine. No matter the number, the issues always concerned troop withdrawal, cease-fire, prisoner release, political settlement, international guarantees, foreign intervention, and reparations, To include details of the talks would take volumes, but the final agreements can be put concisely. Signed on January 27, 1973, in Paris, they include the following provisions: 1) An in-place cease-fire on January 28, 1973; 2) United States forces allowed sixty days to withdraw; 3) prisoners of war be released; 4) establishment of an International Commission of Control and Supervision with a broad charter to handle disagreements between parties to the agreement; 5) provisions for general elections at a later date.

Although the terms of the agreement represented compromises

on both sides, they were not equally acceptable to North and South. Some advantages that the Saigon government had held during the war were altered by the treaty. The most obvious change detrimental to Saigon was the final withdrawal of the United States military. Another major disadvantage to the Thieu government was that North Vietnamese forces were permitted to remain in South Vietnam. In effect, the parts of several southern provinces seized in the Easter Offensive were retained by the North, and that would have considerable significance for the future. The agreement may have been the best the United States could get in the divided political climate at home, but it clearly was not good from Thieu's point of view.

It would be reassuring to be able to bring this examination of Vietnamization to a close by attesting to its success, but subsequent developments made this impossible. Yet it is not necessary to base an assessment solely on the stunning North Vietnamese triumph in the spring of 1975. The short-term results of the program were beneficial. More importantly, the orderly withdrawal of American troops set the stage for the reconstitution of American forces worldwide.

Laird had stated repeatedly throughout his years as secretary that the South Vietnamese would have to develop their national will to retain their independence from the North. He did not predict the eventual fall of South Vietnam, but he recognized clearly that the ultimate outcome could not be decided by the United States alone. The case can be made that the Vietnamization program did accomplish its central purpose—if that purpose was the removal of the United States troops in response to domestic pressure on the American home front. Removal, moreover, occurred over a period of three and one-half years, so that the South Vietnamese had at least a hope of pulling themselves together.

Perhaps the central failure of Vietnamization may be viewed as a recognition that U.S. abilities to control events in the international arena had significantly decreased—at least from what earlier perceptions of U.S. leadership had been. When Secretary Melvin Laird left office at the close of the first Nixon administration, however, the eventual outcome was over two years in the future, and Laird had reason to feel that his central objective—removing U.S. forces from

Vietnam in a way that left South Vietnam a reasonable chance of survival—had been successfully accomplished.

Looking back over the period of the first Nixon administration, one is struck with the central importance that United States activities in and concerning Vietnam assumed in the American political process. In the 1968 campaign candidate Nixon made two important pledges: an end to the war, and an end to the draft. To accomplish the Defense Department's portion of those promises the new president appointed as secretary a man well equipped to understand and deal with the two essential elements that would condition both the nature and pace of the programmatic approach to accomplish those pledges. These elements were an increasingly restive American society and a Congress increasingly inserting itself into foreign and defense policy decision-making.

Melvin Laird, a skilled politician and master of bureaucratic maneuvering, was well suited to the task of defense secretary during the time he served. Sixteen years in the House, including substantial time concerned with defense appropriations, had given him an inside knowledge of the Washington scene and a healthy skepticism concerning the Pentagon bureaucracy as well as the White House staff. It also gave him much more than that: an independent political stature, and a sensitive understanding of the American polity—both of which attributes were to serve him in good stead.

Laird also had a strong view of what the secretary's role should be. Except for a brief interregnum he was successor to Robert McNamara, the first secretary who gained real control of the Pentagon. Laird had no intention of diluting that control, but his approach was different. He practiced something he called participatory management, which was intended to draw the services deeper into the decision-making process. To make it work, McNamara's famous Systems Analysis Office had to be transformed into a supporting office which, although it still provided analysis, now let the services initiate the programs. (Another reason the office had to assume a less salient posture were the congressional sensitivities it had provoked during the McNamara period.) Another of McNamara's favorites, the International Security Affairs office, Laird in fact emasculated, since he wished to play its role himself.

President Nixon made clear from the outset that he himself would direct American foreign policy. The appointment of William Rogers as secretary of state was intended to assist that objective. An old friend, Rogers was installed merely to manage State and to maintain good relations with Congress.

The appointment of Kissinger as assistant for national security affairs was a major step by Nixon. The president intended the position to be more than it had been in the past and wanted the incumbent to assist him significantly in conducting foreign affairs. As time went on, due to the assistant's personal characteristics and to the nature of the times, the role became much more than that. Kissinger eventually became an international figure in his own right, easily overshadowing the secretary of state, and at times even the president.

In the interaction between the presidential assistant and the secretary of defense, the outcome was somewhat different. On matters of defense policy Laird, with his own political base, held his position well. The assistant might be brilliant and powerful, but Laird held firmly to the prerogatives of his office. On most matters, including the pace of Vietnamization, Laird's approach worked well and he generally achieved his policy objectives.

There is, however, an important exception, and that has to do with major operational initiatives connected with the war. On these matters Laird, acting from his keen awareness of the American domestic scene, was perceived by the president as being dovish, or not sufficiently aggressive. One example of this was Laird's opposition to many aspects of the Cambodian Incursion of May 1970 and to the bombing and mining response of early May 1972 to the Communist Easter Offensive. In these cases, final decisions were made in small meetings, essentially between Nixon and Kissinger, with Kissinger's Washington Special Action Group acting as the backup.

Secretary Laird's handling of the Joint Chiefs was skillful and generally successful. Although they opposed the fast pace he wanted for Vietnamization, Laird prevailed by means of bureaucratic manipulation and through his alliance with General Abrams, then American commander in Vietnam. One of Laird's great accomplishments was to convince the senior military that the most prudent thing for American forces was to get out of Vietnam in order to be able to rebuild for the post-Vietnam era. In sum, his handling of the senior military was considerably more successful than Robert McNamara's had been.

Laird's relations with Congress were unique for a secretary of defense. Although there were problems, especially as Congress became more restive and skeptical as the war went on, he was nevertheless quite successful in his dealings with that body. He was, after all, by background one of them, even though he had assumed a potentially adversarial cabinet role.

To redeem the Nixon pledge of ending the war, the administration followed two paths: negotiation with North Vietnam, and unilateral withdrawal under the rubric of Vietnamization. Laird's enthusiastic espousal of the latter was later to cause Nixon to state that his administration undertook the program largely because of Laird's optimism. On the other hand, given the lack of success in negotiations over so many years and considering the campaign pledge to end the war and the disenchantment of the American public and Congress, few other options obtained.

To make the withdrawal succeed Laird invested a good deal of his personal time in overseeing the program. Since he had not been directly involved in previous decisions concerning Vietnam, he was able to bring to the office a fresh perspective. He viewed Vietnamization as the only way to begin to rebuild the sociopolitical structure of the United States, and at the same time perhaps give South Vietnam a chance to survive. Yet, even while focusing on the withdrawal, the secretary remained interested in the negotiations (although he was not directly involved) and always considered them the best approach.

In monitoring Vietnamization through his daily meetings with the Vietnam Task Force, and in various other ways, he frequently reminded others of the program's time constraints. In part this had to do with his concern about the 1972 presidential election, but it also had to do with his reading of Congress and its declining tolerance for continuing the war. Conscious of this time constraint, he pushed faster on the program than the White House at the time wished to go. Kissinger viewed the remaining American presence as a matter of leverage in negotiating with the North Vietnamese. Laird viewed the remaining forces as something to be reduced as fast as possible. Kissinger for his part has been quoted as saying that he never thought Vietnamization would work, and most who lived through the "Great Spring Victory" of 1975 would say it did not work. Still, one could turn it around by saying that it was the negotiations that did not work rather than Vietnamization; for example, by allowing a large military force from North Vietnam to remain in the south, was the settlement not setting the stage for the 1975 debacle?

Secretary Laird was concerned with many strategic concerns that extended well beyond Vietnamization. He worked hard at getting the public, Congress, and bureaucracy to look to the post-Vietnam period. He talked frequently of the Strategy of Realistic Deterrence, a strategy designed to support the Nixon Doctrine, characterized by having our non-European allies supply the manpower in the event of hostilities while we supplied the sea and air power. He accepted the fact of smaller forces but talked of greater readiness in the post-Vietnam environment.

Another project to which he devoted some time, although not with as great an enthusiasm as he embraced Vietnamization, was the All Volunteer Force. The impetus for this program came from the White House and although Laird sensed the opposition of the services who had become accustomed to the relatively inexpensive high quality manpower that the draft had provided, he did put the required pressure on the service chiefs to make the program work, and he was able to announce before leaving office that the draft would soon end.

Like all secretaries of defense, Laird was deeply involved in problems concerning the defense budget. Here his record is somewhat mixed, depending on how one views the problem. In the public arena, he successfully carried the fight to presidential candidate George McGovern in 1972. McGovern was of course an easy mark when he almost casually called for cuts of some twenty billion in the defense budget.

It is evident in the defense budget during the Laird period that there was a definite decline in constant dollars, to the lowest point in about a quarter of a century. For this there were many reasons beyond the control of the secretary of defense. Two are especially important. The first and most important was unforeseen inflation. Some provision was made for this, but in retrospect far less than enough. The second reason was congressional reductions, which averaged about four billion annually during the first Nixon administration.

Melvin Laird served as secretary of defense at a difficult time in the United States. Disengagement in an orderly manner from an unpopular war was no easy task. In doing so he called on his political knowledge and drew on his political base to push along a reluctant military while compromising with an impatient Congress. In this and other matters he had to contend with a White House assistant who was de facto secretary of state and would have been de facto secretary of defense if he could. Laird prevented that.

As successor to the powerful Robert McNamara, he retained McNamara's control of the Pentagon but improved the civilian-military dialogue at top level. Given the times, his interaction with Congress was first-rate. Though the defense budget did not fare as well as many thought it should, probably no secretary could have done better given the times. At least with the forces out of Vietnam the stage was set for a revitalization of American military forces to meet the changing threats of the post-Vietnam times.

Perhaps Laird's greatest contribution was an event that did not happen and that he played a large part in avoiding. There was no crisis in civilian-military relations over the "lost" war and who "lost" it. All in all, history will judge Secretary of Defense Melvin Laird well.

5

James R. Schlesinger
Strategist

James Rodney Schlesinger served as secretary of defense during the last year of the Nixon adminstration and the first year of the Ford administration.[1] The major event of the first part of his term, transcending all issues domestic and international, was Watergate. It will sufficient here merely to highlight certain of the major events concerned with the episode to provide a feeling for the domestic milieu of the last of the Nixon presidential years.

Nixon's second term was hardly under way when the Senate Watergate hearings began that spring. In mid-July the bombshell was dropped that tapes had been made routinely of conversations in the president's office. Though the hearings ended in early August, Nixon's troubles were only beginning. In a matter not directly related, Vice President Spiro T. Agnew became involved as a principal in investigations of allegations of conspiracy, extortion, bribery, and tax fraud. In early August 1973 the story broke, and the administration came under severe fire. By October 10 it was over for Agnew and he resigned as vice president.[2]

Ten days after Agnew's resignation there was another domestic crisis, this time directly involving Watergate. A confrontation developed between the White House and Archibald Cox, special Watergate prosecutor, over Cox's efforts to obtain some of the presidential tapes. On Saturday, October 20, 1973, Cox was fired, and the same day, his two superiors, Elliot Richardson, attorney general, and William Ruckelshaus, deputy to Richardson, both resigned in protest. The "Saturday Night Massacre," as the event became known, touched off a violent wave of anti-Nixon reaction in the press, Congress, and elsewhere.

Between the time of the Agnew resignation and of the Cox firing, the president announced his choice of Gerald Rudolph Ford to be vice president. Ford was approved as vice president by the House of Representatives on December 6 and sworn in on the same day. A couple of months thereafter, the House authorized an impeachment inquiry on Richard Nixon, and closed hearings began on May 9, 1974, before the House Judiciary Committee. The hearings became public and were televised beginning July 24. By July 30 the committee had voted three articles of impeachment. On August 9, 1974, in the face of insurmountable pressure, President Nixon resigned.

Notwithstanding the president's preoccupation with the domestic events just highlighted, the last one and a half years of the Nixon administration also had problems on the international scene. Chief preoccupations were detente with the USSR and the simmering Middle Eastern situation.

If detente had a starting point it probably was the Moscow meeting of May 1972, which Nixon calls Summit I, where the SALT I agreements were signed. There were two later Brezhnev-Nixon summits, the first of which took place in June 1973 in the United States. The later agreements were not as spectacular as those of the previous year, although there was an "Agreement for the Prevention of Nuclear War," which was, however, general in nature. The discussion concerning the Middle East ended on an even vaguer note, the communiqué stating, "Each of the parties set forth its position on this problem."[3] Less than four months later the Middle East was the scene of a major crisis in United States-USSR relations, with the Yom Kippur War. This was a crisis that involved the new defense secretary, James Schlesinger, rather deeply.

On October 6, 1973, Syria and Egypt attacked the Israelis on two fronts: the Golan Heights and along the Suez Canal. United States and Israeli intelligence had been below par and the assaults began with little warning, catching the Israelis not only unprepared but at home totally preoccupied with their religious observances. The fighting along the Suez broke a 1970 United States-mediated cease-fire, and the conflict marked the onset of the fourth major war between the Arabs and Israelis in twenty-five years.

Israeli losses in manpower and materiel were heavy, and U.S. replacement of the latter (not, however, without some Washington bureaucratic infighting) brought a cautionary note from the Soviets, although for their part they were supplying Syria and Egypt with about 700 tons of materiel a day. Soon the tide of battle turned. In the north the Israelis occupied the Syrian Golan Heights, and on the east bank of the Suez they had the Egyptian Third Army on the run, and before long had it encircled.[4]

As events began to turn against Egypt and Syria, the Soviet Union reversed its earlier position and began to work within the United Nations forum to arrange a cease-fire. With U.S. assistance, such a halt was finally secured, but not before the Soviets had done a little saber rattling. First, the Soviets proposed a joint United States-USSR force in the Middle East to maintain the cease-fire. When the United States demurred, the Soviets indicated they might send in forces unilaterally. Since U.S. intelligence knew that the Soviets had reinforced their Mediterranean fleet and had alerted an airborne force consisting of about 50,000 troops, their threat seemed, to the president and Kissinger at least, a real one. The president's decision, which has been considered controversial ever since, was to place all American military forces on a worldwide precautionary alert which lasted from October 25 to 31.

On the day the U.S. alert began, the United Nations Security Council passed a resolution establishing a Peacekeeping Force, and on November 11 Egypt and Israel agreed to a cease-fire. Nixon was to say later of the episode that he did not view it "as a failure of detente but as an illustration of its limitations."

Nixon's final forays in the international field also concerned the Middle East and detente. In June he traveled to Egypt, Saudi Arabia, Syria, Israel, and Jordan on a peace mission—but one, as it turned out, that he could scarcely bring to fruition considering the short time that remained for him in office.

Nixon's final summit with Brezhnev was held in the Soviet Union in late June and early July 1974. The president was later to refer to it as a "holding pattern" summit. He apparently felt that there was no chance of making a major breakthrough on further arms control agreements. He states that there was a convergence of anti-detente forces in the United States by this point, and given his Watergate-weakened presidency he was in no position to take them on. In addition to the liberal and conservative opposition, there was also, he says, the "military establishment and its friends in Congress and the country, who were up in arms over the prospect" that the summit might succeed in producing real gains in arms control.[5] The summit produced a few modest gains, such as further restrictions on antiballistic missiles, but in general it was theater. Richard Nixon left Moscow on July 3 and returned to Washington, to the impeachment hearings and to his resignation from the presidency on August 9.

When Gerald Ford assumed the presidency, the country experienced a brief period of good feeling toward the new incumbent. Even those who opposed his conservative ideology praised him for his straightforwardness. The honeymoon, however, ended abruptly on September 8, when the new president announced that he was pardoning Richard Nixon for any crimes he may have committed while he was in the White House. To the country it smacked of a deal made in advance, although there was no evidence of that being so. Nevertheless, the public's confidence in the new president dropped rapidly. Into the White House poured phone calls, wires, and letters, the enormous percentage of them hostile. The intensity of the reaction in time diminished in the response to new events, but the image remained, to float up again later during the Ford-Carter campaign of 1976.

The main domestic problems that Ford faced in his first year and one-half in the White House, however, were those concerned with the nation's economy. These were economic problems that had developed during the Nixon years; by 1974 they combined to send the United States economy into its worst recession since the Great Depression. Ford attempted to secure congressional and public support for an antiinflation program but without much success, and by the final quarter of 1974 the economy was in a state of general collapse. By this point, unemployment joined inflation as a major issue in the eyes of the American public.

The president acknowledged the seriousness of the situation in his State of the Union address in January 1975. At this point Ford shifted government emphasis from curbing inflation to reducing unemployment by creating more jobs—although not to the extent that the Democrat-controlled Congress would have preferred. The shift of emphasis to countering unemployment in turn required a cut in taxes and therefore an increase in budget deficits, a painful approach for an economic conservative like Ford. It was in light of

these economic realities and the resulting attempt by the administration to hold down the federal budget in order to minimize deficits
and inflation that a battle between Ford and Defense Secretary
Schlesinger over the size of the defense budget took place.

On the international scene as well as the domestic, Gerald Ford
inherited some problems from Richard Nixon. One of the major
problems was in the actual conduct of foreign affairs. As a result of
the Vietnam disaster and the Watergate scandal, Congress had become increasingly aggressive in the conduct of foreign policy. At the
same time it had become highly skeptical of invocation by the chief
executive, or his representatives, of the importance to American
national security of particular foreign policies the president wanted
to pursue.

An excellent illustration is the Cyprus issue, which flared up less
than a month before Ford assumed the presidency. Cyprus, which
had become independent in 1960, had existed between then and
1974 in an uneasy situation because of disputes between the Greek
and Turkish communities and between factions within the Greek
community. On July 15, 1974, the Greek Cypriot National Guard
staged a coup deposing Archbishop Markarios (who had been president of the republic since 1960) and appointed their own president.
Five days later at the request of the Turkish Cypriot leader, the
Turkish army intervened, eventually occupying about 20 percent of
the island.[6] Turkish military action continued spasmodically until
mid-August, when action eventually stopped and their occupation
began on the northern part of the island.

By this point Ford had assumed the presidency, and his secretary of defense was setting forth views on the issue—although it
was not clear whose—according to a *New York Times* article by
Leslie Gelb:

Mr. Schlesinger said that Turkey had gone beyond what any of her "friends
or sympathizers" were prepared to accept in military advances in Cyprus.

While the Secretary termed it "inappropriate" to discuss what pressures
Washington might bring to bear on Ankara, the clear implication was that
he believed Turkey had gone too far, and that Washington should now be
prepared to reassess its provision of military and economic aid to Turkey. . . .

In regard to Mr. Schlesinger's remark about Turkey, a State Department spokesman, John F. King, said he did not know whether Mr.

Schlesinger had checked his remarks with Secretary of State Kissinger or
other State Department officials. The spokesman added that Mr.
Schlesinger had his own views on this subject.[7]

As it turned out, the State Department views prevailed, and the
administration did not cut off military arms assistance to Turkey. A
substantial group in Congress, however, did hold the same views as
Schlesinger and proceeded to challenge the administration.
Throughout the fall of 1974 Congress tried to get a ban on arms
transfers to Turkey as a rider on a continuing resolution, and twice
Ford vetoed the legislation. Finally Congress succeeded in December by attaching such a prohibition to the Foreign Assistance
Act, which the president signed. So against the new president's
wishes, the United States was prohibited from selling arms to its
NATO partner, Turkey.[8]

It was not long before President Ford was trying his own hand at
summitry. In mid-November he was off to the Far East to meet
Emperor Hirohito and Japanese Prime Minister Tanaka in Tokyo, to
call on President Park Chung Hee in Seoul, and to confer with
Leonid Brezhnev in Vladivostok. This latter meeting was concerned
with prospects for a European security conferences[9] and two familiar problems, the Middle East and SALT. This latter issue deserves
some further comment.

The United States and the USSR were still struggling with SALT
II, which, unlike SALT I, a quantitative agreement, was concerned
largely with qualitative issues. Although discussions included qualitative issues, the agreements at Vladivostok were again largely
quantitative,[10] although the aide-mémoire did reaffirm a mutual
interest in negotiating a new agreement that would be effective
through 1985.

Another inherited foreign policy problem for Ford, and one
whose final stages he was to preside over, was the war in Vietnam.
Here, as in the case of Cyprus, he found himself at odds with
Congress, in this case over the amount of aid to be provided the
South Vietnamese government.

After the U.S. withdrawal in early 1973, the initial task for Hanoi
was reconstructing its own economic base at home. The threat
posed by North Vietnamese forces, along with the political contest

with the Viet Cong, kept South Vietnam fully mobilized. As 1973 moved into 1974, it became evident that the North expected to remain permanently in the South. The Ho Chi Minh Trail became an all-weather highway. In time, an oil pipeline appeared. Supplies and weapons were routinely shipped south, as were troop replacements and reinforcements.

The critical arena for South Vietnam became more and more the United States. Congress showed less and less inclination to continue the support of the South Vietnamese government. What this meant over a period of time was that the armed forces of the South survived only by cannibalizing equipment, deferring maintenance, and becoming less and less able to counter an increasingly aggressive and probing enemy. Weaknesses showed themselves especially in the Vietnamese air force's operational capability and in its army's inability to adjust to the changing environment.

Perhaps more important than the problems of material support were the problems of morale, which is the backbone of any armed force. The continued persistence of the North and its suppliers, the dwindling nature of United States support, and the realization that even American airpower would no longer be applied to gross violations of the truce were cumulatively too oppressive, and in the end the South Vietnamese morale cracked.

The year 1975 started quietly in South Vietnam with the expectation that there would be no general offensive by the North Vietnamese but rather a series of probing attacks leading to an all-out effort in 1976. In mid-January, however, the provincial capital of Phuoc Long, one of the eleven provinces in Military Region III surrounding Saigon, fell to the Communists. That was hardly reassuring but not in itself critical.

In March the action that had begun gradually began to build up in earnest. Communist forces attacked along an immense area running down Route 14, a strategic inland road extending from the Central Highlands city of Pleiku all the way to Tay Ninh city northwest of Saigon. Obviously such an attack was a major violation of the Paris peace agreement of two years earlier. The reaction of the United States was predictable, since congressional acts in 1973 had made any United States military intervention virtually impossible. The reaction of a congressional mission just returning from Vietnam, together with public opinion in general, made it highly doubtful that any of the increased military aid that the Ford administration requested would be forthcoming.

The beginning of the collapse itself was the capture of Ban Me Thuot, a remote provincial capital on Highway 14. At this point President Thieu made a critical decision that caught everyone, including United States officials in Saigon and Washington, by surprise. He ordered the withdrawal of South Vietnamese forces from the highlands to the coast—the most difficult of all military maneuvers. Because the South Vietnamese army had never been trained for a war of maneuver in the traditional sense, the outcome of this withdrawal was a military disaster.

At the same time, the North Vietnamese began pressure in the north near the Hue area. This time panic ensued as tens of thousands of civilians crowded the roads, communications were lost, and military units simply disintegrated. A South Vietnamese official was quoted as saying at the time: "Pleiku finis, Kontum finis, Ban Me Thuot finis, Hue finis. Everything finis." So it was.

The events of March and twenty years of struggle were too much; morale was broken, and the end of the Republic of Vietnam was at hand. Officially the war ended on April 30, only hours after the last Americans were helicoptered off the United States Embassy roof, when the flag of the Provisional Revolutionary Government was raised in Saigon.[11]

As his Watergate troubles increased, President Nixon withdrew more and more into problems associated with that scandal, leaving the daily operations of government to General Alexander M. Haig[12] and the foreign policy issues to Henry Kissinger. In September 1973 Nixon appointed Kissinger to replace William Rogers as secretary of state. The new secretary also retained his old office as assistant to the president for national security affairs. While an enviable position for Kissinger, this situation was not so desirable for other cabinet officials, especially for secretary of defense.

After he became secretary of state the locus of decision-making in foreign policy shifted from Kissinger as head of the NSC staff to Kissinger as secretary. Kissinger took with him to State a small number of his key White House advisers. The NSC staff continued to exist, but as a policy-influencing entity it had been considerably weakened. Since Kissinger had both White House and State Department posts he had leverage not only on foreign policy issues but also directly on defense policy issues. Further, when he wished, he could circumvent his own subordinates in State, In the entire history of the NSC system no one ever had a position as powerful as that, and no one is likely to in the foreseeable future.

Schlesinger's nomination in the spring of 1973 to be secretary of defense was directly related to Watergate, as was at least one other appointment (director of the CIA) in the Nixon administration, although perhaps not as directly as this one.

Schlesinger was a 1950 Harvard classmate of Kissinger, likewise staying on to get a Ph.D., in Schlesinger's case in economics.[13] He joined the economics faculty of the University of Virginia in 1955; during the course of his stay he took a six-month leave of absence at the Naval War College where he delivered a series of lectures that were subsequently brought together in a book, *The Political Economy of National Security*.[14] Reviews were mixed but officials at the RAND corporation were impressed, and in due time he left Virginia and joined the RAND staff.[15] Eventually he became director of strategic studies there, serving also as a consultant to the federal Bureau of the Budget.

This was the situation in 1969 when the Nixon administration took office. Schlesinger was apparently considered by Laird to head the Systems Analysis Office, but for one reason or another was rejected. Instead he was named as assistant director of the Bureau of the Budget, specializing in defense matters, even though his policies were not always to the liking of Laird or the air force or navy.[16] When the bureau was transferred into the Office of Management and Budget, Schlesinger stayed on when the new office began operating in 1970. It was at this point that Schlesinger met Nixon for the first time, not an altogether harmonious occasion. "At the first meeting in the Oval Office, Schlesinger was characteristically blunt about some Pentagon requests and after the meeting the President pronounced: 'I don't want to see that guy in my office again.'"[17]

Apparently, as time went on, the president objected less to Schlesinger (who by now had an ally in Alexander Haig)[18] and was ready in the spring of 1971 to nominate him to be under secretary of the interior. There were, however, objections from some western senators, and after a short time in limbo Schlesinger was nominated in July 1971 to head the Atomic Energy Commission (AEC). Here he was caught in the battle between the environmentalists and the utilities-first group, and he did remarkably well. For the first time he got into some direct management activities, reorganizing the agency and appointing some new people to key jobs—moves that were generally perceived as having improved the agency.

A Schlesinger action that improved his standing with Nixon was a memorandum written while he was still in the Office of Management and Budget, one highly critical of the CIA's intelligence production abilities.[19] Shortly after the 1972 election, as a result of Nixon's dissatisfaction with how things were going in the intelligence community, Richard Helms was fired as CIA director.[20] After less than a year and a half as AEC chief, Schlesinger was transferred to the more prestigious post of director of the Central Intelligence Agency.

Schlesinger's tour as CIA director was, however, to be yet another brief one. Although an intelligence "outsider," here again he moved in with apparent confidence, reorganizing and starting some professionals to an early (and as he perceived well-deserved) retirement.

At this juncture, however, Watergate was having such a major effect that Nixon thought it important to improve the image of the Attorney General's office by appointing Elliot Richardson, the current (though only briefly) defense secretary. After having been sworn in as CIA director on February 2, 1973, Schlesinger, on May 10, 1973, was nominated by the president to be the twelfth secretary of defense.

From even this brief sketch of Schlesinger's background it is evident that, in terms of background knowledge, he was probably the most qualified person ever to have assumed the office of secretary of defense. And of all secretaries to that time, he may also have had the most complex personality—and that is saying a great deal.

One thing about Schlesinger that all who knew him agree on—although his personal characteristics may have been more obvious as he became better known, they were already well developed by the time he arrived in Washington in 1969. A summary sketch of

Schlesinger would read as follows: He is professorial in manner, including the usual rumpled appearance attributed to those in that profession; he is described as being brilliant and articulate (although sometimes given to speaking in parables) and as possessing great intellectual insight. Three terms frequently applied in characterizing him are bluntness, arrogance, and abrasiveness. He apparently enjoys intellectual exploration of problems, frequently inserting probing questions, sometimes with a touch of satire. He is also at times rather withering in dealing with subordinates.[21] All in all, these are not the qualities of charm and warmth usually attributed to those who get ahead in Washington. Still, Schlesinger did get ahead; he learned fast about the Washington scene and adapted his personal assets and liabilities to become a very successful secretary of defense.

Secretary Schlesinger's interactions with the White House, the Pentagon, and Congress were complex. The White House situation posed some difficulties for him. There was first the president's preoccupation with Watergate, and then there was presidential adviser Kissinger who was also secretary of state. The Kissinger-Schlesinger adversarial role was a natural one in this situation. One ploy used to close the communication gap was scheduled Friday breakfasts between the two. The two men's differences, however, were ones not of communication but of policy differences, most importantly how to deal with the Russians. One shrewd observer of the scene commented on the interaction between the two this way: "In Jim Schlesinger, Henry Kissinger met his superior as a strategic theorist. But since Henry is a superior bureaucrat, he was able to impose his positions on Jim most of the time."[22]

Schlesinger arrived at the Pentagon with a reputation for toughness based upon the organizational and personnel changes that he had accomplished in short order at the Atomic Energy Commission and the Central Intelligence Agency. But he had something else in mind when he arrived at the Pentagon. Looking at the sheer size of the Pentagon and the power of the military, he decided not to spend much time on organizational or management questions.[23] Rather, he decided to limit his time, energies, and intellectual leadership to a few problems that he considered most important.

First of all, he wanted to restore the military's positive public image. Second, he wanted to rearticulate strategic doctrine to meet the current world situation and particularly to meet the Soviet threat. Finally, he wanted to reverse the downward trend of the defense budget in order to be able to improve the U.S. strategic situation. These objectives should be kept in mind in viewing Schlesinger's approach to running the Pentagon.

Refusing to let the bureaucracy dominate him, Schlesinger detailed most of the management problems to others.[24] His method was to present in conceptual terms what he wanted and let the organization develop and implement the plans that would satisfy his goals. As compared to his predecessors he had relatively few systematic series of staff meetings. Working in this way he was able to reserve a good deal of his time for thinking and for conferring only with those he wished to. Regarding this latter point, Schlesinger kept a roster of people in various areas, not always in the Pentagon, whose views he regarded highly and would seek out. Since some of these individuals were as much as four echelons below him in the hierarchy, naturally this did not sit well with many of those in intermediate echelons.[25]

One routine meeting that Schlesinger found useful was an early morning session with his assistant secretary for public affairs, his assistant for legislative affairs, and others close to him. Sometimes these meetings lasted as long as one and a half hours. The group sat informally around a coffee table, Schlesinger with his coat off, puffing on his pipe. Immediate problems took priority, but the subjects were fairly wide-ranging, including Schlesinger, shaking his head, musing "What is Henry up to?" This informality, however, should not be confused with lack of purpose. Schlesinger was very sensitive to the press and Congress in these sessions and was quick to perceive developing issues, frequently even before his advisers.[26] All this is not to suggest that the formal institutional machinery of the Pentagon was abandoned; it continued to function, but it was not the locus of Schlesinger's decision-making process.

An example of his use of formal institutions is the Systems Analysis Office. Initiated by Robert McNamara, who had made much of it, the office wound up antagonizing the military (although they rapidly adopted the analytical technique themselves) and also their allies in the Congress. Under Laird, the office was kept out of sight, and project initiation passed to the military, though the office remained highly effective in assisting the secretary in analysis of service programs.

Under Schlesinger the office was somewhat upgraded, though not to the McNamara level. To head up the agency he appointed Leonard Sullivan, Jr., who knew his way around the Pentagon, having been in the Defense Research office since 1964 and having had considerable experience in the aerospace industry prior to that. An appointment of this caliber was found to give the office some salience.[27] And soon, at Schlesinger's request, Sullivan was up on Capitol Hill where some of the old antagonisms survived, even though the office was now called Program Analysis and Evaluation.

In time there came conflict with Senator John McClelland, chairman of the Senate Appropriations Committee, and chairman also of its Defense Subcommittee. First, there was a courtesy problem concerning a report that McClelland had called for from Defense but which had been seen in draft form by another committee first. Then a more serious problem arose when Sullivan, at Schlesinger's request, became the point of contact with the newly formed Budget Committees—bound to lead to sensitivities on the part of the Appropriations chairman. McClelland tried to get Sullivan's job canceled by not permitting it to be funded. He did not succeed while Schlesinger was secretary; however, not long after Schlesinger's departure, the position reverted back to director level and Sullivan departed the scene.[28]

One of the more interesting areas of Schlesinger's tour of the Pentagon is his relationship with the military. First, though, these were his expressed feelings about the military on assuming office:

The first question I raise is how do we treat our military. There has been a fair amount of abuse in using the Department of Defense and the military services as a whipping boy for all the frustrations of Vietnam and all the idiocies committed by the civilian leadership. A democratic nation gets about the kind of military establishment that it deserves, and if we continue to abuse these fellows and treat them this way, it is going to have consequences, I am not sure just what. I think that we have—to whatever extent it is a rough analogy—the isolation of the French military during the post-Algerian period. These people have been obedient to civilian direction, and we ought to be very careful to refrain from criticizing them doing what we would have regarded as very reprehensible their not having done. We want them to be responsible to civilian control, but that is the responsibility of the civilians.[29]

Since the tours of the senior military, meaning here the Joint Chiefs of Staff, have no relationship to the tenure of the secretary of defense, each secretary whose tour is of any duration must deal with a fairly large number of varying personalities. Schlesinger's experience was no different. During the twenty-eight months he was secretary, there were two chairmen (Admiral Thomas H. Moorer, who was appointed during Laird's tenure, and Air Force General George S. Brown) and no fewer than nine service chiefs.[30]

One of Schlesinger's weekly meetings was one with the chiefs in the Tank, which is their formal conference room, or in the National Military Command Center, the nerve center for worldwide operations of United States forces.[31] Secretaries of defense have done this in one way or another since Forrestal, and it became routine from the time of Secretary Thomas Gates (December 1959–January 1961) on. Schlesinger's meetings with the chiefs were, however, somewhat different from his predecessors. He frequently was the briefer. Appearing with his own slides, the former professor would proceed to lecture the nation's top military officials. According to one observer, the lectures were "academically outstanding" but were not put in Joint Chiefs' terms, or as some might say, in military bureaucratese.

Apparently the chiefs were intially skeptical of this professor character, with his big ego and analytical ability. After all, the last analyst who held the job was McNamara and some military still recalled that period as a disaster, wondering whether another McNamara was appearing on the scene. It turned out that Schlesinger was not another McNamara. At the outset, Schlesinger himself had reservations about the Joint Chiefs, not so much regarding the individuals as the value of the system. His strategic views were overall similar to theirs, and his budget views were in harmony with their own. So, whatever Schlesinger's personal idiosyncracies (and there were many), the chiefs were in fact supportive of his efforts for the military with Congress and elsewhere.

Schlesinger had a high regard for at least two of the chiefs who were in office when he arrived. One was Creighton W. Abrams, army chief, who had been the commander in Vietnam during most of Laird's Vietnamization program. Had Abrams not been suffering from a terminal illness,[32] he would probably have been Schlesinger's choice for chairman when Admiral Moorer's term expired in June 1974. Schlesinger's actual choice was Air Force Chief George Brown, whom he also highly esteemed.

Brown had graduated from West Point in 1941 and was a bomber pilot in Europe during the war, winning a Distinguished Service Cross on the Ploesti raid over Romania in August 1943. As the years went on he had important commands (the Seventh Air Force in Vietnam and the Air Force Systems Command being the most prestigious) and key staff assignments. Brown was a personable and able chairman, being particularly effective in smoothing over interservice rivalries in the post-Vietnam era with its lower budgets. Brown's one defect, and hence Schlesinger's and the president's, was that he was too outspoken in public pronouncements and had to have his "sails trimmed" by these superiors from time to time.[33] Nonetheless, on internal defense matters, Brown was a strong asset in helping the Schlesinger-Joint Chiefs team function cooperatively.

Schlesinger's relations with Congress deserve some comment at this point. Obviously he did not bring to the Defense Department job the great skill in congressional relations that his predecessor Melvin Laird possessed. But it was a myth that he was not good at relations with Congress. When he arrived in Washington in 1969 he lacked skill in that area, but being a fast learner, in time gained command of the technique of hustling votes on the Hill, although it would be a mistake to believe that all congressmen felt comfortable with his blunt professional approach. He could, however, go to Congress to discuss defense matters in a rational and straightforward way. One senator who was on the Armed Services Committee, while admitting that Schlesinger's arrogance irritated certain of his colleagues, told me that Schlesinger was always perfectly honest and accurate in his answers before the committee and was always well prepared without needing a large backup of staffers.

One technique that he developed was constant personal contacts with congressmen who stressed factual discussion on the issues. Still, even as his technique on the Hill improved, the recollection of his earlier lack of effectiveness continued. Also, some of his public statements did offend certain key members of Congress.

When Gerald Ford became president in August 1974, James Schlesinger had completed thirteen months as secretary of defense. Unlike Nixon, foreign policy was not Ford's strongest area. In fact, he lacked experience in foreign affairs and felt diffident in dealing with issues in that area. He did, however, inherit an experienced and unusually powerful secretary of state, in whom he placed great confidence and with whom he was to work closely.[34] In effect Ford inherited not only a secretary of state but the policies that Kissinger and Nixon had developed, and to which, in order to provide continuity in American foreign policy, the new president subscribed.

The foreign policy initiatives of which Kissinger was most proud during that summer of 1974 were the SALT I agreement with the Soviet Union, the policy of detente, opening up a connection with the People's Republic of China, the disengagement of forces in the Middle East after the Yom Kippur War, and the end of American participation in the war in Vietnam. Of course he was aware of new difficulties that each of these initiatives had introduced and of a long agenda of problems that required new initiatives.

Essentially, the foreign policy of the Nixon administration was embraced by Ford, although not all members of his administration were equally enthusiastic about all those policies. Chief among the doubters was James R. Schlesinger.

If it was clear that Gerald Ford had always considered Kissinger a necessary asset to be kept in his administration should he become president, it was less clear how he felt about retaining Nixon's secretary of defense. Consider the following:

A few days after Mr. Ford became Vice President . . . he had a long conversation with the Secretary of Defense. Mr. Ford was impressed with Mr. Schlesinger's erudition and remarked later to an associate that Mr. Schlesinger seemed extraordinarily versed in the details of the sprawling defense establishment's activities. Yet Mr. Ford also noted, the associate recalled . . . , that he felt uneasy in the company of the self-possessed, professional,—and, some say, almost arrogant—Secretary of Defense. After a quarter-century in Congress, Mr. Ford was accustomed to indulging himself in small talk and to count an easiness in idle repartee as an essential tool of politics. Mr. Schlesinger seemed to him stiff, doctrinaire, and, for all the Secretary's evident ability, incapable of chumminess.[35]

An article the following spring in the *New Republic* touched on Ford's perceptions of Schlesinger from a different perspective:

The Nixon Cabinet member with the big question mark over his name is Secretary of Defense James R. Schlesinger. Ford thinks that Schlesinger is in many respects an excellent Secretary of Defense. He admires Schlesinger as a person and as an official. . . . Ford's reservation about Schlesinger has to do with Congress. In the Vice President's opinion, Schlesinger doesn't understand Congress and doesn't know how to deal with Congress. . . . Ford spent most of the last week of March working on a problem in Congress that, in the Vice President's opinion, Schlesinger simply didn't know how to handle and was not equipped to handle.[36]

At a news conference the day following publication of the *New Republic* article, Ford commented to the effect that whatever reservations he may have had over the effectiveness of Schlesinger as secretary of defense, they had been resolved. Yet the main thrust of Ford's doubts as described in the two preceding quotations (i.e., Schlesinger's personality and Ford's perceptions of Schlesinger's handling of Congress) were to play a part in the defense secretary's future abrupt dismissal.

More important, however, than personality or process, probably were differences that developed on substantive issues. The Ford-Kissinger approach to detente and SALT were on a different track from the Schlesinger Pentagon. Partially as a result of this, but more particularly because of domestic considerations, the president and the defense secretary were on another collision course over what is always the bottom line in national security matters, the defense budget.

From his earlier four years' government experience of working on various aspects of national security policy, Secretary Schlesinger was aware in advance of the problems facing the department whose leadership he assumed in the summer of 1973. The legacy of the Vietnam War hung heavy in the Pentagon: the operating costs of the war had postponed new capital investment and major overhaul work, resulting in serious equipment shortages, especially in combat ships and tanks; research and development had been neglected, again because of the cost of the war; the morale of the armed forces in general, and of the army in particular, was at a low ebb; the implementation of the all-volunteer force, itself a product of the war, had been completed, but the "new military" was faced with major personnel problems because the quality of the volunteer recruits was mediocre; further, the high cost of the pay of the volunteer force was beginning to cut deeply into the defense budget.

Schlesinger approached his job with two goals. First, he was determined to undo the Vietnam legacy, to rebuild the American military machine by improving its morale, its efficiency, and its aging weapons and combat systems. Second, he was committed to revising U.S. strategic policy, whose evolution over the 1960s had disturbed him greatly.

Unlike Robert McNamara, but like James Forrestal, James Schlesinger arrived at the Pentagon with his own world view. He had developed this over a period of many years, and it had been reinforced based upon his experience in government since 1969. Because it is so essential to the kind of strategic policy he wished to see established, I will take some time to develop his views at this point.[37]

The Schlesinger world view never altered either during his term at the head of the Defense Department or afterward. The vision was simple, clear, and unwavering. A single theme connects the early statements with the later ones, and all are built upon a logical progression of ideas. The first principle to be recognized, Schlesinger said, was that armed force constituted one of the basic ordering factors in the international system: "Power remains the ultimate sanction in dealing with potential conflict. Where power exists and is respected, it will not have to be exercised. Through power one can deter the initiation of an unfavorable chain of events. To be sure, military power is not the only form of power, but it remains an irreplaceable element in the total mix of power; without it, the disadvantageous turn in events would be swift and sure."[38]

Given such a world, it followed that the United States, regardless of its diplomatic intentions and nonbelligerent foreign policy goals, needed to maintain military forces. "It is necessary for the United States to participate in the maintenance of a worldwide equilibrium of forces," Schlesinger noted, "and this requires the American people to do what seems to some to be inconsistent: to pursue detente—an alleviation of political tensions—and to maintain an adequate defense capability. We want to have a relaxation of political relations with the Soviet Union, and at the same time our military posture must be sufficiently strong so that we maintain worldwide equilibrium of military forces."[39]

Furthermore, history had, in a sense, treated the United States unfairly. The Second World War had thrust the mantle of free world leadership on the United States; Western Europe's postwar weakness had made America the defender of democracy. Although Americans had not sought such a role, and in fact had attempted to avoid it, Schlesinger now saw no alternative route for the United States:

We now unavoidably have the leading part in the defense arrangements of the free world. There is no substitute among the other industrialized democracies for the power of the United States. Whereas prior to World War II the United States could serve as the arsenal of democracy and its great reserve force, now we constitute democracy's first line of defense. There is no longer any large and friendly shield of defenses behind which we can take two or more years to mobilize our forces. . . . We are not the policemen of the world, but we are the backbone of free world collective security.[40]

During his short stay in the CIA, Schlesinger had taken a close look at intelligence estimates concerning the Soviet Union, and what he saw disturbed him. His own view was that Soviet defense effort was being considerably underestimated. He had the suspicion that people wanted to believe what the Soviets were saying, and some attempt had to be made to get into the intelligence data in a more rigorous way.[41]

To assist on this problem Schlesinger brought to the Pentagon an old friend from the RAND days Andrew Marshall, to head up the Net Assessment Office of the Defense Department.[42] What Schlesinger sought was analyses of a type that other agencies were not engaged in or were doing in ways that could be improved upon, such as comparative costs of U.S. and Soviet military programs; naval balance between the United States and the USSR; political and psychological aspects of military forces—how, for example, does deterrence actually work, viewed from a Soviet perspective?

As Schlesinger studied the Soviets and observed the steady

buildup of their strategic and general purpose forces, he was again and again to return to this idea: "The United States, while remaining the great arsenal and reserve of democracy, had also joined its first line of defense; moreover, it is alone as the superpower of the non-communist world."[43] The more concerned he became about the Soviet's military capabilities, the more he stressed the uniqueness of the American role: "Unless we are prepared to withdraw into the North American continent, the contribution of the United States to worldwide military balance remains indispensable to all other foreign policies. . . . Only the United States can serve as a counterweight to the power of the Soviet Union. There will be no *deus ex machina*; there is no one else waiting in the wings."[44]

Feeling that both the Congress and the American people did not comprehend these realities of the international situation, Schlesinger undertook a personal mission to carry his view of the world to them; he believed that only after they understood the dimensions of the problem would the United States be able fully to meet the challenge posed by free world leadership. He would thus assume the familiar role of the educator, in the hope that it would enable him to function successfully as the renovator of the defense establishment.

Given his views, it is not surprising that Schlesinger would have policy clashes with the detente-minded White House of the Nixon-Ford-Kissinger period. This is particularly so in the case of the ongoing SALT negotiations with the Soviets. The interim offensive missile agreement of SALT I in May 1972 had not been a good one from the United States point of view. Nixon's attempts to improve the accords in his visit to Moscow in the summer of 1974 were halted in part by the efforts of the senior American military and Schlesinger. As Nixon puts it: "The U.S. military opposition to a new SALT agreement came to a head at the meeting of the National Security Council on the afternoon of June 20 when Secretary of Defense Schlesinger presented the Pentagon's proposal. It amounted to an unyielding hard line against any SALT agreement that did not ensure an overwhelming American advantage. It was a proposal that the Soviets were sure to reject out of hand."[45]

Only a few months after the Ford-Brezhnev Vladivostok agreement of late 1974, the defense secretary was voicing his misgivings publicly:

Secretary of Defense James R. Schlesinger has served notice that the United States plans to build up its strategic forces to the levels permitted by the Vladivostok agreement unless the Russians "exhibit restraint" in their own program. What he said could be interpreted in two ways.

Mr. Schlesinger may be making explicit what was only implicit in last November's "agreement in principle" between President Ford and the Soviet leader, Leonid Brezhnev—that the accord puts a cap on the arms race at a level not yet reached by either side but probably planned by both.

Or, Mr. Schlesinger may be telling the Soviet leaders that the Defense Department, having studied the implications of the Vladivostok accord, would prefer a new agreement or understanding for stopping short of the authorized ceilings.[46]

In light of Schlesinger's concerns with broad national policy issues, it was virtually predictable that Schlesinger would be interested more in strategy than in management. No secretary, however, can avoid deep involvement in certain management questions, such as, for example, the time-consuming annual budget cycle or the management of crises, expertise that demands, among other things, cooperative interaction between Defense and State. It will be instructive to examine one example of these occurring during the Schlesinger period, before returning to the theme of his development of strategic policy based upon his world view.

Schlesinger had been in office scarcely three months when Egyptian and Syrian armies launched the Yom Kippur War with their furious attack on Israel on October 6, 1973. In the initial stages, a combination of Israeli unpreparedness and Arab employment of Soviet-built "smart" antitank and antiair weapons caused the Israelis to suffer early battlefield reverses and heavy equipment losses. To turn the tide in what appeared to be developing into a perilous situation, the Israeli armed forces needed a massive infusion of tanks, planes, ammunition, and spare parts. By October 15 the United States government had undertaken to supply that equipment using American military air transport to carry it to Israel and using American naval forces to safeguard the aerial resupply pipeline.

According to Schlesinger, in a *Time* magazine interview, there was no difference of opinion between State, Defense, and the White House on the issue, and the airlift was begun immediately after being ordered.[47] According to two other accounts, however, this government decision was implemented only after some Schlesinger-Kissinger conflict. The account given by Bernard and Marvin Kalb suggests that Schlesinger and the Joint Chiefs of Staff argued against the resupply policy by pointing to possible Arab reprisals against the United States and then deliberately stalled the provision both of supplies and transport aircraft. The Kalbs state that only Henry Kissinger's personal intervention, to instigate a direct order from Richard Nixon to the secretary of defense, started the supplies moving again.[48] Nixon virtually confirms this report.[49]

Admiral Elmo Zumwalt argues that Schlesinger, in dealing with Israel, was the victim of Kissinger's duplicity. Zumwalt states that the secretary of state wanted the Israelis to suffer losses serious enough that they would be completely dependent on the United States and thus vulnerable to diplomatic pressure. Thus, according to this version, Kissinger ordered a delay in the resupply and then, in discussions with the Israelis, blamed the delay on Schlesinger.[50]

What actually transpired has not yet been resolved. Regardless, the experience must have been no end of a lesson for the new defense secretary and a precursor of future interaction between the two secretaries.

To return to the question of Schlesinger's view of the world and the United States' place in it, Schlesinger felt that, given the world situation and U.S. commitments, it was time to reexamine the adequacy of U.S. strategic policy and forces.

Highest priority was accorded the question of the role of nuclear weapons. The McNamara years had been the formative era of American strategic doctrine. With only minor modifications, the United States' plan for strategic war in 1973 was the same as the policy of "assured destruction plus flexible response" which had emerged in 1966. Briefly stated, that policy separated the problem of strategic defense into two areas: deterrence of nuclear attack against the continental United States, and defense of Western Europe against both conventional and nuclear attack.

"Assured destruction" related to the first task. It denoted the theory that the threat of overwhelming retaliation could be relied upon to deter the Soviets from ever launching an attack and declared that the United States would maintain a strategic arsenal of sufficient size and diversity so as to be able, even in the event of a surprise Soviet nuclear attack, to destroy 25 percent of the USSR's population and 75 percent of its industrial base. The policy of assured destruction was also extended to deter the Soviets from launching a nuclear attack on Western Europe or Japan: the American strategic arsenal was thus linked to the prevention of any Soviet nuclear strike on the Western allies.

Under the policy of "flexible response" the United States pledged itself to aid NATO to defend against the Soviet army attack by supplying general purpose forces to the alliance. Should NATO's conventional strength prove incapable of containing the Soviet thrust, the American forces would escalate to the use of tactical nuclear weapons, both for their military effect and as a warning to the Soviets to halt lest the situation escalate further. In the event that the Soviet attack continued, regardless of tactical nuclear weapon use, the United States would employ strategic nuclear weapons to attack targets inside the USSR.

Schlesinger, in his days at RAND, had observed the evolution of this strategic doctrine with great uneasiness. In addition to his basic misgivings about the wisdom of the posture itself, he "became haunted by Strangelove scenarios of accidental nuclear confrontation" and began to hypothesize about alternative strategic postures. When he became secretary of defense he conducted a thorough review of American strategic plans and pronounced them to constitute an unsatisfactory policy.[51]

Schlesinger's criticism was based on several premises. His first argument was that the Soviet Union's achievement, in the early 1970s, of an assured destruction capability against the United States had changed the strategic environment: no longer could the United States employ the ultimate threat of striking at Soviet cities in the event of a Soviet invasion of Western Europe, for the Soviets were now capable of destroying American cities in retaliation. Second, Schlesinger found that United States nuclear options were not carefully conceived. It was therefore possible that the explosion of a single Soviet weapon on United States soil could trigger an American response that would initiate a holocaust. Schlesinger found this unacceptable. Finally, he found the policy of destroying Soviet cities as a punishment for an act of the Soviet government to be "morally defective."

Having identified these flaws, Schlesinger set out to correct them. In addition to his own strongly held views, the impetus for the change was largely extra-bureaucratic; it came from former associates at RAND and elsewhere, but not from within the Pentagon.[52] His supporters in the revision of strategic doctrine were those who were most concerned with the effects of mutual assured destruction on extended deterrence; his opponents were an unusual coalition of "military conservatives and veteran arms controllers" who feared that a move away from the existing policy would make nuclear war more likely.[53]

On January 10, 1974, in remarks to the Overseas Writers Association Luncheon in Washington, Schlesinger announced that "a change [had taken place] in the strategies of the United States with regard to the hypothetical employment of central strategic forces, a change in targeting strategy, as it were." That change, he continued, involved a shift in strategic doctrine itself: "To a large extent the American doctrinal position has been wrapped around something called 'assured destruction' which implies a tendency to target Soviet cities initially and massively and that this is the principal option that the President would have. It is our intention that this not be the only option and possibly not the principal option open to the National Command Authorities."[54]

By far the most complete public presentation of the reasons impelling a new targeting doctrine and the dimensions of that doctrine appeared a little more than a month later in Schlesinger's presentation of the fiscal year 1975 defense budget to Congress. Morality and the Soviet-assured destruction capability were among the points stressed:

Not only must those in power consider the morality of threatening such terrible retribution on the Soviet people for some ill-defined transgression by their leaders; in the most practical terms, they must also question the prudence and plausibility of such a response when the enemy is able, even after some sort of first strike, to maintain the capability of destroying our cities. The wisdom and credibility of relying simply on the preplanned strikes of assured destruction are even more in doubt when allies rather than the United States itself face the threat of a nuclear war.[55]

Further, he told the Congress, the United States must take into account the threat posed by the proliferation of nuclear weapons: "It is even more essential that we focus on the issues that could arise if and when several additional nations acquire nuclear weapons, not necessarily against the United States, but for possible use or pressure against one another. Such a development could have a considerable impact on our own policies, plans, and programs. Indeed this prospect alone should make it evident that no single target system and no stereotyped scenario of mutual city destruction will suffice as the basis for our strategic planning."[56]

Schlesinger's answer to the problems he set out in his statement was a new American approach to strategic planning. It emphasized flexibility and the capability of meeting a limited nuclear provocation at the level of violence of that attack:

But if, for whatever reason, deterrence should fail, we want to have the planning flexibility to be able to respond selectively to the attack in such a way as to (1) limit the chances of uncontrolled escalation, and (2) hit meaningful targets with a sufficient accuracy-yield combination to destroy only the intended target and to avoid widespread collateral damage. If a nuclear clash occurs—and we fervently believe that it will not—in order to protect American cities and the cities of our allies, we shall rely into the wartime period upon reserving our 'assured destruction' force and persuading, through intrawar deterrence, any political foe not to attack cities.... This adjustment in strategic policy does not imply major new strategic weapons systems and expenditures. We are simply ensuring that in our new doctrine, our plans, and our command and control we have—and are seen to have—the selectivity and flexibility to respond to aggression in an appropriate manner.[57]

The introduction of flexible strategic targeting was the heart of Schlesinger's changes in American nuclear planning. It did not, however, constitute the sum total of his effect on strategic doctrine. As he observed the Soviet strategic arms buildup during the course of 1974 and noted that the new generation of Russian missiles were armed with large, potentially "silo-killing" warheads, Schlesinger decided that the United States must react to the quantitative and qualitative challenge. Accordingly, in his *Report to the Congress* for the following fiscal year, he called for increased research and development funds for maneuverable warheads and new intercontinental ballistic missiles, which could carry out counterforce strikes (against enemy nuclear forces). The American strategic forces, he noted in the report, "should have some ability to destroy hard targets, even though we would prefer to see both sides avoid major

counterforce capabilities. We do not propose, however, to concede
to the Soviets a unilateral advantage in this realm. Accordingly, our
programs will depend on how far the Soviets go in developing a
counterforce capability of their own."

In response to critics who stated that counterforce weapons
would destabilize the strategic nuclear balance, Schlesinger argued
that a unilateral counterforce capability was far more destabilizing
than a mutual capability. The research and development work was
approved and went forward. To meet the numerical imbalance that
the Soviet arms program threatened, the secretary of defense urged
that the United States maintain "essential equivalence" in central
strategic systems and that the Russian challenge could not be ignored. The U.S. strategic force, he asserted, must be maintained so
that it possessed "a range and magnitude of capabilities such that
everyone—friend, foe, and domestic audiences alike—will perceive
that we are the equal of our strongest competitors."[58]

Schlesinger firmly believed, however, that successful deterrence was not solely the product of nuclear forces. In fact, notwithstanding the attention that his statements on nuclear strategy
received, he felt that there had been a "long term fascination with
nuclear weapons which had skewed American policy toward over-
reliance on nuclear as opposed to conventional forces."[59] This
preoccupation had led in turn to a neglect of conventional forces,
which were intended to be complementary to the nuclear forces and
which were needed to support the strategic policy underlying
American foreign policy.

As Schlesinger surveyed the state of America's conventional
forces, he was not satisfied that they were in fact complementary.
Unlike his difficulties with the strategic forces, which focused on
planning deficiencies, his criticism of general purpose forces was
directed at actual combat capabilities, both manpower and
hardware. The shortcomings he perceived were due to the changing
international environment; when he was at the Bureau of the
Budget he regarded the nation's military forces as being too large for
the roles they had to play and the enemies they had to meet. As he
later testified to the Congress, during his Budget days, "I thought
the Defense Establishment was too large, and I wished to bring it
back down to roughly the size that had prevailed pre[Vietnam]

war." "It was not until approximately Fiscal Year 1972," he continued, "that we reached a position in which I personally thought we were on the thin side."[60]

The difference between 1969 and 1974 as pertains to the Soviet Union and the United States, Schlesinger argued, was that the United States no longer enjoyed a significant strategic nuclear advantage over its potential enemy. "Any edge in strategic forces previously possessed by the United States has already disappeared or is in the process of disappearing. Whatever inhibiting effect on Soviet exploitation of local conventional superiority that earlier strategic edge provided has now been lost. Nuclear parity continues to provide some restraint, but it is a weakened one. Now that our nuclear advantage has disappeared, we are obliged closely to examine deficiencies in our general purpose forces."[61]

Those deficiencies had become more critical as the Soviet Union embarked, in the late 1960s, on a major upgrading of its own conventional forces, one that included a substantial increase in front-line army manpower, accelerated production of new types of tactical aircraft and armored vehicles, and the continued expansion of the growing Soviet navy. As a result of this buildup, "nowhere on the Eurasian continent is the Soviet position itself threatened by a local imbalance. In all sectors around the periphery, the Soviets possess a clear edge."[62]

Thus, the United States (and its NATO allies), through its conventional force weaknesses, was in essence undercutting its own strategic policy by maintaining not much more than trip-wire forces, lowering the level of the nuclear threshold, and perhaps even inviting a conventional assault.

Schlesinger's plan to improve conventional capabilities called for improving the combat efficiency of the army by altering the "teeth to tail" ratio—the proportion of combat soldiers to support troops. Other Schlesinger ideas in his first budget to help renovate the army were an increase in the production rate of main battle tanks and helicopters and an application "of the lessons of the recent Middle East war by giving high priority to... modern anti-tank weapons, tanks, air defense of land forces and its opposite, defense suppression, improving munitions and larger stocks."[63] The next year's request called for sixteen army divisions, again to be manned through an improvement to existing teeth-to-tail ratios. The budgets made clear that Schlesinger, unlike some of his predecessors, truly meant what he said about improving general purpose force capabilities.

Bolstering American forces and improving their combat efficiency could not, in and of itself, suffice to correct the military imbalance which faced the NATO allies. The European allies had to be energized for a greater effort, he felt, if the imbalance between NATO and Soviet forces were to be corrected.

By 1975, therefore, Schlesinger carried a message to Europe which he had been delivering to domestic audiences for some time. In his self-cast role as "sort of an international missionary for defense," Schlesinger told the twenty-first annual meeting of the North Atlantic Alliance that "the good life must be protected in order to be preserved." The absence of overt conflict with the Soviet Union over a thirty-year period had fostered a psychological climate in Europe, he stated, such that "the Western allies are in danger of falling into the pit of post-war folly because of a feeling that security falls like manna from heaven rather than from collective efforts and sacrifices."[64] This, he warned, was practicing dangerous self-deception. Using the same argument that he had employed for building up American general purpose forces—that the loss of the American strategic nuclear superiority meant that the United States could not permit the Soviet Union to maintain a major advantage in conventional power—Schlesinger declared that NATO must strengthen its conventional forces on the European front. Accordingly, he called on NATO governments to increase their individual defense spending to an equivalent of 4 to 5 percent of their state's Gross National Product.

In addition to his concern over the level of NATO forces, Schlesinger was also troubled by the qualitative problems of the alliance and had been deeply involved with one of them, standardization of equipment—a problem no American secretary of defense is ever going to solve. One example of Schlesinger's approach will suffice here. In 1973 Schlesinger entered into an agreement with German Defense Minister George Leber on a new main battle tank for the alliance: according to the agreement the new German Leopard II tank would be evaluated against the American prototype eventually chosen by the United States Army. The competition between the tanks was to be conducted fairly—"in terms of their capability rather than country of national origin." "At the time the agreement was entered into the understanding, at least in Mr. Schlesinger's mind, was that the winner of the competition between the American and German tanks would be selected as the common battle tank of the two countries." Although the army was opposed to buying the Leopard even if it proved superior to the American models, and interceded with Schlesinger several times to start full-scale production of the American version before the evaluation was conducted, the secretary held firm to his commitment to the West Germans.[65] In the end, however, after Schlesinger's time as secretary, the army won, and there was no common tank.

Schlesinger's thought on the standardization issue also reflected the comparative advantage arguments which were part of his economics training. It was sheer waste, he felt, for the United States to duplicate the weapons developments of its allies. One approach he was reportedly weighing was a proposal that the United States would supply the alliance with such high technology items as aircraft and missiles while turning to European arms manufacturers for ground force equipment.[66] This was a complex subject involving at the core the natural tendency for defense industries in each country to put forward arguments to protect their own sales. It was not a problem Schlesinger could solve, but he did raise the issue.

In the final analysis, Secretary Schlesinger put a good deal of effort into attempting to revitalize NATO. The importance of this effort he summed up rather well after leaving office:

The United States has sought to encourage NATO generally to maintain an adequate balance of conventional forces in Western Europe. This is based on the recognition that the most possible source of the outbreak of nuclear violence would be escalation from a lower level conventional provocation to which a nuclear response seemed inappropriate to a hypothetical aggressor. This renewed emphasis on conventional forces is not based, as in the early sixties, on the concept of a "nuclear firebreak." It is instead based on recognition of an underlying synergy between conventional forces and tactical nuclear forces for purposes of deterrence. For the military security of Western Europe, the mutually reinforcing characteristics of the three legs of the NATO triad of conventional, tactical nuclear, and strategic forces have been explicitly underscored.[67]

In this effort he met with some modest success. More importantly he set the stage for other major efforts in later years.[68]

Obtaining the required resources to provide the manpower and material to give reality to Secretary Schlesinger's view of the United States' role in the world and strategic concepts was another question. In dollar terms, defense spending had not changed much since the peak year of 1968. In terms of the value of the dollar, however, there had been an enormous decline. From the fiscal year 1968, when spending had been $99.6 billion, it had declined during Schlesinger's first year in office to $67.8 billion.[69]

His objective was to reverse that trend. Laird had held the line as best he could, with a Congress disaffected over Vietnam in particular and defense spending in general. But as Schlesinger viewed what he perceived to be deteriorating American military power, coincident with increasing Soviet military strength, he knew the budget would be the major battleground for correcting this growing imbalance.

The first budget he could influence was that for the fiscal year beginning July 1, 1975. There would not be much help from the president on this budget; heavily preoccupied with Watergate, Nixon, though he kept his foreign policy interests, had drifted away from any particular interest in, or close analysis of, defense matters. At his annual meeting with the Joint Chiefs in December 1973, at which defense problems are discussed prior to presidential approval of the defense budget, Nixon was described by one of the military chiefs present as follows: "The President used the ostensible budget meeting to engage in a long, rambling monologue, which at times almost seemed to be a stream of consciousness, about the virtues of his domestic and foreign policy. . . . [He presented] the very disturbing spectacle of a man who had pumped his adrenalin up to such a high pressure that he was on an emotional binge. He appeared to me to be incapable of carrying on a rational conversation, much less exercising rational leadership."[70]

A few days after the meeting with the president, word was leaked in a *New York Times* article that Defense was going to ask for about $85 billion for the coming fiscal year,[71] about a $6 billion increase over the current year.

In February, Schlesinger led off the support of the defense budget by appearing before the Senate Armed Services Committee in a bravura performance. He began, "As the Psalmist tell us, 'Where there is no vision the people perish.'" Then he went on to what the *New York Times* called an extemporaneous seventy-minute talk and did in fact ask for an $85.8 billion dollar budget.[72]

There ensued a torrent of newspaper comment, much of it critical, about the defense budget request. Schlesinger, however, was prepared to stay the course without any apologies. A few weeks after his Senate appearance Schlesinger went before the House Appropriations Committee and was afterward questioned by newsmen:

Q: But you don't give any indication that there's going to be a reduction in the Defense spending from now on, it's just going to keep going up, up up?

A: I think that any further reductions would be imprudent for the United States. We should maintain the same force structure and roughly the same military manpower.

Q: To do that it will cost more money every year?

A: It will cost more money every year, in the same way that I suspect that the payroll costs of CBS or NBC or ABC are going up each year and you fellows are delighted with it.[73]

In the end Congress made some cuts to an $83 billion spending authorization, but it was still the largest military appropriation bill ever passed by Congress. Still, in constant dollars Schlesinger did not reverse the trend. Inflation was still ahead and defense spending in real terms was down about one billion.[74]

By the time serious preparation got under way on the fiscal year 1976 budget, the new White House occupant, Gerald Ford, was already beset with economic problems, especially inflation. Schlesinger, however, basing his estimate on Ford's background as a former pro-Pentagon member of the House Appropriations Subcommittee, was reasonably certain that the defense budget would not bear the burden of any anti-inflation cut. Also, as the year wore on unemployment rather than inflation seemed to loom as the big problem. It seemed possible that the president might conclude that a big shot of defense spending was just what was needed to stimulate employment.

Even though Congress might agree the economy needed stimulating, there were ways to do this other than defense spending. Moreover, the Congress elected in that fall of 1974, especially in the House, turned out to be heavily Democratic and antidefense. Thus, the stage was set for an executive-legislative battle over the 1976 defense budget, one that wore on into the fall of 1975.

In addition to the sheer size of the defense budget, certain criticisms focused on specific defense programs. One of these, on which confrontation was to rage for many years, was the B-1 strategic bomber which was planned to replace the aging B-52.

Despite the many arguments against the B-1 bomber, Schlesinger supported the program fully and was able to keep it under development. His support was based on two points: first, that the existence of a U.S. strategic bomber force complicated the Soviet Union's allocation of defense resources; second, that the bomber force offset the missile advantage given to the Soviets by the 1972 SALT agreement. That pact, he noted, in establishing "lower limits for United States missile forces than those applied to the Soviets, implicitly compensated for a larger number of U.S. bombers. Logically, this points, once again, to the necessity of a bomber follow-on."[75]

Furthermore, Schlesinger believed that bombers, which are incapable of first-strike missions, enhanced strategic stability and were therefore inherently preferable to more destabilizing systems. The final decision to begin full-scale production of the B-1 would, he stated, be based on the plane's performance in a series of rigorous tests and evaluations and would exclude consideration of the aircraft's high unit cost because, as Schlesinger expressed it, "America's strategic nuclear forces were bought not for their specific cost effective contribution to target destruction, narrowly defined, but for their broader contribution to that panoply of power that maintains deterrence."[76]

Schlesinger made his presentation of the fiscal year 1976 budget request to the Senate Armed Services Committee on February 5, 1975. This time he had another biblical quotation to lead off with: " When a strong man armed keepeth his palace, his goods are in peace." To "keep the goods in peace," Schlesinger was asking for $92.8 billion in spending, another record request.

His argument to Congress was similar to his previous year's:

"The way that we will approach the Congress this year will be in broad outline the same as a year ago; to point to the circumstances in which the United States finds itself, the role that the United States plays in the world as the mainstay of free world defenses, and as the necessary ingredient in a world-wide equilibrium of force, which undergirds detente, which we hope to succeed, and which is a prerequisite should there be any faltering in the process toward detente."[77]

This time his approach ran into difficulty with the House of Representatives as a whole. The battle raged into the fall with the House making budget request cuts of $2.6 billion, cuts that Schlesinger felt were unwise. He then took the extraordinary step of writing a letter (which his office subsequently made public) to Senator John McClelland, chairman of the Senate Appropriations Committee, asking that the House cuts be restored.[78] Although Schlesinger appeared to have the backing of the president, who opposed any cut in the defense budget,[79] the tone of Schlesinger's letter to McClelland did not sit well with former Congressman Gerald Ford. In the course of the letter Schlesinger attacked the House action as being "deep, savage, and arbitrary." One of the most powerful legislators in Washington and a close friend of President Ford's, House Appropriations Committee Chairman George Mahon, presumably resented both the public nature and the substance of Schlesinger's attack.[80] Ultimately, although he got another record budget, Schlesinger did not get the figure he wanted, and in terms of constant dollars, the downward trend in the defense budget continued.[81]

Meanwhile, the Defense Department and White House were deeply into their preparation of the fiscal year 1977 budget. On November 1, 1975, the defense secretary met with the president on that subject, and Schlesinger proposed that defense expenditures for the following year total $102 billion, up about $9 billion from the current year.[82] The following year, however, was a presidential election year and Ford's political advisers, at this point at least, had talked him into running on a balanced budget theme. Therefore, at issue that day was a White House-proposed cut in Schlesinger's budget of about $5 billion, documented by a memorandum from his Office of Management and Budget to the effect that the defense budget could indeed take a cut of that magnitude.[83] Schlesinger objected, among other things, that a cut of such magnitude would require an ill-advised decline of 200,000 personnel in active military strength. The meeting concluded without final decisions being made but with Schlesinger implying that he might not be able to support a defense budget slashed as deeply as the White House proposed.

After leaving the meeting, Schlesinger was informed that the president wanted to see him the following day at the White House. The outcome of this and other meetings that day resulted in what was later called the "Sunday Massacre," summarized in *New York Times* headlines on the following day: "Ford Discharges Schlesinger and Colby and Asks Kissinger to Give up His Security Post [national security adviser]"; "Rumsfeld Is Seen as New Defense Chief—Bush for C.I.A."

There have been many explanations for so precipitous a termination of the tenure of the twelfth secretary of defense—as precipitous as that of the first secretary, James Forrestal. Ford himself had one at a press conference on the Monday evening after the firing:

Q: Mr. President, could you tell us why Mr. Schlesinger and Mr. Colby did not fit on your new team?

A: I think any President has to have the opportunity to put together his own team. They were kept on when I assumed office because I wanted continuity. But any President to do the job that's needed and necessary has to have his own team in the area of foreign policy.[84]

While in general terms it is hard to argue with the principle the president was enunciating, in fact the problem went somewhat deeper. Schlesinger himself tied it to the disagreement on the defense budget, which he characterized as the "chief substantive issue" that led to his dismissal. Probably that was the immediate precipitating issue, if one accepts the suggestion that Schlesinger had "pointedly declined to endorse the re-election of President Ford until he saw how the national security issue 'shaped up.'"[85] The president was said to feel that Schlesinger's public position against the budget cuts and his own unwillingness to attack the Congress was making him appear "soft on defense," an especially important point given his challenge for the renomination by conservative Republican Ronald Reagan.[86] It was also suggested that the president considered de-

tente "as the only issue [that he had] for his 1976 campaign" and that
Schlesinger's attacks on that policy were diminishing his major
strategy for reelection.[87]

The detente issue entails another aspect—the Kissinger-
Schlesinger relationship—which is an issue many focus on in explaining Schlesinger's forced resignation. This explanation runs as
follows: Schlesinger's relations with the secretary of state had declined steadily since the Yom Kippur War period. This was due to
Schlesinger's increasingly skeptical view of Kissinger's detente policy, based on his perceptions that the Soviets were not living up to
the provisions of SALT I, that they were embarked upon an expansionist foreign policy, and that Kissinger's approach to negotiations
offered too many unilateral U.S. concessions. In June 1974
Schlesinger and Kissinger had disagreed over a proposed SALT II
package to be submitted to the Soviets at the Moscow summit. The
proposal was deferred, resulting in another clash between the two
men before the Vladivostok meetings in December of that year. The
dispute became increasingly public: the *Annual Department of Defense Report for FY 1976 and FY 197T*, published in February 1975,
contained political analysis stating, in implicit contradiction to Kissinger's position, that the Soviet view of detente was that of an
adversarial relationship.[88] In early October 1975 the Pentagon cir-
culated an intelligence assessment, said to have Schlesinger's approval, that stated the Soviets were "using the policy of detente to
gain dominance over the West in all fields."[89]

The role of the White House Chief of Staff Donald Rumsfeld in
Schlesinger's firing is also seen as problematical. The Kissinger-
Schlesinger antagonism was, of course, an uncomfortable one for
Ford, and no president would wish to go into an election year with
his principal advisers on national security policy and foreign policy
disagreeing on issues as important as detente and SALT. There is no
doubt that Rumsfeld was seriously concerned over the rift between
the two advisers.[90] Since he replaced Schlesinger as secretary of
defense, however, some have raised the question whether his part
(whatever it was) was one of concern for Ford's future or
Rumsfeld's.[91]

Another explanation of the dismissal has to do with relations
between Schlesinger and Congress. Schlesinger's October letter
that attacked the House for its cuts in his fiscal year 1976 budget

obviously alienated many of Ford's former colleagues. It is also true that Schlesinger was disliked merely for his abrasive manner by certain members of both houses. In general, however, Schlesinger had been quite effective with Congress, especially on a one-to-one basis. It is possible that certain members of Ford's White House staff convinced the president that Schlesinger was fumbling in his relations with Congress.[92]

Finally there was the matter of the Ford-Schlesinger personality conflict. Ford was never comfortable with Schlesinger and never really understood his mode of operation. Schlesinger, for his part, was disconcerted by Ford's method of compromising on issues in a nonrational manner. In short, Schlesinger, in sharp contrast to Ford, was not preeminently political in outlook. And at a more basic level, Ford resented Schlesinger's constant lecturing.[93]

Probably the real explanation is some combination of the foregoing. In any case, the firing was a political error on the part of the president. Rather than present the image of being in charge, the firing created an image of a White House in disarray. More important, it conveyed the impression of a president who was soft on defense matters and who wanted to cut into U.S. defenses. In one of those strange swings of American public opinion there was suddenly a shift of support for a greater defense effort.

Schlesinger for his part transferred from his big office in the Pentagon to a scholar's office in Johns Hopkins School for Advanced International Studies in Washington. Using that as a base, he became a popular lecturer, taking his case on the need for greater defense effort to the campuses, to the business world, and to the people. Schlesinger's evangelism came at a time extremely awkward for Ford, because it coincided with preparations by Ronald Reagan, whose position on defense and most other issues was right of Ford's, to challenge the appointed president for the Republican nomination.

The outcome of all this was ironic. In January 1976 the new secretary of defense, Donald Rumsfeld, went before Congress defending a budget fairly close to the one that had brought Schlesinger to his final confrontation with Ford. While Congress did not go along with the entire request, it did reverse, for the first time since 1968, the downward trend in real defense spending.[94] James R.

Schlesinger, strategist, did achieve his budgetary goal, though at the cost of his office.

The years 1973–1975 were hard times to be the secretary of defense. There was that crisis in American government known by the code name Watergate. There was the resignation not only of a president but also of a vice president. It was an unhappy economic time for America—the most unhappy since the Great Depression. The international scene was no less disturbing. Most traumatic was the winding down of the most unpopular war in American history, one that had cost 50,000 American lives and $150 billion. Detente also seemed to be less than it was billed. How else to explain, for instance, the Soviet-supported, if not inspired, Yom Kippur War?

In those turbulent years came along an unknown scholar-bureaucrat—James Schlesinger—propelled by Watergate onto the national scene to be the secretary of defense. Certainly, no one who has held the office was technically more qualified for the position, although in terms of having the proper political skills, and necessary political sensitivity, many of his predecessors were more qualified. Still, history will doubtless judge that Schlesinger was a man who came along at the right time.

His view of the world was a stern one and, despite their diverse personal dissimilarities, not unlike that of John Foster Dulles, secretary of state in the 1950s. Schlesinger was above all else logical, and eminently distrusting of the Soviet leadership. Brilliant, blunt, informed, arrogant, and abrasive, he was not interested in the Metternichian world of Kissinger.

It was, he felt, a time to rethink and rearticulate American military strategy, which had been too long dinned out by the distracting and, in the long run, meaningless noises of Vietnam. Operating from the intellectual base he had laid at RAND in the 1960s, Schlesinger set out to redirect U.S. strategy and simultaneously to obtain the resources to support that strategy. He knew he faced an American public and Congress alienated toward defense matters by Vietnam and highly cynical as a result of Watergate. Schlesinger saw his mission as being to educate them in the realities of international life in the mid-1970s—notwithstanding that Nobel Peace Prize winner and soothsayer, Henry Kissinger.

The White House of this era was not an easy one to deal wtih. Initially preoccupied with Watergate, and later with economic uncertainty, there was always the overriding problem of the presence of that super bureaucrat and public relations expert, Kissinger. Determined to be the overwhelming power in international affairs, Henry in addition could handle the press more effectively than anyone else on the Washington scene. In the early days of the Nixon administration, Kissinger had not perceived Schlesinger to be a threat, but by the time Schlesinger was ensconced in the Pentagon Kissinger knew better and was smart enough never to tangle in public with Schlesinger on substantive issues.

In this contest between two monstrous egos, over the issue of the nature of American security policy, one president had lost control and his successor did not really know what it was all about. These situations, combined with a post-Vietnam War assertiveness on the part of Congress, made that body vital to Schlesinger's plan to reinvigorate America's military strategy and secure the resources to implement the revitalized strategy. Admittedly, Schlesinger lacked Laird's skill and experience in handling Congress. Yet while he never fully solved the problem of dealing with Congress, he became skillful at it, and the myth that he had bad relations with that body was overall just that, a myth.

The senior military were a bit skeptical of the pipe-smoking academic at first. His strong-armed tactics at the Atomic Energy Commission and at the Central Intelligence Agency had not helped his reputation when he arrived at the Pentagon. At Defense, however, Schlesinger provided intellectual rather than the managerial leadership; he became a strategist, not a manager. And since his strategic ideas, the Joint Chiefs soon learned, were intelligent and, in general, pretty much the same as theirs, he could obtain concord with them on strategic matters.

Any fair evaluation of Schlesinger's twenty-eight months at the Pentagon requires an outstanding rating. For the first time since the early McNamara period an American military strategy was articulated in a public forum and, even if not embraced by all elements of the polity, was ultimately accepted as a better course of action for America than passively continuing to wring our hands over Southeast Asia.

For one of his major goals, rebuilding the U.S. military establishment in the post-Vietnam era, he receives high marks. He provided the intellectual and philosophical direction, as well as the congressional support, that permitted the American military establishment to regroup and rebuild after the Vietnam turmoil.

In another major objective, redirecting strategic doctrine, he succeeded also. His rearticulation of nuclear strategy was, if initially misunderstood, masterful and long overdue. His real emphasis, however, was on developing a stronger conventional force; here he met at least with a fair degree of success. An element of this was his concern about the state of NATO. By the time he left office, he had become "something of a 'guru' to the defense ministers of Western Europe, supplying them with philosophical arguments to defend their military programs and reinstilling some sense of purpose within the NATO alliance."[95]

His public positions on detente and the defense budget were taken with a definite purpose in mind. As Schlesinger noted: "Why do I make this a cause? Because that is the responsibility of my position. If we are to maintain a position of power, the public must be informed about the trends. Some years from now, somebody will ask the question why were we not warned, and I want to be able to say, indeed you were."[96] In this, too, he was successful. Within months of his departure from office, proposed budget cuts had been restored, the policies of the Soviet Union were being viewed with increasing public skepticism, and domestic political opinion had accepted the call for an increase in U.S. military strength. Thus, in the short term, we must conclude that Schlesinger's impact was indeed major. The long-term assessment of his policies, however, must await the judgment of later years. Our perspective is still too fresh, we are still too close to the events, to undertake that task now.

6

The Secretary of Defense in Retrospect

The experiences of World War II and the increased role of America on the world scene were the impetus for the 1945–1947 debate on how best to restructure the executive branch to cope with national security matters. As pertains to the defense establishment, the unification debate was deeply rooted in the differing strategic views and pride of service of the army, navy, and the soon-to-be air force, as well as of their respective supporters both in and out of Congress. The resulting National Security Act of 1947 was of necessity a compromise attempt to begin unification, and the outcome, insofar as it pertained to the National Military Establishment, can be described as a federated structure.

The first secretary of defense, James Forrestal, soon learned that the "general direction, authority and control" he was to exercise over the services provided him with inadequate authority. This was especially true in his efforts to "supervise and coordinate the preparation of budget estimates," an area where, particularly in a period of increasing competition for a reduced defense budget, the service secretaries retained too much authority for Forrestal to make his office effective.

Forrestal saw this before he left office, as did others such as the Hoover Commission. The result was the 1949 legislative amendments to the National Security Act, which established a Department of Defense; increased the authority of the secretary of defense, especially over the budget; and reduced the service secretaries to subcabinet level officials. Finally, there was created a chairman of the earlier (1947) established Joint Chiefs of Staff. These amendments provided adequate leverage for Truman's remaining three secretaries, Louis Johnson, George Marshall, and Robert Lovett. Since most of this period coincided with the Korean War, however, increased wartime budgets reduced to a minimum interservice debate over resources. Before Lovett left office, he wrote outgoing President Truman a letter outlining the need for additional authority for the defense secretary.

In the same year that Dwight Eisenhower became president, he put into effect the 1953 Reorganization of the Defense Department. This further centralized the functions in the secretary's office and correspondingly reduced the power of the services. In addition, the role as chairman of the Joint Chiefs of Staff was strengthened in an attempt to cause that body to adopt a broader strategic outlook as compared to a recognized tendency to represent service views.

The Eisenhower period was unique insofar as Eisenhower performed, in many ways, as his own secretary of defense. Nonetheless, as he watched his secretaries, Charles Wilson and Neil McElroy, struggle with the services to keep the lid on his relatively austere defense budget, Eisenhower was convinced that additional authority had to be given to the office of secretary of defense. This belief was further supported by the public furor over Sputnik, the interservice rivalry involving new missile technology, and the apparent need for tighter coordination over research and development.

In 1958 Eisenhower sponsored another Reorganization Act, one that was rather far-reaching, though not as much so as he would have liked. The act vested new authority in the secretary and definitely subordinated the military departments to him. It made the United States worldwide operational commands directly responsible to the secretary of defense and the president. It was the major, and last, legislative step toward a truly centralized defense establishment.

Although President-elect Kennedy considered additional centralization legislation, he decided, on the recommendation of his new secretary of defense, Robert McNamara, to rely instead on the already considerable powers granted to the secretary by the 1958 act. The new secretary found it possible within that legislative framework to introduce managerial innovations.

McNamara's imprint on the Pentagon was indeed made through

management techniques, and his tenure marked the high point of central control by a secretary. His approach accomplished, for the first time since World War II, true civilian control of the Pentagon below the presidential level.

Among the mangement concepts introduced by McNamara were the Planning Programming Budgeting System, a system of assessing major programs that cut across service lines; the Five Year Defense Program, designed to project defense expenditures; and an Office of Systems Analysis, designed to provide civilian decision-makers with an analytical tool for judging the logic and cost comparisons of various force, materiel, or training options. Naturally these changes caused charges by the services, and their supporters, of overcentralization by the defense secretary and too deep a civilian intrusion into strategic concepts, which had hitherto been the province of the military services. Such criticisms notwithstanding, McNamara's tenure represented a fulfillment of the authority given the secretary by Eisenhower's 1958 Reorganization Act.

Lingering criticism of McNamara's management mode, as well as a normal tendency for a new administration to take a management look at defense led to President Nixon's appointment, in 1969, of a Blue Ribbon Defense Panel. The panel's major recommendations, such as removing the Joint Chiefs of Staff from the operational chain, were, however, never implemented, primarily because they were too far-reaching to secure wide support.

Nixon's first defense secretary, Melvin Laird, was a skilled politician with long service in the House and extensive experience in defense issues. He also had a strong view of what the secretary's role should be. He considered himself McNamara's successor and had no intention of diluting McNamara's control of the Pentagon, even though his approach was different. Laird introduced what he called "participatory management," a structure intended to draw the services deeper into the decision-making process. The initiation of programs was now returned to the services, and McNamara's Systems Analysis Office, even though it still provided analysis, was transformed into a supporting office.

Like all secretaries of defense, Laird was deeply involved in problems concerning the defense budget. Here his record is somewhat mixed, depending on how one views the problem. In the public arena, he successfully carried the fight to presidential "peace" candidate George McGovern in 1972 whose proposals for reducing the defense budget were extreme. The defense budget during the Laird period, however, shows a definite decline in constant dollars, to the lowest point in about a quarter of a century; for this there were two reasons beyond the control of the secretary of defense: inflation to an extent not foreseen and congressional and public disenchantment with the Defense Department in the late Vietnam War period.

Laird's major successor, James Schlesinger, was, in terms of background and knowledge, probably the most qualified person ever to assume the office. He arrived at the Pentagon with a reputation for toughness based upon organizational and personnel changes that he had accomplished in short order at the Atomic Energy Commission and the Central Intelligence Agency. But he had something else in mind for the Pentagon. Looking at the sheer size of the operation and the power of the military, he decided not to spend much time on organizational or management questions. Rather, he decided to limit his time, energies, and intellectual leadership to a few problems that he considered most important. First of all, he wanted to restore the military's positive public image. Second, he wanted to rearticulate strategic doctrine to meet the current world situation and particularly to meet the Soviet threat. Finally, he wanted to reverse the downward trend of the defense budget in order to be able to improve the U.S. strategic situation. Refusing to let the bureaucracy dominate him, Schlesinger detailed most of the management problems to others. His method was to present in conceptual terms what he wanted and let the organization develop and implement the plans that would satisfy his goals.

When Schlesinger left office in November 1975, his substantive accomplishments, considering the relatively short period of his tenure, were formidable. His intellectual and philosophical direction permitted the American military establishment to regroup and to rebuild after the Vietnam turmoil, and he secured congressional support in the process. His articulation of nuclear strategy was masterful and long overdue. But his greatest emphasis was on developing a stronger conventional force, and here he met with a fair degree of success. His intense struggle to reverse the downward budget trend (a struggle that led to his departure from office) was successful within a few months after he left the Pentagon.

Three themes emerge from this study which can be discussed as conclusions: the central role of the defense budget as a determinant of strategic policy and the importance of the domestic context in shaping the size of that budget;[1] variations in presidential interest and style in managing national security affairs and the resultant variations in the manner in which the secretary of defense carries out the roles of his office;[2] and the declining nature of the influence senior military have on major defense issues.[3]

It seems quite clear from our examination of the Forrestal period (1947-1949) that President Truman was deeply concerned with the need to complete the conversion of the U.S. economy from a war to a peace situation. He was determined to balance the budget and to keep defense spending to the level needed to achieve that goal. Of central importance was Truman's underlying assumption of a fixed limit to what the country could spend on defense based upon domestic political realities, such as continuing inflation and related labor unrest. Yet looking at the international situation, as it appeared to Washington policymakers then, the predominant theme was the deteriorating relationship between the United States and the USSR and the unfolding of the cold war. The main debate about the kind of defense posture the United States was to have focused on the budgetary process.

The defense budget for fiscal year 1950 is illustrative. Acting during one of the most intense periods of the early cold war (during the Berlin Blockade), the president nevertheless set a defense budget ceiling of $15 billion, which neither Secretary Forrestal nor the Joint Chiefs considered adequate. Moreover, Forrestal did not get the balanced forces he wanted, nor did the air force get the forces it estimated necessary (seventy groups) to provide compensating air-heavy strategy in lieu of balanced forces.

When Eisenhower assumed the presidency in 1953 he inherited the Korean War and a fairly high defense budget (almost $50 billion) brought about by that war. Although three of Eisenhower's major campaign promises had been oriented toward the domestic context, their implementation had a significant influence on U.S. strategic policy. These promises were to liquidate the Korean War, to balance the budget, and to reduce taxes. Liquidation of the war (along with additional slashes in land forces) did result in a reduced budget and, a year after taking office, the Eisenhower administration was able to reduce taxes.

In subsequent years President Eisenhower was determined that his conservative economic views be reflected in the budget, particularly the defense budget, even though on the international scene the perceived adversary was growing increasingly stronger—militarily and economically.

On the domestic scene, the Korean War approach had been rejected and the Truman administration's last pre-Korean War look at strategy had received a mixed reaction from President Eisenhower. It was accepted insofar as Eisenhower agreed America should provide leadership to the non-Communist world; it was rejected in that military force was not to be based on Forrestal's concept of balanced forces but on the strategic deterrent (at a time, moreover, when the adversary would soon be moving toward strategic parity).

Kennedy had campaigned hard on the inadequacies of the Eisenhower defense program. To overcome these alleged inadequacies Kennedy proposed an improved limited war capability and an improved nuclear deterrent system. Obviously, these changes were going to require an increased defense budget; according to McNamara, Kennedy told the new defense secretary to develop the forces necessary "without regard to arbitrary budget ceilings" but to operate the force at "the lowest possible cost." It would appear on the surface that Kennedy's world view prevailed somewhat over the domestic context. But the question is, to what extent?

A study of the Kennedy defense budgets shows an increase over the Eisenhower years averaging about six billion in constant (fiscal year 1972) dollars. When examining the service estimates and the eventual outcome, however, budget ceilings were obviously applied as they had been for the previous administration, whatever the rhetoric. For example, service requests for fiscal year 1963 totaled $63 billion of which the president eventually asked Congress for $51.6 billion; for fiscal year 1964 the comparative figures were $67 billion and $53.7 billion. Although the Kennedy defense budgets were somewhat more generous and there were some force improvements, the differences from the Eisenhower period do not seem great. The external context did play a more important role, but the domestic context was controlling.

The major international event involving President Johnson and Secretary McNamara was the Vietnam War. Like the Korean War early in the previous decade, this was also the major event influencing the defense budget. In the early stages of the American buildup beginning in 1965, supplemental budget requests followed each other rapidly. The peak war budget was reached in fiscal year 1968, that budget being the highest in constant dollars since World War II.

One must examine this period in somewhat different terms from the peace periods. There is no question that the war caused a dramatic increase in the defense budget. But if one leaves aside resources employed in prosecuting that war, did these increased budgets improve the U.S. strategy posture worldwide? The answer is no. Fighting the Vietnam War without mobilizing the reserves and the concomitant personnel turbulence due to one-year tours in Vietnam in time virtually destroyed the strategic reserves in the United States and the American forces in NATO.

There were also shortages of military equipment worldwide except in Vietnam. The domestic context indeed governed in all except Vietnam itself. President Johnson continued his Great Society programs. The approach was guns and butter—not guns to improve the U.S. strategic position worldwide but guns to prosecute the war in Vietnam. In fact a major reason not to mobilize the reserves was to avoid the ensuing debate in Congress which might have jeopardized the Great Society by causing congressional scrutiny of the guns and butter approach.

Secretary Melvin Laird was well attuned to the domestic context by virtue of his congressional background. He was especially conscious of the need for withdrawal from Vietnam by the time President Nixon faced the 1972 campaign. Laird was also aware of the public's disenchantment with defense matters in general, especially with the size of the defense budget. No question that during Laird's tenure at the Pentagon the domestic context shaped budgets and strategic policy.

Vietnamization alone would have driven down the size of the defense budget, but an increasingly severe and unforeseen inflation served to drive up the budget. In constant dollars, however, each successive Laird budget was less than the last. Part of Laird's success in getting the Joint Chiefs to go along with him on Vietnamization was his thesis that in an increasingly constrained budgetary environment it was better to improve U.S. forces worldwide than to continue to invest in the Vietnam War.

Through his generally good relations with Congress he probably prevented catastrophic erosion of the defense budget, but the time was not propitious for any turnaround of the downward trend. The American public had turned inward as a result of the Vietnam War. In one area he held his own on the defense budget and that was in countering the McGovern 1972 campaign call for a reduction in the defense budget of between $20 and $30 billion. Obviously this was an irresponsible proposal.

When James Schlesinger became secretary of defense in 1973 he brought with him a stern world view. Distrustful of both the Soviet leadership and detente, he felt it was time to rethink and rearticulate American strategic policy which for too long had been confused by the Vietnam War. He set out to redirect U.S. strategy and to obtain the resources to support that strategy. He set out first to provide the intellectual and philosophical base to permit the American military establishment to regroup and rebuild. Simultaneously he worked at redirecting American strategy by putting increased emphasis on conventional forces.

In securing increased defense budgets to support his world and strategic views he was less successful. Eventually the issue merged with the 1976 Republican primary, where conservative Republican candidate Reagan argued the case for increased defense spending. In this context President Ford's firing of Schlesinger over the issue of the size of the defense budget was a political error. Shortly Ford had to reverse himself and in fact the first post-Schlesinger defense budget was, in effect, the budget Schlesinger was proposing when he was dismissed.

By the time Schlesinger took office the turning inward had gone too far and the domestic context had become overcontrolling in defense matters, both budgetary and strategic. Schlesinger's efforts, the Reagan critique, and changing times all helped to realign public opinion. This realignment brought to an end the real-dollar decline in defense spending and marked the beginning of post-Vietnam armed forces and strategic policies. All this was still shaped mainly by domestic considerations but not as unreasonably so as had been true during the Laird period.

Clearly in the Truman, Eisenhower, Nixon, and Ford periods the domestic context was controlling with differing degrees of intensity. The external context impinged to a greater degree during the Kennedy period but not as powerfully as one might at first think. The Johnson period is more complex; Vietnam was after all a fairly large-scale war. Apart from Vietnam, however, there is no question that the domestic context governed the nature of U.S. worldwide strategic policies.

In regard to the theme of presidential style in managing national security affairs, President Truman appears to have guarded jealously his prerogatives in controlling major defense decisions. It is true that his hopes in 1945 to have a highly centralized defense establishment were frustrated by Congress. But it was Truman's navy secretary, James Forrestal, who was the most forceful advocate of the federalized type of organization that was eventually established in 1947. During Forrestal's tenure as secretary of defense, it is evident that Truman kept a tight control on major defense issues. Using the defense budget ceiling as his tool, Truman obtained the kind of military forces and defense policies he wanted.

Truman's relationship with Forrestal was correct but not close, and the first secretary of defense was frequently undercut by "end runs," in particular by Air Force Secretary Stuart Symington. Forrestal for his part was loyal to the president's guidance on the defense budget, though not in agreement with it. This placed him in the role of arbitrator between Truman and the Joint Chiefs, but there was no real arbitration. Truman always won.

There is no evidence that Truman paid a great deal of attention to the National Security Council prior to the Korean War. He did make it clear, however, that the NSC staff was his staff and that he was somewhat suspicious of the NSC itself; he did not want any of his decision-making powers usurped.

Dwight Eisenhower, war hero and father figure, and a conservative in his economic outlook, assumed the presidency with long experience as an executive. He put great emphasis on organization and systematic procedures. His principal secretaries of defense were functionalists, and Eisenhower viewed their primary function as one of keeping the Pentagon programs within the budgetary ceilings important to the carrying out of his conservative fiscal goals. On strategic matters, Eisenhower in effect dealt directly with the chairmen of the Joint Chiefs of Staff and thus usurped to himself an important portion of the secretary of defense's role. He respected the secretaries as businessmen but insisted on being his own strategist.

The NSC had an important function during the Eisenhower period, but the function was somewhat different than is usually attributed to it. It was an ideal forum in which to achieve consensus and coordination and to give an impetus to the implementation of decisions. Certainly the planning process, especially on lesser papers, promoted a healthy interaction among the agencies and departments concerned with strategic policy. It forced appropriate officials to confront major issues of national security and to evaluate the options. Whether the procedures were too elaborate or there was too much paper should not be of much concern. Eisenhower had a use for the NSC, but it is not true, as some critics have maintained, that it was an overly elaborate system which slowed down the decision-making process excessively.

John Kennedy came to office with a legislative background and as an activist in foreign policy matters. He was determined to run the State Department in a policy sense. On the other hand, the secretary of defense (who accepted Kennedy's world view) was left to run his own department and in the process frequently found himself deeply involved in foreign policymaking.

Kennedy's management approach was quite different from Eisenhower's. He relied on task forces consisting of his top advisers focusing on specific problems, the best known being the EXCOMM, which he used during the Cuban Missile Crisis. Early in his administration Kennedy disestablished the committee structure that Eisenhower had set up under the National Security Council. There is considerable evidence that Kennedy did not feel comfortable with the council and hence his participation in that body, even for discussion purposes, was considerably less frequent than Eisenhower's.

When Johnson assumed the Kennedy mantle, he also accepted wholeheartedly Kennedy's secretary of defense. There is little question that McNamara, then at the peak of his powers, became an influential official in the Johnson administration. By 1967 when McNamara's dovishness over the war became evident, the president still retained a high regard for McNamara's abilities, although not in all cases for his views.

Johnson was oriented toward domestic matters more than Kennedy and hence was somewhat dependent on his advisers on foreign policy issues. Like Kennedy, however, he disliked the formal NSC forum for dealing with current problems and instead substituted the Tuesday Luncheon forum. The principals were there (Rusk, McNamara, in time Chairman Earle Wheeler, CIA director Richard Helms, and Special Assistant Walt Rostow), but not the subordinates. Also, the forum tended to emphasize operational rather than policy issues.

When the Nixon administration took over in 1969 the new secretary of defense, Melvin Laird, had a political base of his own based upon sixteen years in the House of Representatives. Henry Kissinger arrived on the national scene, first as assistant for national security affairs and in time as secretary of state. We have Nixon's word for it that he intended to direct foreign policy from the White House and this he did, normally with the close assistance of Henry Kissinger.

Laird never had a close relationship with Nixon but he was a strong secretary of defense. His political background and clout permitted him to oppose the White House when he felt it necessary. Perceived to be a bit dovish, he was sometimes bypassed by the White House during operational crises such as the Cambodian Incursion in 1970. On defense budget and on policy matters, however, he was much involved and highly effective.

As for the National Security Council, the approach used initially by Nixon was superficially similar to Eisenhower's. The council was used routinely (as during the Eisenhower period), with more emphasis on presentation of options and alternatives than Eisenhower would have wished. A strong committee structure from the NSC staff and the departments, especially State and Defense, was established to support the NSC.

After the early period of the administration the actual process tended to be somewhat different. Increasingly the White House took a closer control of foreign policy and walled itself off from the State and Defense bureaucracy, especially on major matters, such as the diplomatic initiative toward the Peoples Republic of China.

The role of Henry Kissinger as assistant for national security affairs went well beyond any of his predecessors. He was a more powerful official than the secretary of state (which indeed he became in the second Nixon term) and fully as important as the secretary of defense. In terms of rapport with the president, he was considerably closer to Nixon than either the secretary of state or the secretary of defense.

In 1973 Kissinger became secretary of state, retaining the role of White House assistant; even though he had shifted his locus of decision-making from the White House to State, his personal influence continued unparalleled. Earlier that year Schlesinger had taken over in the Pentagon. Although he never gained a close rapport with the Watergate-preoccupied president he was, nevertheless, due to his background and personality, a strong secretary of defense. His principal adversary (as in the case of Laird) was Henry Kissinger.

When Gerald Ford assumed the presidency in 1974 he was highly dependent on Secretary of State Kissinger and somewhat skeptical of the secretary of defense. In time Schlesinger's lack of rapport with Ford, among other matters, cost him his job, but in the meanwhile he was an effective secretary. Ford employed the National Security Council system in a manner not greatly different from Nixon's; after Schlesinger's departure, however, as a result both of Ford's close rapport with incoming Secretary Donald Rumsfeld and Ford's grooming of his own White House advisers, Kissinger, by now without his White House post, dominated the system less.

Generally, presidents, where they wished to intrude into major defense issues, have done so with effectiveness. Certainly the president's relationship with the secretary of defense influences that cabinet official's manner of functioning. Still, the record seems to indicate that even without a close personal relationship with the president, a defense secretary, given favorable circumstances, can be quite effective. For example, Melvin Laird's independent power base gave him a degree of independence from the Nixon-Kissinger White House he would not otherwise have had. And Watergate-preoccupied Nixon permitted Schlesinger a degree of maneuverability he might not otherwise have achieved.

The National Security Council's employment followed presidential wishes in all the cases we have examined, and in most instances the Council itself was not the decision-making forum. What is perhaps more interesting is the steady growth, since the time of Truman, in the bureaucratic power of the National Security Council Staff and especially in the power of its head, the assistant for national security affairs. This reached its apogee under Kissinger, but given the right combination of personalities and events, the same situation could occur again.

Finally, I would like to comment on the declining influence of the senior military on major defense issues. The high point of military influence on presidential decisions was, without a doubt, World War II. During that conflict President Roosevelt regarded the then nonstatutory Joint Chiefs as directly responsible to him in his role as commander-in-chief. When the Joint Chiefs of Staff were established by the Act of 1947 and began to operate within the framework of the Department of Defense, there was a major reduction from their wartime influence. Still, the wartime prestige of the early chiefs, such as Eisenhower, Spaatz, and Nimitz, carried over, and the group was highly influential, enjoying a strong adversarial relationship with the first secretary of defense. Controversies involved not only their losing battle with Truman over the defense budget but also the important question of the missions of each service. Forrestal was able to achieve a compromise of sorts on this latter issue in the form of the Key West Agreement of 1948. Experience with this and the budget battles convinced Forrestal that his office needed greater authority and the Joint Chiefs themselves needed a chairman. The result was the amendments to the National Security Act of 1949. This plus the Eisenhower amendments of 1953 and 1958 set the statutory basis for a strong secretary of defense and a greater role for the chairman of the Joint Chiefs of Staff.

By 1958 the role of the Joint Chiefs and their chairman had pretty well been set. As the defense secretary became stronger and his staff support increased, the influence of the senior military decreased. There were occasional JCS chairmen who were highly influential—Admiral Radford in the Eisenhower period and General Taylor in the Kennedy/Johnson period being the prime examples—but generally the senior military became more and more an element of the Defense Department.

Another trend was the rising prominence of the chairmen as contrasted to the chiefs as a body. To the public and to Congress the chairman became the most visible of the Joint Chiefs and the only one not identified with a particular service. Still, his power resides in his capacity as the representative of the corporate chiefs.

By law the Joint Chiefs as a group are the military advisers to the president, the National Security Council, and the secretary of defense. The political and bureaucratic realities since McNamara are that the chiefs are advisers to the defense secretary. This function is based not only on the powerful role of the secretary but also on the sophisticated analytical and budgetary systems within the department, controlled by the secretary. The point should not be overstated though; there are occasional expressions of disagreement in the National Security Council forum between chairmen speaking for the chiefs and the defense secretary.

With regard to the lessened influence of the senior military on policy decisions, the rise of other influential groups should be taken into account. The increased influence of Congress on defense policy is one such reality. This has been occasioned by political events, such as the public reaction to the Vietnam War, and also by their increased staff support in the defense area. Another reality is the permanent and powerful staff supporting the National Security Council and the importance of the presidential assistant for national security affairs, who heads the staff.

The office of secretary of defense is now more than thirty years old and has had fourteen incumbents under seven presidents. By comparison to most other cabinet positions, this is a relatively short span of time. But those thirty years were tumultuous ones for the United States, involving two wars.

Notwithstanding the rapidly changing context with which each secretary had to contend, there are certain characteristics of the national security environment which they shared. First is the supreme importance to the nation of national security itself. Second is the problem of sorting out long-range security needs from the immediate day-to-day problems that constantly intrude. Third is the problem of dealing with the many competing interests—bureaucratic and otherwise—that become involved in national security matters in the American polity. Finally is the frequent requirement to make crisis recommendations to the president, often with inadequate information on the matter at hand.

Given the relative newness of the organization, its early compromise nature between central control and federation, and the changing international and domestic contexts, it is understandable that faced with the security environment just characterized there would be considerable organizational evolution in the department. Overall, this evolution can be described as a gradual transfer of authority away from the services to the secretary of defense and his office.

In the course of this evolution the question of the adequacy of civilian control has frequently been raised, primarily in the context of the proper relationship between civilians with appointive positions and military professionals. At the level of presidential decision-making on national security problems, there is no definite line of demarcation between military and civilians. Yet the senior military have not always had access to the president on major controversial issues. The McNamara period is probably the best illustration. When a member of the Joint Chiefs of Staff was made to feel "like a spectator" during the Vietnam War and was told not to expose the president to disagreements, it might be said that this was an example of civilian overcontrol.

By and large we have been fortunate in the caliber of men who have served in the position of secretary of defense. It is a demanding job requiring great dedication and certainly is no place for either an amateur manager or amateur strategist. Whether the issue is the size of the defense budget, the place of the carrier task force in U.S. strategy, or the best way to solve the manpower needs of the services, the president needs a secretary of defense who can provide him the best advice from a dedicated military-civilian team.

Appendix 1
THE SECRETARIES OF DEFENSE

James Vincent Forrestal (September 1947–March 1949). Born Mattewan, New York, February 15, 1892. Princeton, 1915. Joined Dillon, Read, and Company, 1916. Served in the navy in World War I. President of Dillon, Read, 1938. Under secretary of the navy, 1940–1944. Secretary of the navy, 1944–1947. Secretary of defense, September 1947 to March 1949. Died May 22, 1949.

Louis Arthur Johnson (March 1949–September 1950). Born Roanoke, Virginia, January 10, 1891. LL.B., University of Virginia, 1912. Law practice, Clarksburg, West Virginia. Member of West Virginia House of Representatives, 1917. National commander of American Legion, 1932–1933. Civilian aide to secretary of war, 1933–1937. Assistant secretary of war, 1937–1940. Personal representative of the president in India, 1942. Secretary of defense, March 1949 to September 1950. Died April 24, 1956.

George Catlett Marshall (September 1950–September 1951). Born Uniontown, Pennsylvania, December 31, 1880. Graduated Virginia Military Institute, 1901, and Infantry-Cavalry School at Fort Leavenworth, 1907. Graduated from and later instructed at Army Staff College of Fort Leavenworth, 1908–1910. Chief of staff, United States Army, 1939–1945, and General of the Army. Special representative of the president, with ambassadorial rank, to China, 1945–1947. Secretary of state, 1947–1949. Secretary of defense, September 1950 to September 1951. Died October 16, 1959.

Robert Abercrombie Lovett (September 1951–January 1953). Born Huntsville, Texas, September 14, 1895. B.A. Yale, 1919. Attended Harvard Law School and Harvard Business School, 1920–1923. Employed Brown Brothers and Company, 1923, partner in the firm, 1926–1940. Assistant secretary of war (for air), 1940–1945. Under secretary of state, 1947–1949; deputy secretary of defense, 1950–1951. Secretary of defense, September 1951 to January 1953. Consultant to the president, 1961–1963.

Charles Erwin Wilson (January 1953–October 1957). Born Minerva, Ohio, July 18, 1890. Graduated Carnegie Institute of Technology,

1909. Employed by Westinghouse Corporation, 1909–1919. Joined General Motors Corporation, 1919, president of the company, 1941–1953. Secretary of defense, January 1953 to October 1957. Died September 26, 1961.

Neil Hosler McElroy (October 1957–December 1959). Born Berea, Ohio, October 20, 1904. B.A. Harvard, 1925. Joined Procter and Gamble Company, 1925, president of the company, 1948–1957. Chairman, White House Conference on Education, 1954–1955. Chairman, National Industrial Conference Board, 1956. Secretary of defense, October 1957 to December 1959. Returned as chairman of Procter and Gamble, 1959. Died November 30, 1972.

Thomas Sovereign Gates, Jr. (December 1959–January 1961). Born Philadelphia, Pennsylvania, April 10, 1906. Graduated from the University of Pennsylvania, 1928. Joined Drexel and Company, 1928, partner in the firm, 1940. Under secretary of the navy, 1956–1957. Secretary of defense, December 1959 to January 1961. President of Morgan Guaranty Trust Company and chairman of the board, 1961–1965. Head of Peking liaison, 1976–1978.

Robert Strange McNamara (January 1961–February 1968). Born San Francisco, California, June 9, 1916. Graduated from the University of California at Berkeley, 1937. Received M.B.A. Harvard Graduate School of Business Administration, 1939. Served in United States Army Air Force, World War II. Employed by the Ford Motor Company, 1946–1960, served briefly as president of the company, 1960. Secretary of defense, January 1961 to March 1968. Appointed president of the World Bank, 1967.

Clark McAdams Clifford (March 1968–January 1969). Born Fort Scott, Kansas, December 25, 1906. LL.B. Washington University, Saint Louis, 1928. Employed by the legal firm of Holland, Lashly, and Donnell, 1928, partner of the firm, 1938. Served as President Truman's naval aide, 1946; special counsel to the president, 1946–1950. Senior partner in the law firm, Clifford and Miller, Washington, D.C., 1950–1968. Secretary of defense, March 1968 to January 1969. Returned to law practice, 1969. Special envoy to Cyprus, Department of State, 1977.

Melvin Robert Laird (January 1969–January 1973). Born Omaha, Nebraska, September 1, 1922. B.A. Carleton College, 1942. United

States House of Representatives, 1953-1969 (Seventh Congressional District of Wisconsin). Secretary of defense, January 1969 to January 1973. Served as counselor for domestic affairs to Presidents Nixon and Ford, 1973-1974. Employed as senior counselor to *Reader's Digest* subsequently.

Elliot Lee Richardson (January 1973-May 1973). Born Boston, Massachusetts, July 20, 1920. Harvard, B.A. in 1941 and LL.B. in 1947. Employed by Ropes, Gray, Boston; partner in the firm, 1961-1964. Under secretary of state, 1969-1970. Secretary of health, education, and welfare, 1970-1973. Secretary of defense, January 1973 to May 1973. United States attorney general, May 1973-October 1973. Ambassador to Great Britain, 1975-1976. Secretary of commerce, 1976-1977. Ambassador at large and representative to the Law of the Sea Conference, 1977.

James Rodney Schlesinger (July 1973-November 1975). Born New York, New York, February 15, 1929. Harvard, B.A. in 1950, Ph.D. (economics) in 1956. Senior staff member for the RAND Corporation until 1969. Assistant director, Office of Management and Budget and the Bureau of the Budget, 1969-1971. Chairman, Atomic Energy Commission, 1971-1973. Director, Central Intelligence Agency, 1973. Secretary of defense, July 1973 to November 1975. Secretary, Department of Energy, 1977-1979.

Donald Henry Rumsfeld (November 1975-January 1977). Born Chicago, Illinois, July 9, 1932. B.A. Princeton, 1954. United States House of Representatives, 1963-1969 (Thirteenth Congressional District of Illinois). Director, Office of Economic Opportunity, 1969-1970. Director, Cost of Living Council, 1971-1972. Ambassador to the North Atlantic Treaty Organization, 1973-1974. Assistant to President Ford in charge of White House operations, 1974-1975. Secretary of defense, November 1975 to January 1977. President, G. D. Searle and Company, 1977.

Harold Brown (January 1977-). Born New York, New York, September 19, 1927. Columbia, B.A. in 1945, Ph.D. (physics) in 1949. Director of defense research and engineering, Department of Defense, 1961-1965. Secretary of the air force, 1965-1969. President, California Institute of Technology, Pasadena, 1969-1977. Delegate to Strategic Arms Limitation Talks, Helsinki, Vienna, and Geneva, 1969-1977. Secretary of defense, beginning January 1977.

Appendix 2 NATIONAL SECURITY

President	Year	Secretary of State	Secretary of Defense	Chairman JCS
TRUMAN	45	James F. Byrnes 7/45		(Fleet Admiral William D. Leahy, chief of staff to the commander-in-chief, 42-49)
	46			
	47			
	48	George C. Marshall 1/47	James V. Forrestal 9/47	
	49			
	50	Dean Acheson 1/49	Louis A. Johnson 3/49	Omar N. Bradley 8/49
	51		George C. Marshall 9/50	
	52		Robert A. Lovett 9/51	
	53			
EISENHOWER	54	John F. Dulles 1/53	Charles E. Wilson 1/53	Arthur W. Radford 8/53
	55			
	56			
	57			
	58		Neil H. McElroy 10/57	Nathan F. Twining 8/57
	59			
	60	Christian A. Herter 4/59	Thomas S. Gates, Jr. 12/59	
KENNEDY	61			Lyman L. Lemnitzer 10/60
	62	Dean Rusk 1/61	Robert S. McNamara 1/61	
	63			Maxwell D. Taylor 10/62
	64			
JOHNSON	65			Earle G. Wheeler 7/64
	66			
	67			
	68			
	69		Clark M. Clifford 3/68	
NIXON	70	William P. Rogers 1/69	Melvin R. Laird 1/69	
	71			Thomas H. Moorer 7/70
	72			
	73		Elliot Richardson 1/73	
	74			
FORD	75	Henry A. Kissinger 8/73	James R. Schlesinger 7/73	George S. Brown 7/74
	76			
	77		Donald H. Rumsfeld 11/75	
CARTER	78	Cyrus R. Vance 1/77	Harold R. Brown 1/77	
	79			David C. Jones 7/78
	80	Edmund S. Muskie 5/80		

LEADERSHIP SINCE WW II

Chief of Staff Army	Chief of Naval Operations	Chief of Staff Air Force	Commandant Marine Corps
George C. Marshall to 11/45	Ernest J. King to 12/45		Alexander A. Vandegrift to 12/47
Dwight D. Eisenhower 11/45	Chester W. Nimitz 12/45		
Omar N. Bradley 2/48	Louis E. Denfeld 12/47	Carl Spaatz 9/47	Clifton B. Cates 1/48
		Hoyt S. Vandenberg 4/48	
J. Lawton Collins 8/49	Forrest P. Sherman 11/49		
	William M. Fechteler 8/51		Lemuel C. Shepherd 1/52
Matthew B. Ridgway 8/53	Robert B. Carney 8/53	Nathan F. Twining 6/53	
Maxwell D. Taylor 6/55	Arleigh A. Burke 8/55		Randolph McC. Pate 1/56
		Thomas D. White 7/57	
Lyman L. Lemnitzer 7/59			David M. Shoup 1/60
George H. Decker 10/60	George W. Anderson 8/61	Curtis E. LeMay 6/61	
Earle G. Wheeler 10/62	David L. McDonald 8/63		Wallace M. Greene 1/64
Harold K. Johnson 7/64		John P. McConnell 2/65	
William C. Westmoreland 7/68	Thomas H. Moorer 8/67		Leonard F. Chapman 1/68
	Elmo R. Zumwalt 7/70	John D. Ryan 8/69	
Creighton W. Abrams 7/72		George S. Brown 9/73	Robert E. Cushman 1/72
Frederick C. Weyand 9/74	James L. Holloway 7/74	David C. Jones 7/74	
Bernard W. Rogers 9/76			Louis H. Wilson 7/75
Edward C. Meyer 7/79	Thomas B. Hayward 7/78	Lew Allen 7/78	Robert H. Barrow 7/79

NOTES

CHAPTER 1

1. Truman preferred to leave the word *military* out. He apparently convinced himself that the training was not military, even though the army would administer it. Rather he conceived it as training for citizenship and personal development.

2. For contrasting perspectives, see chapters by Robert H. Ferrell and Lloyd C. Gardner, in Richard S. Kirkendall et al., *The Truman Period as a Research Field: A Reappraisal, 1972* (Columbia: University of Missouri Press, 1974), pp. 11–74.

3. This was a group formally established at the Potsdam Conference that consisted of the foreign ministers of the United States, the USSR, Great Britain, France, and sometimes China. The meetings, held in Europe and the United States, were interminable and had few results.

4. General George C. Marshall, army; Admirals Harold R. Stark (until March 1942) and Ernest J. King, navy; and General Henry H. Arnold, air force.

5. The best study of the unification struggle, which took place mainly from 1945 to 1947, remains Demetrios Caraley, *The Politics of Military Unification* (New York: Columbia University Press, 1966).

6. General Collins states that a navy official named it the Collins plan. In reality, he said, it was Marshall's plan, but in those days Marshall was so prestigious that it would have been difficult to criticize a plan that bore his name. (Discussion during conference at Marshall Library, Lexington, Va., March 26, 1977).

7. There was a brief interruption during World War I, when he served as a naval aviator.

8. Forrestal is a fascinating study, both as a successful financier and as a government leader. Arnold A. Rogow's *James Forrestal* (New York: Macmillan, 1963) examines his personality in depth. One aspect of his life that played a significant part in his outlook was his marriage in 1926 to Josephine Ogden, a divorcee and a *Vogue* editor at the time. Although they remained married until his death, the marriage did not work and essentially they led

separate lives. Forrestal's life-style was oriented toward exceptionally long hours of work, including weekends, and eventually this took its toll.

9. Harry S. Truman, *Years of Trial and Hope* (New York: Doubleday, 1956), p. 60.

10. Interviews: Marx Leva; Wilfred J. McNeil; John Ohly.

11. Interview: Marx Leva. Truman played down the service secretaries' cabinet rank by not inviting them to cabinet meetings.

12. Interview: Wilfred J. McNeil.

13. The case of interservice competition, which focuses on the defense budget (sometimes directly, sometimes in terms of strategic policy, and sometimes in terms of roles and missions), was selected because it is central to understanding the problems faced by the first secretary of defense. The problem was, of course, not solved in Forrestal's time and the reader may be left with a sense of frustration. One, however, should not overlook Forrestal's many positive accomplishments in getting the new department under way. These included, for example, reinstitution of the badly needed draft; a thrust in research and development in missiles and other areas; a beginning to the reconstitution of the reserve forces; and initial attempts toward articulating a new strategic doctrine in the early period of the atomic era.

14. *Public Papers of the Presidents,* 1947 (Washington: Government Printing Office), pp. 385-86; hereafter cited as *Public Papers.*

15. *New York Times,* August 29, 1947.

16. This memorandum, dated September 16, 1947, is contained in the private papers of Wilfred J. McNeil, one of Forrestal's three special assistants (hereafter cited as McNeil Papers). Forrestal had high hopes for the War Council and in the early months of his tenure he found it quite useful. As time went on, however, this forum did not tackle the real issues and the group began to deal with rather trivial matters, such as whether the air force should have a dress uniform. There were exceptions, as during the Berlin Air Lift of 1945-1949, when the council provided a useful discussion forum. On such occasions, the head of the State Department's Policy Planning staff and the executive secretary of the National Security Council were in attendance. Interview: John Ohly.

17. Walter Millis, ed., *The Forrestal Diaries* (New York: Viking Press, 1951), p. 352; hereafter cited as Diaries.

18. Forrestal Collection, Princeton University, Box 93. Memorandum dated October 17, 1947.

19. U.S. President's Air Policy Commission, *Survival in the Air Age* (Washington, D.C.: Government Printing Office, 1948), pp. 8, 25. The precise rationale for seventy groups is not clear, but by the time the commission picked it up, it already had a life of its own. The seventy groups were composed of the following types: twenty strategic bombardment; six strategic reconnaissance; four tactical reconnaissance; five light bombardment; twenty-two day fighters; three all-weather fighters; four heavy troop carriers; and six medium troop carriers. There was also a Congressional Aviation Policy Board (the Brewster-Hinshaw Board) that studied the air

problem at about the same time. Its report was published about two months after the Finletter Commission Report and relied heavily on the testimony given to that commission. Findings relative to air power were about the same.

20. Described in Diaries, pp. 374–77.

21. The entire message is contained in Diaries, p. 387.

22. Robert Cutler, No Time for Rest (Boston: Little, Brown, 1966), p. 244.

23. New York Times, article by Harold B. Hinton, March 12, 1948.

24. Diaries, pp. 389–94. About the time of the conference Jan Masaryk, foreign minister of Czechoslovakia, a well-liked person in Western circles, fell or was pushed from a window in his official residence. The shock further intensified the crises brought about by the coup of the previous month. European reaction to the increasingly tense situation was the agreement on March 14 to the Brussels Pact, a fifty-year treaty of mutual defense between Britain, France, Belgium, The Netherlands, and Luxembourg.

25. Diaries, p. 394.

26. The address to Congress and the Saint Patrick's Day address are items 52 and 53 respectively Public Papers, 1948.

27. A fascinating account of the fiscal year 1949 supplemental is told from Cutler's perspective in No Time for Rest, chapt. 15.

28. New York Times, March 26, 1948.

29. When the details were worked out on Forrestal's position, it would support the air force at fifty-five groups rather than seventy.

30. No Time for Rest, pp. 257, 258.

31. Arnold A. Rogow, James Forrestal (New York: Macmillan, 1963), p. 295.

32. This figure is contrasted to the $11 billion the president had initially proposed in his budget message to Congress in January. Congress also authorized reinstitution of the draft. Universal military training was not approved and was eventually abandoned.

33. Forrestal, the three service secretaries, the three military chiefs, James Webb, the budget director, and McNeil, Forrestal's assistant. Actually the memorandum had been prepared by McNeil, based on presidential guidance and edited subsequently by Webb.

34. Excerpts are from a talking paper for the president contained in the McNeil Papers. Wording is about the same as Diaries, pp. 435–38. The $15 billion ceiling from the services point of view was really $14.4 billion, since about $0.6 billion was included for stockpiling. Webb, having in effect won out over Forrestal in holding the line on the supplemental, now wanted to protect his victory. There is included in the McNeil papers a memorandum from McNeil to Forrestal dated May 13, 1948, in which Webb suggests that Forrestal comment to the assemblage after the president's reading that "any mention of today's meeting in the press would be extremely injurious to our foreign policy." There is no evidence that Forrestal took this suggestion.

35. B-295 were identified as planes capable of carrying atomic weapons.

36. Memorandum for the Joint Chiefs of Staff dated July 19, 1948, McNeil Papers.

37. This group became known as the McNarney Board. The other members were Vice Admiral Robert B. Carney (navy), and Major General George J. Richards (army); Diaries, p. 450.

38. I am not attempting to make Symington the villain of the piece. He was the air secretary in the formative period of the Department of Air Force and much credit for the early postwar development of United States air power must be given to him. He was, however, a strong adversary whom Forrestal, perhaps because of their long friendship going back to New York days, found difficult to handle. Some comments by Forrestal's assistants on Symington: "I was summoned to Symington's office, where I found the Secretary highly excited because Forrestal had in the course of testimony on the Hill that day stated that two-thirds of the earth's surface was covered with water. The inference Symington took was that Forrestal was pushing the Navy and undercutting the Air Force. We finally found a solution which Symington said was 'marvelous.' I suggested that when we edited the transcript of the hearings I add, 'but above all the water and above all the land is the air.'" "Symington was making a terrific effort to be Secretary of Defense." "Symington was a great burden to Forrestal." "He should have resigned and carried on his campaign for increased air power outside of government."

39. This episode is contained in Diaries, pp. 462–65.

40. This had been helped along early in 1948 through a speech by retired Fleet Admiral Chester W. Nimitz, in which he spoke of bombing Russia with naval aircraft from super aircraft carriers. This controversy was to reach its peak during the tenure of Forrestal's successor, Louis Johnson, in the famous "Revolt of the Admirals." The story of this controversy is expertly told by Paul Y. Hammond, "Super Carriers and B-36 Bombers" in *American Civil-Military Decisions*, ed. Harold Stein (Birmingham: University of Alabama Press, 1963).

41. This memorandum is contained in the James V. Forrestal diaries in the Princeton University Library. It, like a number of other papers, was declassified on June 28, 1973. It seems obvious that Walter Millis used these papers in editing the Diaries in 1951. In this case, see Diaries, p. 476, which summarizes this memorandum.

42. There are two memoranda for record on this conference dated August 23, 1948, contained in the Forrestal Diaries at Princeton. Again, these were declassified on June 28, 1973.

43. The first two decisions were the only ones touched upon in the press release on the conference. The second decision still begs the issue of which service should perform a function that both could do.

44. Subsequently Field Marshal Montgomery was commander-in-chief of such a headquarters. Later the headquarters became Supreme Allied Headquarters Europe, with Eisenhower appointed as first supreme commander in December 1950. This was in the aftermath of the shock of the

communist invasion of South Korea in the summer of 1950 and in effect made operational in a military sense the NATO Alliance signed in April 1949.

45. This was the first budget in which the organization established by the National Security Act of 1947 was able to play a part from the beginning to the end of the budget cycle. The development of this defense budget has been exhaustively covered in Warner R. Schilling, "The Politics of National Defense: Fiscal 1950," in Warner R. Schilling, Paul Y. Hammond, and Glenn H. Snyder, *Strategy, Politics, and Defense Budgets* (New York: Columbia University Press, 1962).

46. McNeil Papers, memorandum dated September 24, 1948. Although he was very loyal to the president in attempting to live within the imposed ceiling, Forrestal during the fall of 1948 explored higher alternatives. In an interview with George Fielding Eliot during the summer of 1948 (but not published until 1950), Forrestal stated that a budget of some $18 billion for fiscal 1950 would be required. When asked if he thought he could convince the president, Forrestal replied: "No, I think I'm going to be overruled." *American Legion Magazine* (September 1950), p. 55.

47. Diaries, p. 498.

48. Diaries, p. 499.

49. McNeil Papers, memorandum for the Joint Chiefs, dated 8 October 1948.

50. Diaries, pp. 500–502.

51. This meeting was apparently transcribed and is contained in some eleven pages of notes in the Forrestal Diaries at Princeton. It was declassified on June 28, 1973.

52. Diaries, p. 507.

53. The NATO Alliance was not formally established until shortly after Forrestal left office.

54. Diaries, p. 511.

55. Forrestal Papers, Princeton, Box 95, telegram dated November 3, 1948.

56. Defense-minded Johnson, a former national commander of the American Legion, was assistant secretary of war from 1937 to 1940. He was more interested in rearming than his chief, Secretary Harry Woodring. Their feud indirectly led to Johnson's departure from the War Department. Following the 1948 election, early newspaper speculation was to the effect that Forrestal would stay on. At a White House news conference on December 2, Truman stated that Secretary of State Marshall and Defense Secretary Forrestal had been asked to remain in office and had expressed willingness to do so. *Washington Post*, December 5, 1948.

57. There were disagreements about specifics. For example, within the navy's $4.6 billion, they planned on operating nine carriers. The army thought six would be enough, while the air force thought four would do the job.

58. McNeil Papers. Memorandum from McNeil to Forrestal, dated 13 November 1948.

59. Interview: Wilfred J. McNeil.

60. Who had just warned Truman that new taxes would be required to balance the planned fiscal 1950 budget, even without any increase in defense expenditures.

61. Forrestal was instrumental through Senator Henry Cabot Lodge in shaping the Lodge-Brown Act, which established the commission. Forrestal was offered the vice-chairmanship but declined, serving instead as a member of the commission.

62. He also set forth his views in the first Annual Report of the Secretary of Defense, published at the end of December 1948, and in testimony before a Senate Committee in late March 1949.

63. The organizational problem was solved for the moment by Public Law 216 of August 10, 1949. The key provisions of the law were: The National Military Establishment became the Department of Defense, with the secretary exercising direction, authority, and control; the service secretaries lost their places on the NSC and in the cabinet (by failing to invite them to meetings, Truman had already excluded them from the cabinet); a JCS chairman was authorized, but he had no vote; the numerical limitation on the Joint Staff was raised from 100 to 210 officers; and the services were protected by requiring that they be administered separately and by providing that their combatant functions not be transferred and that their noncombatant functions not be reassigned without first informing Congress.

64. On January 7 the resignation of George Marshall and his under secretary, Robert Lovett, who was one of Forrestal's closest friends, was announced. Marshall was replaced by Dean Acheson and Lovett by Forrestal's budget adversary, James Webb.

65. Diaries, p. 546.

66. Rogow, *James Forrestal*, p. 307.

67. Diaries, pp. 548-51.

68. As to the irony of his having led the forces who wanted a secretary without strong powers, Marx Leva, one of his assistants, had this to say in an interview with me: "I think he would have felt, even in retrospect, that you probably had to go through the National Military Establishment phase in order to get to the Department of Defense phase." Wilfred McNeil, another assistant, stated in an interview with me that if Truman had supported Forrestal in his confrontation with Symington, the centralization trend set in effect by the 1949 amendments could have been avoided.

69. Truman had three other secretaries of defense during his remaining years as president. Louis Johnson, with the president's support, chopped away at the military budget with apparent enthusiasm and a good deal of bombast. His biggest controversy began a month after he took office, when he canceled the navy's flush-deck carrier, for which the keel had just been laid. The secretary of the navy resigned and the "revolt" of the admirals was on. When the Korean War broke out in June 1950, it soon exposed the sad state of the American armed forces, especially land forces. Economizer Johnson had to pay the price and resigned in September 1950. The prestige of the office and of the military had to be restored. The president again

called on the prestigious George Marshall, who in turn persuaded his former under secretary of state Robert Lovett to come back to government service, this time as the deputy secretary of defense (a position created by the 1949 amendments, which had first been occupied by Stephen T. Early under Johnson). Marshall was past his peak at this point, and knew it, and essentially let Lovett run the department. Lovett succeeded Marshall in September 1951 and served out the remainder of the Truman years with distinction. In the Korean War period budgets were no longer the central problem and the services came close to satisfying their perceived needs. Relations between Defense and State became strained during the Johnson tenure but were restored under Marshall and Lovett.

CHAPTER 2

1. These dollar objectives had been agreed to by Eisenhower with the conservative wing of the Republican party—specifically, with its leader Robert Taft, shortly after Eisenhower's nomination. He was thoroughly in sympathy with the objectives, however, except that he thought they were "perhaps too ambitious in timing."

2. John S. D. Eisenhower, in correspondence with me, indicated that his father's economic views began to be formed during his first duty tour in the Army General Staff from 1927 to 1935. For an interesting account of how they were nurtured during the period from 1948 to 1952 by a number of Republicans who wanted Ike to run for president, see Peter Lyon, *Eisenhower: Portrait of the Hero* (Boston: Little, Brown, 1974), pp. 381–439.

3. Cutler, *No Time for Rest*, pp. 296–98.

4. John S. D. Eisenhower, *Strictly Personal* (New York: Doubleday, 1974), pp. 204–6. Andrew J. Goodpaster transcript, Columbia Oral History Project. John S. D. Eisenhower, unpublished manuscript in JSDE's private papers.

5. Best set forth in Henry M. Jackson, *The National Security Council* (New York: Praeger, 1965).

6. Sherman Adams transcript, Dulles Oral History Project (DOH), Princeton University. Dwight D. Eisenhower, *Waging Peace* (New York: Doubleday, 1965), pp. 367–68.

7. Adams transcript (DOH). Robert Bowie transcript (DOH).

8. Maxwell D. Taylor, *Swords and Plowshares* (New York: Norton, 1972), p. 170.

9. Carter Burgess transcript, Columbia Oral History Project, and transcripts of Sherman Adams, Arthur Radford, and Thomas Gates in DOH.

10. Dwight D. Eisenhower, *Mandate for Change* (New York: Doubleday, 1963), pp. 96, 455 n.

11. Ibid., passim. John S. D. Eisenhower unpublished manuscript, Arthur Radford transcript DOH. Maxwell D. Taylor, *The Uncertain Trumpet* (New York: Harper, 1959), passim.

12. President Truman's outoing secretary of defense, Robert A. Lovett,

had sent Truman a letter on November 18, 1952, in which he highlighted his own comments on organizational problems of the Department of Defense. This was made public on January 8, 1953, in a Department of Defense press release.

13. This is a twice-told tale, with the best accounts still being Samuel P. Huntington, *The Common Defense* (New York: Columbia Press, 1961), and Glenn H. Snyder, "The New Look of 1953," in *Strategy, Politics and Defense Budgets*, ed. Warner R. Schilling, Paul Y. Hammond, and Glenn H. Snyder (New York: Columbia University Press, 1962).

14. The five categories of forces were nuclear retaliatory; land and air forces overseas; naval and marine forces at sea; continental air defense units; and strategic reserve forces in the United States. Eisenhower, *Mandate for Change*, p. 45.

15. This meeting was an outstanding exception to Eisenhower's customary use of the NSC.

16. Column by Joseph and Stewart Alsop, *New York Herald Tribune*, February 22, 1954, p. 10.

17. This paper is now available as part of the Pentagon Papers: The Defense Department, *History of United States Decision-Making on Vietnam*, ed. Theodore Gravel, 5 vols. (Boston: Beacon Press, 1971), 1:412 ff.

18. "Local defenses must be reinforced by the further deterrent of massive retaliatory power. . . . The basic decision was to depend primarily on a great capacity to retaliate, instantly, by means and at places of our choosing." The last sentence quoted was penned onto page 10 of a draft of the speech (located in the Dulles Papers in the Firestone Library at Princeton) which had been sent to the president for comment, in what appears to be Eisenhower's handwriting. Eisenhower himself addressed the matter of commenting on Dulles's speeches in *Waging Peace*, p. 365. "He would never deliver an important speech or statement until after I had read, edited, and approved it; he guarded constantly against the possibility that any misunderstanding could arise between us." Louis Halle (*The Cold War as History*, p. 281), is wrong when he says that Dulles showed the speech only to a State Department lawyer in advance of its delivery.

19. This remarkable body of literature, most of which was produced from 1956 until 1960, was largely the work of academics. Since the logical fallacies of massive retaliation were too obvious to be overlooked, its opponents included about every strategic thinker of any importance. Some of the better known were Bernard Brodie, William W. Kaufmann, Henry A. Kissinger, Oskar Morgenstern, Robert E. Osgood, and Albert Wohlstetter. Early emphasis was on limited war, whereas toward the end of the period stable deterrence was emphasized. In aggregate, the argument was for a wider spectrum of options than massive retaliation seemed to allow. There is no evidence that Eisenhower paid much attention to all this, but the literature did provide theoretical support for his opponents in the bureaucracy and in Congress. It was also the basis for the Kennedy defense platform and later for the McNamara strategy.

20. NATO still had to be brought on board, and this was accomplished at the ministerial meeting in December 1954 when the NATO Council approved M.C. 48, which made the primary strategy of NATO dependent on nuclear weapons. Dulles's approach with the council was rather heavy-handed. However, since the Allies, like the United States, perceived that they needed economies, they accommodated to the new U.S. strategy.

21. By mid-1956 the administration had abandoned any notions of nuclear superiority over the growing nuclear capability of the USSR, opting instead for a goal of "sufficient deterrence." As set forth by Deputy Defense Secretary Quarles, deterrence rested not so much on the relative strategic strength of both sides as on their absolute ability to inflict unacceptable damage to each other.

22. McElroy transcript, *Columbia Oral History Project*.

23. Nathan F. Twining, *Neither Liberty nor Safety* (New York: Holt, Rinehart, 1966), p. 148.

24. Memorandum of Conference with the President (hereafter MCP), February 24, 1955. Note entries in this chapter such as these refer to meetings with the president on which notes were taken by his staff. These notes, which were converted into documents, are not classified but as of early 1980 are still in some cases considered privileged. I was permitted to examine the documents and take notes. Where quotations are used, they are direct quotes of the speaker cited.

25. Letter from Edward L. Beach to Kinnard, August 17, 1972.

26. Ken Jones and Hubert Kelley, Jr., *Admiral Arleigh (31-Knot) Burke* (Philadelphia: Chilton, 1962), pp. 166-277.

27. The percentage breakdowns of the defense budget by service were remarkably constant from 1955 until the end of the Eisenhower administration: air force, 46 percent; navy, 27 percent; and army, 23 percent.

28. MCP, July 10, 1957.

29. He records his overall reaction in Eisenhower, *Waging Peace*, pp. 210-12.

30. MCP, October 9, 11, 1957.

31. MCP, October 30, 1957.

32. MCP, November 22, 1957.

33. MCP, November 4, 1957.

34. Eisenhower, *Waging Peace*, pp. 244-45.

35. *MCP*, January 30, 1958.

36. Eisenhower, *Waging Peace*, p. 250. MCP, April 9, 1958.

37. MCP, June 23, 1958.

38. MCP, April 21, 1958.

39. Eisenhower, *Waging Peace*, p. 252.

40. Ibid., pp. 385-86.

41. MCP, March 7, 1958. As Schlesinger points out in *The Imperial Presidency*, Eisenhower in 1955 had added an almost unlimited category of information deniable to Congress at the presidential will, i.e., material generated by the internal deliberative processes of government. This was a

claim of executive privilege going far beyond the president's immediate aides to the executive branch as a whole, pp. 156–59.

42. MCP, November 28, 1959.
43. MCP, December 3, 1958.
44. Taylor, *Uncertain Trumpet*, p. 72.
45. The interested senators were Lyndon B. Johnson, Richard B. Russell, Stuart Symington, Henry M. Jackson, John Stennis, and Carl Hayden. The representatives were George Mahon, Robert Sikes, Daniel Flood, Gerald Ford, Melvin Laird, Carl Vinson, and Paul Kilday.
46. MCP, Feb. 9, 1959.
47. In some ways, the most spectacular hearings that spring, though not related directly to the appropriation process were those of Lyndon Johnson's Preparedness Subcommittee. There is no doubt that the hearings were politically embarrassing to the administration, and were so designed. There was no question, either, of the breakdown of public consensus within the administration, which had started earlier with the testimony of the army and navy in the House. There was an unusual interest by the subcommittee in exactly how the Eisenhower defense budget had been developed. Budgetary ceilings, which were denied, and the role of the Bureau of the Budget seemed to hold the greatest fascination for the senators. Probably the primary motivation for these hearings was the 1960 presidential campaign. From that perspective, the hearings were perhaps successful, in that they were of some significance in setting the stage for the defense debate of the 1960 presidential campaign. For an interesting perspective on Johnson's revitalization and political use of this subcommittee commencing with Sputnik, see George E. Reedy, *The Twilight of the Presidency* (Boston: Houghton Mifflin, 1973), p. 52.
48. Eisenhower's final secretary of defense, Thomas Gates, was different than Wilson or McElroy. A generalist, by outlook, he established good rapport with the Joint Chiefs. His service as secretary (December 1959–January 1961) was too brief to be treated in this chapter.

CHAPTER 3

1. This talk, entitled "The Communist Doctrine of Wars of Liberation," is contained in U.S., Department of State, *American Foreign Policy Current Documents* 1961. (Washington, D.C.: Government Printing Office, 1965), pp. 555–58.
2. W. W. Rostow, *The Diffusion of Power* (New York: Macmillan, 1972), chapts. 15, 16.
3. Another U.S. intervention in the spring of 1965 was that into the Dominican Republic. This caused considerable public debate, in a sense foreshadowing the subsequent debate on Vietnam.
4. Interview: Roswell Gilpatric.
5. Rostow, *Diffusion of Power*, p. 162.

6. Ibid., p. 168.

7. McNamara and Gilpatric picked their own immediate assistants, and subsequently the assistant secretaries chose their own assistants, who became known as the "Whiz Kids," both for their youth and for their management innovations. Kennedy kept his agreement about giving McNamara a free hand in appointments. Only one appointee was forced on McNamara, an under secretary whose level of competence was such that the service in which he worked had to "design around him." Interview: Roswell Gilpatric.

8. At the outset of the administration McNamara and Gilpatric each developed a list of major problems and the courses of action that might be taken to solve them. Gilpatric came up with forty-three and McNamara with sixty-seven, including most of those on Gilpatric's list. Interview: Roswell Gilpatric.

9. Robert S. McNamara, *The Essence of Security* (New York: Harper and Row, 1968), p. x.

10. Roswell L. Gilpatric from January 1961 until January 1964; Cyrus R. Vance from January 1964 until June 1967; and from July 1967 Paul Nitze who remained after McNamara left, working under Clark Clifford until the change in administrations in January 1969.

11. To be fair, there is no evidence that Lemnitzer was any more reponsible for the debacle than any other of the principals involved; indeed, I would submit he was less so than Kennedy or McNamara. It seems clear, however, that the event made Kennedy somewhat more skeptical of the senior military as a group than he had been. One interesting aspect of this CIA-sponsored event is that the Defense Department was brought in on the plan fairly late. When McNamara and Gilpatric received their initial briefings by Allen Dulles, director of the CIA, he did not even mention that there was a Cuban invasion plan. Interview: Roswell Gilpatric. Although this event was planned during the Eisenhower period, I seriously doubt that Eisenhower would have permitted this operation to be executed, and if he had, certainly not in the form that it took.

12. Interview, Harold K. Johnson.

13. Ibid.

14. Interview by Paul L. Miles, Jr., with Earle G. Wheeler.

15. As for the services, McNamara felt strongly that they were not independent agencies but an integral part of the Department of Defense. Naturally, the services did not agree. Paul Nitze, former secretary of the navy, put it this way speaking at a conference at the Marshall Library in Lexington, Va., in March 1977: "McNamara had the wrong idea when he thought the service Secretary should represent him rather than his service."

16. Interview by Paul Miles, Jr., with Earle G. Wheeler.

17. There is some contrary evidence on this point. A former deputy secretary of defense (Roswell Gilpatric) told me in an interview that he felt Wheeler was very careful in dealing with the secretary of defense to present the varying views of the chiefs. What is not clear is on what range of issues he took this care.

18. Interview.

19. Records were kept, but they were erratic until late 1966, when the deputy press secretary was given the task. These records are still classified at this writing and are in the Lyndon Baines Johnson Library at Austin.

20. For an insider's view of the Tuesday luncheon, see Rostow, *Diffusion of Power*, pp. 358–60. An interesting account of this forum, based on interviews with the principals, is contained in Henry F. Graff, *The Tuesday Cabinet* (Englewood Cliffs, N.J., Prentice Hall, 1970).

21. Rostow, *Diffusion of Power*, pp. 361, 362.

22. A representative sample of this literature includes: Alain C. Enthoven and K. Wayne Smith, *How Much Is Enough?* (New York: Harper and Row, 1971); Clark A. Murdock, *Defense Policy Formation* (Albany: State University of New York Press, 1974); James M. Roherty, *Decisions of Robert S. McNamara* (Coral Gables, Fla.: University of Miami Press, 1970); Ralph Sanders, *The Politics of Defense Analysis* (New York: Dunellen, 1973); Samuel A. Tucker, ed., *A. Modern Design for Defense Decision* (Washington: Industrial College of the Armed Forces, 1966).

23. This was the Air University Black Book of Reorganization Papers. The Symington Task Force set up by Kennedy during his 1960 campaign also used this book. Some of the Task Force proposals were quite far-reaching, as were some in the Black Book, such as proposing a single chief of staff for the armed forces. This kind of approach was rejected by McNamara.

24. McNamara, *Essence of Security*, p. 88.

25. Military forces also were an element of programming and were projected over an eight-year period.

26. Strategic Retaliatory Forces, Continental Defense Forces, General Purpose Forces, Airlift and Sealift, Reserve and Guard, Research and Development, General Support, Retired Pay, Military Assistance. Congress required the budget in resource categories (rather than mission categories)—i.e., Military Personnel, Operation and Maintenance, Procurement, Research and Development, and Military Construction. This was budgeting by service rather than across services, but it was more meaningful and useful to Congress in resource categories.

27. The FYDP consisted of summaries of each program element (for example, a tactical fighter such as the F-202), together with all the supporting information on that element, such as force descriptions, procurement lists, and facilities lists.

28. The services had also been provided earlier with Tentative Force Guidance tables that could also form the basis for PCRs.

29. Systems Analysis did not review all service proposals. Some were reviewed by other offices, such as Installation and Logistics and Research and Engineering.

30. Some well-known military figures who subsequent to their retirements made strongly adverse comments were General Thomas White, air force chief until 1961, his successor General Curtis LeMay, and Admiral George Anderson, chief of naval operations until 1963.

31. See Stanley M. Barnes, "Defense Planning Processes," *United States Naval Institute Proceedings*, SC (June 1964), pp. 32, 33; the address by W. J. McNeil excerpted in *Army, Navy, Air Force Journal and Register*, June 30, 1964.

32. McNamara's speech in September 1967 supporting a light deployment to counteract the potential Chinese threat comes to mind. Based on previous analysis, a speech had been written rejecting the ABM. Johnson did not want to get caught in the 1968 election with an ABM "gap" comparable to the missile "gap" (invented) with which he and Kennedy had plagued the Republicans in 1960. Hence, a presidential decision was made to go for some ABM deployments. In this case, the same rejection speech was enabled to be used merely by adding the rationale for a light deployment at the end of the text.

33. Henry Trewhitt closes his book *McNamara* (New York: Harper and Row, 1971), with this sentence: "What a splendid time it would have been without Vietnam." McNamara's unparalleled grasp of the details of managing the Pentagon, his success in enabling the U.S. Armed Forces to respond to a greater spectrum of conflict, and his revamping of NATO strategy, along with encouraging greater participation by the other NATO countries in developing that strategy, were enormous accomplishments. In considering Vietnam as the case to develop in the McNamara period, there is no intent to detract from his many accomplishments as secretary of defense. But the Vietnam War, which cost the United States $150 billion and almost 50,000 American lives, must be considered the major event in which McNamara participated while secretary of defense. References to the Pentagon Papers refer to the Gravel Edition and will simply show the volume and page numbers after the abbreviation PP. In this case, NSC 48/2 (December 1949) and NSC 64 (February 1950), vol. 1, pp. 82, 83.

34. NSC 124/2, PP, vol. 1, pp. 384-90.

35. The headquarters of the United States Commander in Chief Pacific (whose area of military surveillance included Southeast Asia) is located in Honolulu.

36. Interview: William P. Bundy.

37. *New York Times*, Feb. 19, Feb. 20, 1962.

38. On which President Kennedy commented, "It is a heartening indication that . . . semingly insoluble international problems can in fact be solved" (*New York Times*, July 24, 1962).

39. In a summary treatment of a subject this complex, some important aspects must be omitted. For example, while the focus here is on the war itself, there was simultaneously under way a pacification effort that changed in emphasis and title during the long drawn-out struggle. During the time period we are now considering, it was called the Strategic Hamlet Program. Earlier the rubrics were Civic Action (1955-1956), Land Development Centers (1957-1959), and Agrovilles (1959-1961). Later rubrics were Hoptac, Chien Thang, and the New Life Hamlets (1964-1965), Rural Reconstruction (1965-1966), and, beginning in 1966, Revolutionary Development.

40. PP, vol. 2, pp. 162, 163.

41. PP, vol. 2, pp. 166, 167. International Security Affairs became an important Pentagon agency during the McNamara period. Sometimes called the Pentagon's State Department it was established at Eisenhower's suggestion in 1953 to develop and coordinate policies and plans in the political-military field and foreign economic affairs. McNamara had great faith in the three assistants who headed that office during his tenure: Paul Nitze, 1961–1963; John McNaughton, 1964–1967; and Paul Warnke, 1967–1969. It was the focal point of McNamara's staff support on Vietnam policy analysis. Systems Analysis, on the other hand, worked primarily on force packages for Vietnam and related logistical matters. There were exceptions, of course, such as in the spring of 1967, when the office got deeply involved in supporting McNaughton who was developing an alternative to a Westmoreland troop request. On a minor level, beginning about 1967, Systems Analysis periodically published a Southeast Asia Analysis Report. This was an unofficial report and was frank in its criticisms of the conduct of the war. Although many thought it served a useful purpose, the chairman of the Joint Chiefs was not one of them. On one occasion he recommended to the secretary of defense that the report, which was widely disseminated, be limited to the secretary's staff.

42. PP, vol. 2, p. 164.

43. On January 27, 1964, Secretary McNamara testified before the House Armed Services Committee. An extract from his testimony gives the tone. "The survival of an independent government in South Vietnam is so important to the security of all of Southeast Asia and to the Free World that I can conceive of no alternative other than to take all necessary measures within our capability to prevent a Communist victory." New York Times, January 30, 1964.

44. PP, vol. 2, p. 412.

45. My source on this was an interview, but Westmoreland tells the same story in slightly different words in William C. Westmoreland, A Soldier Reports (New York: Doubleday, 1976), p. 67.

46. We cannot treat the air war in any detail. The approach favored by McNamara, which was adopted, was a slow deliberate increase in pressure against North Vietnam, at the same time maintaining open communications with Hanoi in the hope of negotiating a settlement. The air war was tightly controlled by McNamara and the president and went through a great number of phases involving intensity, areas targeted, and the nature of the targets themselves.

47. For Johnson's perspective on the early build-up decision, see Lyndon Baines Johnson, The Vantage Point (New York: Holt, Rinehart, and Winston, 1971), chapt. 6.

48. Not all external forces in Vietnam were American. Washington perceived a need to show flags of friendly countries in South Vietnam similar to the situation in Korea during the war there. Under pressure from the United States, four "Free World" countries, as they were termed, contributed combat forces that aggregated at a peak strength of 70,000 troops in

1969. The countries were Korea, Australia, New Zealand, and Thailand.
49. In a later memorandum, this became 394,000 by June 1967.
50. PP, vol. 4, pp. 622, 623. McNamara had raised the pause issue with the president the previous July.
51. Johnson, *Vantage Point*, chapt. 19.
52. Interview: William P. Bundy.
53. Ibid.
54. PP, vol. 4, p. 348.
55. This notion apparently originated with Roger Fisher of Harvard Law School and came to McNamara in late winter 1966 through Assistant Secretary (ISA) McNaughton. The concept of a barrier, along with other aspects of the war, was studied in the summer of 1966 by a group of scientists and others and referred to as the Jason Summer Study. The reports (submitted in late August 1966) were held quite closely, since one of the conclusions was that the bombing of the north was ineffective. The report then went on to recommend a barrier as an alternative way of checking infiltration. The study, especially as pertained to bombing effectiveness, made a definite impact on McNamara and was clearly reflected in his report to the president. The barrier was first announced to the public by McNamara on September 7, 1967.
56. PP, vol. 4, p. 357.
57. Ibid., p. 401. There was also beginning some real pressure, although less concentrated, from the opposite direction. As U.S. forces were increasingly committed in late 1966 and early 1967, casualties began to mount and questions began to be asked by the public and in Congress about the worthiness of the U.S. effort.
58. PP, vol. 4, p. 427.
59. About the time of Westmoreland's cable, President Johnson met with President Thieu, Premier Ky, General Westmoreland, and others at Guam. The main purpose was to accelerate pacification and to introduce two new members of the Saigon team—Ambassador Ellsworth Bunker, replacing Lodge, and Robert Komer, who was to be Westmoreland's deputy for pacification. There was little discussion of the military situation, which was assumed to be in such a good state that it required no particular attention from the conferees.
60. PP, vol. 4, p. 442. The exact numbers were hard to keep up with. They changed frequently in the course of considering various proposals. Some of these changes were real adjustments, while other were of a bookkeeping variety.
61. Ibid., pp. 477-89. This was to be McNaughton's final official word on the war. In July, as he was preparing to take over the post of secretary of the navy, he was killed in an airplane accident.
62. During that same summer, Clark Clifford and General Maxwell Taylor were sent by the president to visit the other countries contributing troops in Vietnam (Korea, Thailand, Australia, New Zealand, and the Philippines) to solicit additional contributions. The additional increment was minimal. Probably of more importance was the discovery of the lack of

importance with which these countries viewed the war in terms of the future security of their own areas.

63. The best inside account of these hearings is Philip G. Goulding, *Confirm or Deny* (New York: Harper and Row, 1970, chapt. 6.

64. Johnson, *Vantage Point*, p. 267. McNamara, Paul Nitze (by now McNamara's deputy), and Paul Warnke (McNaughton's replacement), along with some outside assistance, developed the exact wording of the formula.

65. Ibid., pp. 372-77.

66. Reproduced in ibid., pp. 600, 601.

67. Trewhitt, passim.

68. Clark Gifford, McNamara's successor at the Pentagon became deeply involved in reassessing the Vietnam situation in light of Westmoreland's request for 206,000 additional troops (stimulated more by Wheeler than Westmoreland, who wanted to reconstitute the strategic reserve). Eventually Westmoreland was authorized an increment of just under 25,000, to bring the final total to 549,500. This increment did occasion a small but troublesome reserve call-up. In the process of looking into the situation, hawk Clifford turned against the war and held the line against any escalation. On March 31, 1968, Lyndon Johnson made his abdication speech, in which he announced that he had ordered the bombing of North Vietnam halted except in areas contiguous to the Demilitarized Zone and proclaimed his willingness to negotiate. This offer did lead to negotiations, although with no tangible results for many years. How the United States eventually disengaged is covered in the next chapter, on Secretary Laird.

69. For an informed, interesting, but dated and somewhat polemical account of this, see William W. Kaufmann, *The McNamara Strategy* (New York: Harper and Row, 1964).

70. Westmoreland, *A Soldier Reports*, p. 121.

71. Henry Brandon, *Anatomy of Error* (Boston: Gambit, 1969), p. 164.

72. Quoted in Bernard Brodie, *War and Politics* (New York: Macmillan, 1973), p. 439.

CHAPTER 4

1. Further clarified in Nixon's Report to Congress of February 18, 1970: *United States Foreign Policy for The 1970's*. The Kalbs point out that the section of this report on Communist China was a signal concerning what later became Nixon's China initiative. Marvin and Bernard Kalb, *Kissinger* (New York: Dell, 1974), p. 263. See also Richard Nixon, *The Memoirs of Richard Nixon* (New York: Grosset and Dunlap, 1978), p. 545.

2. Nixon, *Report to Congress*, p. 343.

3. Subsequently during 1970 a U.S. study (NSSM 84) and a NATO study (AD 70) were conducted on NATO strategy for the 1970s. The outcome was an increased European NATO resource commitment to the alliance and a Nixon decision, in the fall of 1970, not to cut U.S. troop strength in Europe.

4. For a brief discussion of the "shocks" in the context of the American

foreign policy process, see I. M. Destler, "The Nixon 'Shocks' to Japan
1971" in Appendix K (Vol. 4), *Report of the Commission of the Government
for the Conduct of Foreign Policy* (Washington, D.C.: Government Printing
Office, 1975).
    5. Nixon tells his version of SALT in his memoirs. The clearest articula-
tion of the military's reservations concerning SALT I are in Elmo Zumwalt,
Jr., *On Watch* (New York: Quadrangle, 1976). The best work on SALT I
remains John Newhouse, *Cold Dawn: The Story of SALT* (New York: Holt,
Rinehart, and Winston, 1973).
    6. This supporting role was not to include U.S. land forces and was to
be defined more precisely after attainment of a cease-fire agreement.
    7. Earlier strong public revulsion toward the war had come in mid-
1969, with exposure of the My Lai massacre, an event that had occurred in
March 1968, but had, apparently at some level within the American division
involved, been covered up.
    8. For some interesting insights into the condition of the U.S. military
forces in 1971-1972 by a journalist see Stuart H. Loory, *Defeated: Inside
America's Military Machine* (New York: Random House, 1973).
    9. As of 1980 questions were being raised about the quality, costs,
long-term viability, and impact on reserve units of the volunteer force. The
most complete discussion of the establishment of the volunteer force that I
have encountered is Gus C. Lee and Geoffrey Y. Parker, *Ending the Draft:
The Story of the All Volunteer Force, Final Report* (Alexandria, Va.: Human
Resources Research Organization, 1977).
    10. The Vietnam War was a major factor in this, but not the only one.
President Johnson's Great Society programs were still in the implementation phase and were being financed in part by deficit spending.
    11. Nixon, *Memoirs*, p. 533.
    12. Although the Watergate break-in occurred on June 17, 1972, too
little was known of the full implications by November to have any real effect
on the election. Subsequently, Watergate became a code word for a whole
host of abuses by the Nixon administration and did play a major role during
the second Nixon administration.
    13. Nixon himself states: "Against McGovern . . . it was clear that the
less I did, the better I would do." Nixon, *Memoirs* p. 533.
    14. George S. McGovern, *Toward a More Secure America: An Alterna-
tive National Defense Posture* (Washington: McGovern Campaign Headquarters, 1972).
    15. Nixon, *Report to Congress*, pp. 17-23.
    16. After a presidential decision was made a National Security Decision
Memorandum was issued.
    17. WSAG grew out of the April 1969 crisis surrounding the downing
of an American EC-121 intelligence-gathering plane by the North Koreans
over the Sea of Japan.
    18. The DPRC was established in October 1969. Other committees
were the Senior Review Group for general foreign policy issues and the
Verification Panel for arms control issues.

19. Melvin R. Laird, *A House Divided: America's Strategy Gap* (Chicago: Henry Regnery, 1962).

20. Nixon, *Memoirs*, p. 338.

21. Ibid., p. 289.

22. The panel was hampered from the outset by an unrealistic charter. The final report was too mild to satisfy the defense critics and controversial enough to concern defense supporters. Under these circumstances there was little overall congressional support for the report.

23. See, for example, the testimony of Secretary of the Air Force Robert C. Seamons in U.S., Congress, Senate, Subcommittee of the Committee on Appropriations, *Department of Defense Appropriations Hearings FY 1970*, 91st Cong., 1st sess., 1969, pt. 4, p. 36.

24. James W. Canan, *The Superwarriors* (New York: Weybright and Talley, 1975), p. 89. Bernard Brodie, *War and Politics* (New York: Macmillan, 1973), p. 409.

25. See Alain C. Enthoven and K. Wayne Smith, *How Much Is Enough?* (New York: Harper and Row, 1971).

26. Interviews with Charles Rossotti, Ivan Selin, and Gardiner Tucker.

27. Interview with William Baroody, Jr.

28. ISA functions include coordinating defense participation in the NSC system; arms control; policy guidance to Defense Department representatives on U.S. missions; policy guidance to the Security Assistance Program; policy guidance for NATO; negotiating and monitoring of agreements with foreign governments on military facilities, operating rights, and status of forces.

29. Melvin R. Laird, *Final Report to the Congress* (Washington, D.C.: Government Printing Office, 1973).

30. Ibid., p. 17.

31. Interviews with Carl Wallace and Robert Pursley.

32. There was, however, no shortage of policy guidance from the White House. During Nixon's first four years in office there were 127 formal National Security Decision Memoranda (NSDM) issued. One of the best known, NSDM 3, established the policy of the United States being able to fight one major and one minor war simultaneously.

33. Zumwalt, *On Watch*, p. 335.

34. Ibid., p. 336.

35. Nixon, *Memoirs*, pp. 433, 434.

36. Kalb, *Kissinger*, p. 329.

37. Not all agree that Laird was successful in establishing a position of trust with the senior military. See for example William C. Westmoreland, *A Soldier Reports*, p. 387. "Laird appeared to distrust the Joint Chiefs, seemingly unable to accept as a consummate politician himself that we were apolitical." On the other hand, Admiral Zumwalt in *On Watch* speaks highly of Laird in his role as secretary of defense.

38. Interview with Carl Wallace. Canan, *Superwarriors*, p. 41.

39. It should be noted that Laird's relationships with all congressmen were not rosy; he did have clashes with Senators William Fulbright and

William Proxmire. See A. Ernest Fitzgerald, *The High Priests of Waste* (New York: W. W. Norton, 1972), pp. 264, 265.

40. Interview.

41. NSSM 1 is contained in U.S., Congress, *Congressional Record*, vol. 118, pt. 13, May 4–11, 1972 (Washington, D.C.: Government Printing Office, 1972).

42. For a perceptive discussion of the bureaucratic differences and the reasons therefor see Edwin A. Deagle, Jr., "NSSM 1" in Appendix K.

43. Interview. Subsequently the secretary of defense did direct "the goal of developing the RVNAF [Republic of Vietnam Armed Forces] with the capability to cope successfully with the combined Viet Cong–North Vietnamese Army threat."

44. Nixon, *Memoirs*, p. 392.

45. Interview with Robert Pursley.

46. General Robert Pursley who receives high marks from many interviewees as to his competence and influence. He had previously held the same position with Secretary McNamara.

47. H. R. Haldeman, *The Ends of Power* (New York: Times Books, 1978), p. 98. The president himself, however, was quite conscious of what he perceived to be the long-range implications of an improper exit of the United States from Vietnam. Speaking to a gathering of chiefs of mission in the American Embassy in Bangkok in late July 1969, Nixon stated, "If the Vietnam War goes sour, there would be an escalation of not just get out of Vietnam sentiment but get out of the world sentiment. This would be disastrous." (Interview.)

48. U.S., Department of Defense, *Statement of Secretary of Defense Melvin Laird* (before a Joint session of Senate Armed Services and Appropriations Committees) (Washington: Government Printing Office, 1970), p. 11.

49. Interview with Philip O'Deen.

50. Nixon, p. 390.

51. Ibid., p. 393.

52. The demonstrators were not all students by any means. Page one of the *New York Times* of October 10 carried an article concerning war critics in Congress which began: "A group of Congressional critics of the Vietnam War laid plans today to keep the House of Representatives in an all-night session next Tuesday, October 14, in symbolic support of the nationwide anti-war demonstrations scheduled the next day."

53. Nixon, *Memoirs*, pp. 407, 408.

54. Details of Vietnam Task Force meetings (hereafter VTF Notes) are based upon informal notes made by one of the participants which were made available to me. The notes, in most cases, however, paraphrase what was said.

55. The Phung Hoang or Phoenix Program stemmed from a Government of Vietnam presidential decree of July 1968 and included an intelligence program to identify members of the Viet Cong Infrastructure, an operational program to apprehend them, and a "legal" program to confine

them. The program operated at each level of administration—national, provincial, district, and village. Dossiers were developed on suspects, but the information in them was, in many cases, considered highly unreliable. From its inception in 1968 until United States participation was closed out in late 1972, the United States supported the program with almost four million dollars. In addition, United States advisers participated in the program, with a peak strength of about 700 being reached in 1970. During the course of the program, over 81,000 Viet Cong were "neutralized." Of this total, over 26,000 were killed and the remaining either came in on their own and were released, or were captured and detained.

56. Interviews with Gardiner Tucker and Philip O'Deen.

57. VTF Notes.

58. This was part of his participatory management program and went beyond the budget itself into weapons development and procurement for example. Canan, *Superwarriors*, p. 81.

59. Although Westmoreland says that Laird "appeared to distrust the Joint Chiefs" (*A Soldier Reports*, p. 387), Zumwalt offers an opposing view (*On Watch*, p. 267). Laird publicly addressed the question himself in an article in the *New York Times* of December 2, 1969, concerning a recent ban by the president on biological and chemical warfare which quotes him as follows: "I think we've had better cooperation between the military and civilian leadership than we have had in many years around here. There are certain differences that exist when you look at anything from a military position without looking at the political considerations. They understand that. So do I" (p. 24).

60. Interviews with Daniel Henkin, Philip O'Deen, and Ivan Selin.

61. See Henry A. Kissinger, *American Foreign Policy* (New York: W. W. Norton, 1974), p. 133, where he states: "But why should Hanoi accept such an approach [to peace negotiations]? The answer is that partly it has no choice; it cannot bring about a withdrawal of American forces by its own efforts."

62. Charles Cooke, who had previously been an air force major.

63. See U.S., Congress, House, Subcommittee of the Appropriations Committee, *FY 1971 Appropriations Hearings*, Pt. 1, pp. 367-71.

64. Interview with Rady Johnson. For an example of a confrontation between Laird and certain congressmen over Vietnamization see the *New York Times*, October 23, 1969, p. 1: "Defense Secretary Melvin R. Laird, rebuffing the Republican and Democratic leaders of the Senate opposed today any cease-fire in Vietnam that was not part of an agreement with North Vietnam."

65. Nixon, *Memoirs*, p. 447. Other good accounts of decision-making leading up to the Cambodian Incursion are contained in the Kalbs' book *Kissinger* and in William Safire, *Before the Fall* (New York: Doubleday, 1975).

66. *New York Times*, May 6, 7, 1970, p. 1.

67. VTF Notes. Normally the deputy secretary of defense, David Packard, was the Defense Department representative to WSAG.

68. Nixon, *Memoirs*, p. 450.

69. Interviewees corroborate this story.

70. Some of the doubts pertained to the progress statistics themselves and some about how they were being interpreted. An official in the Saigon Embassy had this to say privately concerning a document prepared for Ambassador Ellsworth Bunker to use in briefing President Nixon at an NSC session: "The documents speak for themselves. The analysis has been considerably modified. The result is a totally misleading and unbelievably optimistic view of the local elections. This kind of dangerous diplomatic apologetics is what got us into Vietnam, and will one day make Vietnam an American tragedy. The genre of tragedy no bureaucrat or general will be able to disguise."

71. Peak American strength was reached in the spring of 1969 at just below 550,000. By May 1971 it was at 284,000, with another 100,000 scheduled for withdrawal during the remainder of the year.

72. Department of Defense News Release No. 342-71, April 21, 1971.

73. So named, according to Laird, because it took into account the major realities facing America, i.e., the strategic reality of growing Soviet strength; the fiscal reality of inflation and congressional pressure to reduce defense spending; the manpower reality of the heavy cost of personnel; and the political reality of domestic constraints and international constraints caused by both allies and adversaries.

74. Interview with Daniel Henkin and VTF Notes.

75. VTF Notes.

76. Interview. VTF Notes.

77. *New York Times*, October 1, 1971, p. 40.

78. In the course of the summer came the release of the Pentagon Papers. Although they concerned decision-making on Vietnam before the Nixon administration, Laird nevertheless found them troublesome because they raised the issue of "why and how we got into Vietnam and away from why Vietnamization." VTF Notes.

79. *New York Times*, November 9, 1971, p. 8.

80. Good accounts of Washington decision-making during the Easter Offensive are contained in Kalb, *Kissinger*, Chapt. 11; Nixon, *Memoirs*, pp. 586-95, 599-608; William Safire, *Before the Fall* (New York: Doubleday, 1975), pp. 417-31. Zumwalt, *On Watch*, pp. 379-89.

81. Nixon, *Memoirs*, p. 590.

82. Ibid., pp. 594, 595, 599, 600.

83. Zumwalt, *On Watch*, p. 380. Zumwalt mentions Laird's ability to frustrate Kissinger's Southeast Asia initiatives over a period of time. This in turn, says Zumwalt, caused Kissinger to cultivate relations with Chairman Moorer and, in certain instances, to bypass Laird. Westmoreland recalls a Joint Chiefs of Staff meeting with Laird the day after the beginning of the Easter Offensive, in which the offensive was not discussed in any way. Interview with Lt. Col. Paul Miles.

84. Safire, *Before the Fall*, p. 422.

85. Nixon made no mention in this speech of two items that had previously been routine in discussing the war: his confidence in the South Vietnamese army and his confidence in Vietnamization.

CHAPTER 5

1. Melvin Laird's immediate successor was Elliot Richardson, but in the spring of 1973, as Watergate increasingly involved the president, Nixon felt Richardson could do more for the administration as attorney general. In the resulting shift, Schlesinger was appointed secretary of defense. Richardson's time as defense secretary was so short that he made no impact on the office or the Defense Department, and his time as secretary therefore is not treated in this book.

2. Pleading nolo contendere, Agnew received a fine and a sentence to probation, based upon one count brought against him for failing to report income for tax purposes.

3. Nixon, *Memoirs*, p. 886.

4. In the course of all this, the Arab nations placed an oil embargo on the United States, making the following winter of 1973-1974 a trauma for a U.S. public not used to being required to conserve fuel. More important, however, was the economic fact that between the time the embargo was imposed and the time it was lifted (March 1974), American economic output declined by fifteen billion dollars, and the cost of fuel skyrocketed.

5. Nixon, *Memoirs*, p. 1024. That he thought his secretary of defense James Schlesinger was also one of those aligned with the military, he makes quite clear.

6. Although Cyprus is only sixty miles from Turkey, this was a risky operation, since Turkey does not have a strong naval force. It was perceived, however, by that government as necessary to protect the Turkish community and to prevent Greece from taking over the island. Subsequently, the Turkish army remained as a bargaining chip for purposes of establishing a type of political arrangement which the Turks thought they were agreeing to when the republic was established in 1960

7. *New York Times*, August 19, 1974, p. 1.

8. The following year this was modified to release some arms already in the "pipeline," and each year thereafter some modification was made. But it remained a major problem in U.S.-Turkish relations well into the Carter administration.

9. This conference did in fact take place in Helsinki, in late July and early August 1975. Ford met in Helsinki with the leaders of thirty-four other nations to sign the final act of the Conference on Security and Cooperation in Europe. The declaration, among other things, formalized post-World War II territorial boundaries in Europe.

10. A limit for each side of 2,400 strategic nuclear delivery vehicles (i.e., land and underwater missiles, as well as heavy bombers). A limit for

each side of 1,320 MIRV (multiple independently targetable reentry vehicles) systems. Many did not feel that these high limits marked much of an arms control agreement.

11. As it turned out, American involvement in the conflict was not quite ended. On May 12 President Ford ordered U.S. troops to recapture the American merchant ship *Mayaguez* and its crew of thirty-nine which some Cambodian Communists had seized. The incident provided the fourth use of the provisions of the 1973 war powers resolution, which required the president to consult with Congress before committing U.S. troops overseas. The first three uses of the law took place during the evacuation of South Vietnam and Cambodia earlier. Generally Congress was supportive, but a few members of Congress questioned whether Ford had fully complied with the consultation provision during the *Mayaguez* affair. The issue, however, was left open, since the White House never conceded that the law applied to any of the four incidents.

12. Haig came to work in the White House at the beginning of the first Nixon administration, as a serving army colonel, and assistant to Henry Kissinger. His influence with Kissinger and, later, Nixon gradually increased and he became Kissinger's deputy, ascending rapidly through the general officer ranks. For a short time he returned to the army as vice chief of staff, but shortly returned to the White House to replace H. R. Haldeman, when Haldeman, because of his involvements in Watergate, was forced to resign as head of the White House staff in April 1973.

13. Schlesinger was born in New York City, February 15, 1929. He attended Horace Mann School, graduating in 1946 and entered Harvard in that year.

14. James R. Schlesinger, *The Political Economy of National Security* (New York: Praeger, 1960).

15. RAND, an acronym for Research and Development, is a think tank, with headquarters in Santa Monica, California. It had made its way on government contracts, in those days, almost always from the U.S. Air Force.

16. Canan, *Superwarriors*, p. 107. Schlesinger was instrumental in killing the air force's Manned Orbiting Laboratory. He was less successful on the navy's Trident submarine.

17. Leslie H. Gelb, "Schlesinger," *New York Times Magazine*, August 4, 1974, p. 9.

18. Interview with Joseph Laitin. Another strong Schlesinger supporter was Senator Henry M. Jackson, who knew Schlesinger before he left RAND for the government.

19. The president had apparently, for some time, been unhappy with the poor information furnished him by the intelligence community. The Schlesinger memorandum, based on a study he had supervised, led to "a number of management steps to improve the efficiency and effectiveness" of U.S. intelligence. One change gave the CIA director the right to review budgets of other parts of the intelligence community, such as, for example, in defense. Another change worked the other way, by placing overall

supervision over U.S. intelligence in the National Security staff (i.e., the assistant for national security affairs). Victor Marchetti and John D. Marks, *The CIA and the Cult of Intelligence* (New York: Knopf, 1974), pp. 101–3.

20. Ibid., p. 103. There were also Watergate-related problems between the CIA and the Nixon White House. For example, shortly after Helms's departure it became known that the CIA had been cooperating with the White House in helping to organize a plan for domestic surveillance.

21. Most of this is contained in public literature, especially newspaper articles. In addition, I interviewed over twenty individuals who were associated with or in frequent contact with Schlesinger during his Pentagon days.

22. Zumwalt, *On Watch*, p. 432.

23. Interviews with William Brehm, Fritz Ermath, and Henry Gaffney.

24. Ibid.

25. Interviews with Reginald Bartholomew and Robert Ellsworth.

26. Interview with John Maury.

27. In February 1974 Schlesinger had the position promoted to the assistant secretary level from the director level to which it had sunk in April 1973.

28. According to Sullivan, he was fired by Secretary of Defense Donald Rumsfeld, after Rumsfeld had spent the morning with McClelland. Interview with Leonard Sullivan.

29. Quoted in Canan, *Superwarriors*, pp. 235, 236.

30. See Appendix 2 for names and tour lengths.

31. He also met weekly with the Armed Forces Policy Council, the highest level of civilian and military officials in the Pentagon.

32. Abrams died in September 1974. In addition to Abrams's illness there was also the problem that the army had held the chairman's position, which in some rough way is supposed to rotate, from 1960 until 1970.

33. A couple of samples of better known Brown comments from the *Los Angeles Times*, April 29, 1977, p. 1: At Duke University in 1974: "The Israeli lobby... 'own... the banks in this country, the newspapers. You just look where the Jewish money is in this country.'" In 1976, Brown said: "The Shah of Iran was building a military force of much greater power than was needed for his country's defense, and that Britain's military force had deteriorated to the point that 'all they have got are admirals, generals and bands.'" In an off-the-record lecture at the National War College, 1976: "If any citizen of this country is so concerned about his presence in a meeting being noted, I'd say we ought to read his mail and we ought to know what the hell he has done."

34. Not all observers were sanguine about Ford's dependency on Kissinger. Wrote John Hersey in 1975: "And now this idea suddenly bothers me, and even alarms me... that the United States foreign policy should be transacted man-to-man between Henry Kissinger and Gerald Ford. I have seen endless meetings of six, eight, ten advisers sitting with the President to hammer out policy on the economy and energy and Congressional tactics and everything else under the sun; there the President has heard numerous

advisory voices. But foreign policy is apparently of a different order. Of course, Dr. Kissinger has the whole weight of the State Department behind him, and I am told that he does occasionally appear at senior staff meetings to brief the President's advisers; but in the formulation of settled policy, this President, who had a minimal exposure to foriegn affairs before he came to office, hears, I am told, only one voice, and a mercurial voice it is, Henry Kissinger's. Yes, this is the most alarming thought I have had all week." John Hersey, *The President* (New York: Knopf, 1975), pp. 120, 121.

35. James M. Naughton, "The Ford Upheaval and Some Explanations," *New York Times*, November 6, 1975, p. 14.

36. John Osborne, "The Nixon Watch: Ford's Future," *New Republic* (April 13, 1974), p. 11.

37. The first of three lectures, given by Schlesinger at Princeton University on November 29, 30, and December 1, 1976, entitled "The Setting for America's International Role," sets forth his world view in rather specific terms.

38. James R. Schlesinger, "A Testing Time for America," *Fortune* (February 1976), p. 77.

39. Schlesinger, as quoted in "Arming to Disarm in the Age of Detente," *Time* (February 11, 1974), p. 24.

40. James R. Schlesinger, "U.S. Defense and the International Situation," *Commander's Digest* 15, no. 11 (March 14, 1974):5.

41. Interview with Andrew Marshall.

42. This office was started by Laird in late 1971 to do comparative analysis of U.S. and Soviet military programs. The original motivation may have been to counter Kissinger's net assessment activity within the National Security Council staff. Its formal origins came as a result of an approved recommendation from the Report of Laird's Blue Ribbon Defense Panel of 1970. The Report stated: "A Net Assessment Group should be created for the purpose of conducting and reporting net assessments of United States and foreign military capabilities and potentials. This group should consist of individuals from appropriate units in the Department of Defense, consultants and contract personnel appointed from time to time by the Secretary of Defense, and should report directly to him."

43. James R. Schlesinger, *Annual Defense Department Report FY 1976 and FY 1977* (Washington, D.C.: Government Printing Office, February 5, 1975), I-6.

44. Schlesinger, as quoted in John W. Finney, "Schlesinger Gets Outgoing Honors," *New York Times* (November 11, 1975), p. 9. Almost the exact same phrase appears in Schlesinger's February 1976 article in *Fortune*.

45. Nixon, *Memoirs*, p. 1024.

46. *New York Times*, February 16, 1975. Schlesinger's private views at the time were that SALT I and Vladivostok were a setback for serious arms control negotiations. He felt that they were agreements for agreement's sake and did not provide an adequate stabilizing mechanism. (Question and

answer session, Woodrow Wilson School, Princeton University, November 30, 1976.)

47. "Schlesinger and the Resupply Crisis," *Time* (July 1, 1974), p. 33.

48. Kalb, *Kissinger*, pp. 530–40.

49. Nixon, *Memoirs*, p. 924.

50. Zumwalt, *On Watch*, pp. 432–35.

51. The best single overview of Schlesinger's strategic nuclear policy review is Lynn E. Davis, "Limited Nuclear Options: Deterrence and the New American Doctrine," *Adelphi Paper No. 121* (London, 1976). Two interesting articles on the subject of revising nuclear doctrine written before the Schlesinger policy review was made public are Fred C. Ikle, "Can Nuclear Deterrence Last Out the Century?" *Foreign Affairs* (January 1973), and Wolfgang Panofsky, "The Mutual Hostage Relationship between America and Russia," *Foreign Affairs* (October 1973). Other discussions of the new strategic plans include Colin Gray, "Rethinking Nuclear Strategy," *Orbis* (Winter 1974); Herbert Scoville, Jr., "Flexible Madness," *Foreign Policy* (Spring 1974); Ted Greenwood and Michael Nacht, "The New Nuclear Debate: Sense or Nonsense," *Foreign Affairs* (July 1974); the fall 1974 issue of *Orbis;* and Bernard S. Albert, "Constructive Counterpower," *Orbis* (Summer 1976).

52. James R. Schlesinger, Remarks to a seminar, Woodrow Wilson School, Princeton University, November 30, 1976. Excluding previous Pentagon bureaucratic study seems somewhat of an exaggeration. For a discussion of interest and planning for greater flexibility in nuclear weapons going back to the early days of the Nixon administration, see Davis, "Limited Nuclear Options," pp. 3, 4.

53. Schlesinger seminar statement cited above. For the substance of the debate concerning the new doctrine see Davis, "Limited Nuclear Options," pp. 9, 10.

54. Remarks by Secretary of Defense James R. Schlesinger at Overseas Writers Association Luncheon, Washington, D.C., January 10, 1974. These remarks set off a wave of newspaper articles and editorials. It was evident from most of these that Schlesinger had not made his points clearly. Accordingly, he held a news conference on January 24 to clarify his remarks.

55. James R. Schlesinger, *Annual Defense Department Report, Fiscal Year 1975* (Washington: Government Printing Office, 1974), p. 35.

56. Ibid., p. 32.

57. Ibid., p. 5. The implementation of this new doctrine was relatively easy because it involved largely only the creation of the new flexible war plans. Additionally, the targeting mechanism of the Minuteman III missiles was modified so that each of those 550 weapons could be retargeted in thirty-six minutes. The modifications also allowed the entire Minuteman fleet to be completely retargeted in twenty-four hours. Both the doctrinal and software changes were completed well before Schlesinger left the Pentagon and involved relatively minor expenditures.

58. James R. Schlesinger, *Annual Defense Department Report, Fiscal*

Year 1976 and 197T (Washington: Government Printing Office, February 1975), pp. I-13, 14.

59. Lecture, "The Design of U.S. Forces," by James Schlesinger, Princeton University, December 1, 1976.

60. James R. Schlesinger, as quoted in U.S. Congress, House of Representatives, 93/2, Defense Appropriations Subcommittee, *Department of Defense Appropriations for 1975* (Washington: Government Printing Office, 1974), pp. 317, 318.

61. James Schlesinger, "The Military Balance," *Newsweek* (May 31, 1976), p. 9.

62. Ibid.

63. James R. Schlesinger, "U.S. Defense and the International Situation," *Commander's Digest* (March 14, 1974), p. 6.

64. John W. Finney, *New York Times*, September 27, 1975, p. 10.

65. John W. Finney, *New York Times*, September 29, 1975, p. 1; July 15, 1976, p. 6; July 18, 1976, sec. 4, p. 3.

66. Interview.

67. Lecture, "The Role of Nuclear Weapons," by James Schlesinger, Princeton University, November 30, 1976.

68. During Secretary of Defense Harold Brown's tenure in the Carter administration, Robert Komer, Brown's chief assistant on NATO matters, developed a plan that included many programs whose origins went back to Schlesinger's earlier efforts.

69. Both figures are in fiscal year 1972 dollars.

70. Zumwalt, *On Watch*, pp. 460, 461.

71. John W. Finney, "Schlesinger's Impact on the Pentagon is Yet to Be Felt," *New York Times*, December 25, 1973. It was not many days later that *Pravda* was assailing Schlesinger's budget as a "threat to detente," *New York Times*, January 5, 1974, p. 1.

72. These extemporaneous talks of Schlesinger's were in fact well rehearsed and involved a great deal of theater. Interview.

73. Department of Defense Press Release, February 26, 1974.

74. In 1972 dollars from $67.8 billion to $66.7 billion.

75. Schlesinger, as quoted in Robert A Wright, "Prototype of B-1 Is Shown on Coast," *New York Times*, October 27, 1974, p. 43.

76. Schlesinger, as quoted in *Miami* (Fla.) *Herald*, October 27, 1974. Lest one get the impression that Schlesinger supported all military initiatives, it should be noted that Schlesinger took issue with the trend of building ever larger, ever more costly naval aircraft carriers and directed the navy to produce a set of plans for a new, smaller carrier, one displacing only 50,000 tons—a distinct contrast to their latest design, an 82,000-ton supercarrier. In conjunction with his demand for the "midi-carrier," Schlesinger insisted on the design of an airwing composed of lightweight aircraft, rather than the more complex, more expensive, and heavier aircraft that the air admirals wanted. A navy study, predictably enough, showed that the midi-carrier would cost as much as a large carrier but would be a far less effective combat ship, and the navy counterproposed that plans for the

midi-carrier be scrapped. The issue remained unresolved at the time Schlesinger left office.

77. James R. Schlesinger, News Conference, Pentagon, January 14, 1975.

78. There was at the same time an internal battle going on in the Senate between the Appropriations Committee and the new Budget Committee, chaired by Edmund Muskie, which had set a ceiling on the defense budget for fiscal year 1976 even lower than the amount appropriated by the House.

79. *New York Times,* October 13, 1975, p. 27.

80. Gerald R. Ford, *A Time to Heal* (New York: Harper and Row, 1979), p. 320.

81. From $66.7 billion to $64.4 billion in 1972 dollars.

82. *New York Times,* November 24, 1975, p. 1.

83. Interview with F. J. West.

84. *New York Times,* November 4, 1975, p. 24.

85. *New York Times,* November 24, 1975, p. 1.

86. *New York Times,* November 6, 1975, p. 14.

87. Ibid., p. 41.

88. Schlesinger, *Annual Report FY 1976,* p. I-8.

89. *New York Times,* October 9, 1975, p. 15.

90. Interview with Martin Hoffmann.

91. See, for example, John J. Casserly, *The Ford White House* (Boulder: Colorado Associated University Press, 1977), p. 223.

92. Interview with F. J. West.

93. Interviews with Jerry Friedheim, Joseph Laitin, and F. J. West.

94. Up from 64.4 billion to 65.2 billion in 1972 dollars.

95. *New York Times,* November 5, 1975, p. 21.

96. *New York Times,* November 4, 1975, p. 26.

CHAPTER 6

1. This theme also emerges in Bernard Brodie, *War and Politics* (New York: Macmillan, 1973), pp. 121, 292; Alain Enthoven and K. Wayne Smith, *How Much Is Enough?* (New York: Harper and Row, 1971), pp. 13–20; James Schlesinger, "Quantitative Analysis and National Security," *World Politics* 15 (January 1963): 295–315; Morton Halperin, *Bureaucratic Politics and Foreign Policy* (Washington, D.C.: Brookings Institution, 1974), pp. 65–76; Samuel Huntington, *The Soldier and the State* (Cambridge, Mass.: Harvard University Press, 1957), pp. 394, 407, 445; Morris Janowitz, *The Professional Soldier* (New York: Free Press, 1971), p. 363; Douglas Kinnard, *President Eisenhower and Strategy Management: A Study in Defense Politics* (Lexington: University Press of Kentucky, 1977), pp. 4–16, 36, 120–24; Bruce Russett, *What Price Vigilance?* (New Haven, Conn.: Yale University Press, 1970), p. 12; Lawrence Korb, *The Joint Chiefs of Staff: The First Twenty-five years* (Bloomington: Indiana University Press, 1976), p. 129.

240   NOTES TO PAGE 196

2. Others developing this idea include Halperin, *Bureaucratic Politics,* pp. 17, 111, 306; Thomas Schelling, *Arms and Influence* (New Haven, Conn.: Yale University Press, 1966), p. 40; James Roherty, *Decisions of Robert S. McNamara* (Coral Gables, Fla.: University of Miami Press, 1970), p. 46; Kinnard, *President Eisenhower,* pp. 16, 17, 18-24, 121, 122, 130; Paul Y. Hammond, *Organizing for Defense* (Princeton, N.J.: Princeton University Press, 1961), pp. 353-70; Janowitz, *Professional Soldier,* p. 366; Richard F. Haynes, *The Awesome Power* (Baton Rouge: Louisiana State University Press, 1973), pp. 43, 144-45; Richard Neustadt, *Presidential Power* (New York: Science Editions, 1962), pp. 5, 179; Graham Allison, *Essence of Decision* (Boston: Little, Brown, 1971), pp. 166, 215; Korb, *Joint Chiefs,* p. 7; Andrew J. Goodpaster, "Four Presidents and the Conduct of National Security Affairs," *Journal of International Relations* 2 (Spring 1977), pp. 26-37; Keith C. Clark and Laurence Legere, *The President and the Management of National Security* (New York: Praeger, 1969), pp. 123, 176-78, 234.

3. Other works that develop this theme in various ways are Demetrios Caraley, *The Politics of Military Unification* (New York: Columbia University Press, 1966), p. 284; Huntington, *Soldier and State,* pp. 395-99; Clark and Legere, *Management of National Security,* pp. 4, 21; Janowitz, *Professional Soldier,* pp. 347-50; Paul Y. Hammond, "A Functional Analysis of Defense Decision-Making in the McNamara Administration," *American Political Science Review* 62 (March 1968), pp. 57-69; Russett, *What Price Vigilance?* pp. 185-87.

SELECTED BIBLIOGRAPHY

The primary original sources used in this book are the interviews. Relevant memoirs are listed. However, because of the vast amount of literature related to this general subject only those public documents and secondary works necessary to begin exploration of the field are listed.

INTERVIEWS

Chapter 1: W. Averell Harriman (May, 1977), Marx Leva (March, 1977), Wilfred J. McNeil (April, 1977), John Ohly (March, 1977).

Chapter 2: Dean C. Allard (April, 1972; August, 1972), Graham T. Allison (March, 1972), Edward L. Beach (August, 1972), Thomas Belden (April, 1972), Robert R. Bowie (March, 1972), T. Edward Brasswell (January, 1973), Arleigh Burke (April, 1972), Vincent Davis (June, 1971), Charles H. Donnelly (August, 1972), John S. D. Eisenhower (March, 1972; January, 1973; July, 1976), Eileen Galloway (April, 1972; August, 1972), S. Everett Gleason (April, 1972), Francis S. Hewitt (January, 1973), Samuel P. Huntington (March, 1972), Roger Jones (January, 1973). William W. Kaufmann (March, 1972), George B. Kistiakowski (March, 1972), Lawrence J. Legere (August, 1972), Maurice Matloff (April, 1972), Richard E. Neustadt (March, 1972), Samuel R. Preston (August, 1972), Arthur W. Radford (April, 1972), R. C. Richardson (August, 1972), Max Rosenberg (April, 1972), Robert L. F. Sikes (January, 1973), Stuart Symington (January, 1973), Maxwell D. Taylor (August, 1973).

Chapter 3: McGeorge Bundy (November, 1976), William P. Bundy (November, 1976), Harlan Cleveland (November, 1976), Clark M. Clifford (October, 1976), Alain Enthoven (October, 1976), Henry Gaffney (October, 1976), Leslie Gelb (January, 1977), Roswell L. Gilpatric (September, 1976), Robert N. Ginsburg (October, 1976), W. Averell Harriman (May, 1977), H. K. Johnson (October, 1976), Paul H. Nitze (October, 1976), Dean Rusk (May, 1977. (By Tp.), Stuart Symington (October, 1976), Cyrus R. Vance (October, 1976), Paul Warnke (October, 1976).

Chapter 4: William Baroody, Jr. (May, 1977), Daniel Z. Henkin (January, 1977), Rady Johnson (March, 1977), Bob Montague (December, 1976), Phil O'Deen (December, 1976), Robert Pursley (January, 1977**), Charles Rossotti (December, 1976), Ivan Selin (December, 1976), Gardiner Tucker (January, 1977**), Carl S. Wallace (December, 1976).

**Interviewed by Stephen Strom

Chapter 5: Reginald Bartholomew (March, 1977), William Brehm (March, 1977), Leslie Brown (February, 1977), Donald Cotter (March, 1977), Philip Drennan (February, 1977), Robert Ellsworth (March, 1977), Fritz Ermath (March, 1977), Jerry Friedheim (March, 1977), Henry Gaffney (February, 1977), Martin Hoffmann (February, 1977), Randy Jayne (February, 1977), William Kaufmann (May, 1977), Joseph Laitin (March, 1977), Patrick Leahy (August, 1978), Andrew Marshall (March, 1977), James Martin (March, 1977), John Maury (March, 1977), Donald Rumsfeld (February, 1977), Leonard Sullivan (February, 1977), F. J. West (March, 1977), William Whitson (March, 1977).

PUBLIC DOCUMENTS

Donnelly, Charles H. *United States Defense Policies since World War II.* U.S. Congress, House: 85-1: H. Doc. No. 100, 85-2: H. Doc. No. 436, 86-1: H. Doc. No. 227, 86-2: H.̇ Doc. No. 432, 87-1: H. Doc. No. 207.

Hewes, James E., Jr. *From Root to McNamara: Army Organization and Administration, 1908–1963.* Washington, D.C.: Government Printing Office, 1975.

Lee, Gus C., and Parker, Geoffrey Y. *Ending the Draft: The Story of the All Volunteer Force.* Final Report, Human Resources Research Organization, Alexandria, Va. April 1977.

The Pentagon Papers: *The Defense Department History of United States Decision-Making on Vietnam.* Senator Gravel Edition. 5 vols. Boston: Beacon Press, 1971.

Smale, Gordon F., ed. *A Commentary on Defense Management.* Washington, D.C.: Industrial College of the Armed Forces, 1967.

Tucker, Samuel A., ed. *A Modern Design for Defense Decision.* Washington, D.C.: Industrial College of the Armed Forces, 1966.

U.S. Blue Ribbon Defense Panel. *Report to the President and the Secretary of Defense on the Department of Defense.* Washington, D.C.: Government Printing Office, July 1970.

U.S. Congress. Senate. Committee On Naval Affairs, *Unification of the*

War and Navy Departments and Postwar Organization for National Security. Senate Committee Print, 79th Cong., 1st sess., 1945.

U.S. Congress, Report of the *Congressional Aviation Policy Board,* March 1948. (Brewster-Hinshaw Board)

U.S. Department of Defense. *Annual Posture Statements FY 1964–FY 1978.*

U.S. Department of Defense. *The Department of Defense 1944–1978.* Historical Office, D.O.D. Washington, D.C.: Government Printing Office, 1979.

U.S. President's Air Policy Commission, *Survival in the Air Age.* Thomas K. Finletter, Chairman. Washington, D.C.: Government Printing Office, 1948.

U.S. President. *Public Papers of the Presidents of the United States.* Washington, D.C.: Office of the Federal Register, National Archives and Records Service, 1947–1975.

U.S. President. *United States Foreign Policy for the 1970's.* Washington, D.C.: Government Printing Office, 1970.

MEMOIRS

Acheson, Dean. *Present at the Creation.* New York: Norton, 1969.

Adams, Sherman. *First-Hand Report.* New York: Harper, 1961.

Crankshaw, Edward. *Khrushchev Remembers.* New York: Bantam, 1971.

Cutler, Robert. *No Time for Rest.* Boston: Little, Brown, 1965.

Eisenhower, Dwight D. *Mandate for Change.* New York: Doubleday, 1963.

Eisenhower, Dwight D. *Waging Peace.* New York: Doubleday, 1965.

Eisenhower, John S. D. *Strictly Personal.* New York: Doubleday, 1974.

Ford, Gerald R. *A Time To Heal.* New York: Harper and Row, 1979.

Haldeman, H. R., with DiMona, Joseph. *The Ends of Power.* New York: Times Books, 1978.

Hughes, Emmet John. *The Ordeal of Power.* New York: Atheneum, 1963.

Johnson, Lyndon Baines. *The Vantage Point.* New York: Holt, Rinehart, and Winston, 1971.

Kennan, George F. *Memoirs.* Boston: Little, Brown, 1967.

Kennan, George F. *Memoirs 1950–1963.* Boston: Little, Brown, 1972.

Kennedy, Robert. *Thirteen Days.* New York: W. W. Norton, 1969.

Kissinger, Henry. *White House Years.* Boston: Little, Brown, 1979.

Larson, Arthur. *Eisenhower, the President Nobody Knew.* New York: Popular Library, 1968.

Leahy, William D. *I Was There.* New York: McGraw Hill, 1950.

Macmillan, Harold. *Riding the Storm.* New York: Harper, 1971.

Millis, Walter, ed. *The Forrestal Diaries.* New York: Viking Press, 1951.

Nixon, Richard. *Six Crises.* New York: Doubleday, 1962.

Nixon, Richard. *The Memoirs of Richard Nixon.* New York: Grosset and Dunlap, 1978.

Safire, William. *Before the Fall.* New York: Doubleday, 1975.
Strauss, Lewis. *Men and Decisions.* New York: Doubleday, 1962.
Truman, Harry S. *Memoirs—Vol. 1, Year of Decisions.* New York: Doubleday, 1955.
Truman, Harry S. *Memoirs—Vol. II, Years of Trial and Hope.* New York: Doubleday, 1956.
Twining, Nathan F. *Neither Liberty nor Safety.* New York: Holt, Rinehart, 1966.
Westmoreland, William C. *A Soldier Reports.* New York: Doubleday, 1976.
Zumwalt, Elmo R., Jr. *On Watch.* New York: Quadrangle, 1976.

BOOKS

Aliano, Richard A. *American Defense Policy from Eisenhower to Kennedy.* Athens: Ohio University Press, 1975.
Branyan, Robert L., and Larsen, Lawrence H., eds. *The Eisenhower Administration 1953–1961.* 2 vols. New York: Random House, 1971.
Caraley, Demetrios. *The Politics of Military Unification.* New York: Columbia University Press, 1966.
Casserly, John J. *The Ford White House.* Boulder: Colorado Associated University Press, 1977.
Clark, Keith C., and Legere, Laurence J. *The President and the Management of National Security.* New York: Praeger, 1969.
Davis, Lynn Etheridge. "Limited Nuclear Options: Deterrence and the New American Doctrine," *Adelphi Paper No. 121.* London, 1975.
Enthoven, Alain C., and Smith, K. Wayne. *How Much Is Enough?* New York: Harper and Row, 1971.
Futrell, Robert Frank. *Ideas, Concepts, Doctrine: A History of Basic Thinking in the United States Air Force 1907–1964.* 2 vols. Aerospace Studies Institute, Air University, 1971.
Gavin, James M. *War and Peace in the Space Age.* New York: Harper, 1958.
Goulding, Philip G. *Confirm or Deny: Informing the People on National Security.* New York: Harper and Row, 1970.
Graff, Henry F. *The Tuesday Cabinet.* Englewood Cliffs, N.J.: Prentice-Hall, 1970.
Hammond, Paul Y. *Organizing for Defense.* Princeton, N.J.: Princeton University Press, 1961.
Haynes, Richard F. *The Awesome Power: Harry S. Truman as Commander in Chief.* Baton Rouge: Louisiana State University Press, 1973.
Hitch, Charles J., and McKean, Roland N. *The Economics of Defense in the Nuclear Age.* Cambridge, Mass: Harvard University Press, 1960.
Hitch, Charles J. *Decision Making for Defense.* Berkeley: University of California Press, 1965.

Huntington, Samuel P. *The Common Defense.* New York: Columbia University Press, 1961.
Huntington, Samuel P. *The Soldier and the State.* New York: Random House, 1964.
Kalb, Marvin, and Kalb, Bernard. *Kissinger.* New York: Dell, 1975.
Kaufmann, William W. *The McNamara Strategy.* New York: Harper and Row, 1964.
Kinnard, Douglas. *President Eisenhower and Strategy Management: A Study in Defense Politics.* Lexington: University Press of Kentucky, 1977.
Kinnard, Douglas. *The War Managers.* Hanover, N.H.: University Press of New England, 1977.
Korb, Lawrence J. *The Joint Chiefs of Staff: The First Twenty-five Years.* Bloomington: Indiana University Press, 1976.
Korb, Lawrence J. *The Fall and Rise of the Pentagon: American Defense Policies in the 1970's.* Westport, Conn.: Greenwood Press, 1979.
Lyon, Peter, *Eisenhower: Portrait of the Hero.* Boston: Little, Brown, 1974.
McNamara, Robert S. *The Essence of Security: Reflections in Office.* New York: Harper and Row, 1968.
Parmet, Herbert S. *Eisenhower and the American Crusades.* New York: Macmillan, 1972.
Rockefeller Brothers Fund. Report of Panel II. *International Security, The Military Aspect.* New York: Doubleday, 1958.
Roherty, James M. *Decisions of Robert S. McNamara.* Coral Gables, Fla.: University of Miami Press, 1970.
Rostow, W. W. *The Diffusion of Power.* New York: Macmillan, 1972.
Schilling, Warner R., Hammond, Paul Y., and Snyder, Glen H. *Strategy, Politics, and Defense Budgets.* New York: Columbia University Press, 1962.
Schlesinger, Arthur M., Jr. *A Thousand Days.* Boston: Houghton Mifflin, 1965.
Sorensen, Theodore C. *Kennedy.* New York: Harper & Row, 1965.
Stein, Harold, ed., *American Civil-Military Decisions: A Book of Case Studies.* Birmingham: University of Alabama Press, 1963.
Taylor, Maxwell D. *The Uncertain Trumpet.* New York: Harper, 1959.
Taylor, Maxwell D. *Swords and Plowshares.* New York: Norton, 1972.
terHorst, Jerald F. *Gerald Ford and the Future of the Presidency.* New York: Joseph Okpatu Publishing Company, 1974.
Trewhitt, Henry L. *McNamara.* New York: Harper and Row, 1971.

INDEX

Abrams, Creighton W.: replaces
Westmoreland as Vietnam com-
mander, 127; role of, in Vietnamiza-
tion, 130, 141, 144, 149, 167; relations
with Laird, 132, 134, 137
Anderson, George W., 80
Antiwar movement (Vietnam), 75-76,
116, 120-30, 136
Arab-Israeli relations: during Truman
years, 20; during Eisenhower years,
53; 1967 war, 103-4; 1973 Yom Kippur
War, 154-55, 173-74
Armed services, positions on formation
of Defense Department, 15, 16, 25.
See also Interservice competition;
Joint Chiefs of Staff
Atomic weapons. *See* Nuclear weapons

Bay of Pigs, 72, 79, 91
Berlin, 91: crises in, 26, 30, 34, 39; air-
lift, 30, 33; wall erected in, 72-73
Bonesteel, Charles H., 82
Bradley, Omar N., 23, 48-49, 62
Brandon, Henry, 110, 111
Brezhnev, Leonid, 116, 154, 158
Brown, George S., 166, 167
Bundy, McGeorge, 77, 78, 85, 95-96,
100, 106
Bunker, Ellsworth, 106, 140-41
Burke, Arleigh A., 55, 57, 63-64, 80
Byrnes, James F., 11, 12, 13, 21

C. *Turner Joy* (U.S. destroyer), attack
on, 94
Cambodia: incursion, 116, 136; bombing
of North Vietnamese sanctuaries in,
129; movement of North Vietnamese
troops into, 135; U.S. decision-making
about, 137-38, 139
Carney, Robert B., 50, 51, 56-57

Central Intelligence Agency (CIA), 85,
162, 171; proposed, 16; established by
National Security Act, 18
China, 21, 34, 91, 110: explodes nuclear
device, 74; Nixon's initiative toward,
115; visited by Nixon, 115, 142; new
U.S. relationship toward, 123, 168
Chou En-Lai, 115
Clay, Lucius D., 26, 30, 34, 82
Clifford, Clark, 106
Colby, William, 186
Cold war, 8, 12-13, 30
Congress: and Truman's draft proposal,
10; Forrestal's relations with, 23, 28,
41; and defense budget, 28-29, 60-61,
67-69, 151, 182-85, 188; and Defense
Department reorganization, 61,
63-65; increases foreign and defense
decision-making, 67-68, 148, 157,
205; Johnson's relations with, 75;
McNamara's relations with, 83-84;
and Vietnam War, 95, 116, 139, 158;
Laird's relations with, 125, 134, 150,
152; Schlesinger's relations with, 165,
167, 172, 182-85, 187-88, 190
Containment policy, 14, 39
Conventional warfare: U.S. capability
for, 73, 174, 178; Soviet capability for,
179
Cuban missile crisis, 73, 201
Cutler, Robert, 27-28, 78
Cyprus, 157-58
Czechoslovakia: Communist coup in, 26;
and March Crisis, 26

Decker, George H., 79
Defense, Department of (Pentagon):
reasons for new department, 14-15;
Marshall's proposal for unification, 15;
other proposals for organization,